BACK TO GOOD TEACHING

KU-683-384

LIBY END/001

WP 0892208 X

Also available from Cassell:

C. Clark: *Thoughtful Teaching*
G. Claxton: *Teaching to Learn*
B. Creemers: *The Effective Classroom*
A. Hargreaves and M. Fullan: *Understanding Teacher Development*
E. Hoyle and P.D. John: *Professional Knowledge and Professional Practice*
T. Humphreys: *A Different Kind of Teacher*
I. Lawrence (ed): *Education Tomorrow*
S. Ranson: *Towards the Learning Society*
E. Sotto: *When Teaching Becomes Learning*

Back to Good Teaching

Diversity Within Tradition

John Halliday

UNIVERSITY OF WOLVERHAMPTON
LIBRARY

Acc No.	CLASS
892208	371.
CONTROL	
0304335479	102
DATE	SITE
-4. APR 1996	WL HAL

CASSELL

Cassell
Wellington House
125 Strand
London WC2R 0BB

215 Park Avenue South
New York
NY 10003

© John Halliday 1996

All rights reserved. No part of this publication may be reproduced or transmitted in any form or by any means, electronic or mechanical including photocopying, recording or any information storage or retrieval system, without prior permission in writing from the publishers.

British Library Cataloguing-in-Publication Data
A catalogue record for this book is available from the British Library.

First published 1996

ISBN 0–304–33547–9 (hardback)
      0–304–33548–7 (paperback)

Typeset by Mayhew Typesetting, Rhayader, Powys
Printed and bound in Great Britain by Redwood Books Ltd, Trowbridge, Wilts

Contents

Preface

This book is about good teaching. It may be of interest to those involved with school- or college-based programmes of teacher education. It offers support to those who believe that no amount of administrative development, curricular development, management reorganizations, quality audits or anything else of a similar kind is so important to education as the promotion and maintenance of a tradition of good teaching. The idea that goodness in teaching can somehow be assured by attempting to standardize practice is rejected. Instead it is argued that good teaching consists in a set of diverse practices that are sustained by professional discourse and that are subject to democratic accountability.

The book is written to appeal to a general readership interested in the logic of teaching practice and the threat to good teaching that is posed by what might be called 'quality through standardization'. One of the major themes that has informed educational developments world-wide recently has been the move towards professional accountability. The idea that increasing amounts of the taxpayer's money should be spent on education systems without some form of rigorous mechanism for accounting for that money has been rejected. There have been moves for example to devise standards of teacher competence and to link these with the notions of quality, efficiency and effectiveness. The complexity of these moves, however, combined with the sheer difficulty of conceptualizing the values that inform educational development in a pluralistic society make education systems difficult to understand. It is far from clear for example just who is supposed to be accountable to whom and for what. While there are many books that attempt to explain particular parts of education systems and many more that are targeted at an academic readership, there are few that attempt to be both general in scope and appeal.

This is worrying for it is argued that ultimately educational claims are validated in the course of ordinary human conversations. Yet I believe that professionals have not been as good as they might have been at explaining their practice and that is one of the reasons why the (in my view) misguided project of trying to ensure accountability through standardization has gained momentum. No one expects an education system to be easy to understand. Nor do many people expect teaching to pander to narrow interests and immediate desires. Moreover no one expects every aspect of education to be describable in mathematical terms so that all aspects are accounted for through measures of performance. It does however seem reasonable that teachers, policy-makers and other professionals should be able to explain what they are trying to do.

I believe that it is important now for all interested parties to consider critically whether recent moves to try to standardize teaching practice are not likely to submerge a tradition of good teaching beneath a mountain of paper and administrative controls. I have not met many good teachers who get enthusiastic about the ticking of boxes on a checklist and the rest of the paraphernalia that attends moves to standardize their practice. If we continue as we are then we run the risk of encouraging teachers who can conceive of their practice only as the administering of set workbooks according to a prescribed method. For them success can only be measured by the speed at which they can get out of the classroom in order to do better-paid administration designing the next set of guidelines for teachers to follow. Thus we run the risk of attracting entrants to the teaching profession who see teaching as a technical activity designed to achieve some predetermined objective that is supposed somehow to be independent of the interests of particular students.

I may be wrong of course in my view of good teaching. Nevertheless there is considerable academic work to support my view[1] and not a lot of evidence that parents, students and industrialists actually want teachers of the type described above.[2] It is ironic at a time when public services generally are supposed to be more responsive to their 'customers', that those who control public education systems should promote moves towards what are sometimes called 'control by checklist' and 'accountability through statistics'.[3]

No doubt some readers may accuse me of oversimplifying matters in a book that is as wide ranging as this one. Well there are many other books around for those who seek to follow up particular interests. I refer to some of these books through a series of endnotes so that readers who are interested in following up particular points may be guided to suitable texts. In that way the flow of the narrative is not interrupted by frequent reports of who wrote what and when. This book has a particular purpose and that is to give an overview of educational developments from a philosophical perspective and to make that overview reasonably accessible. The book does not, however, take the form of yet another introduction to the philosophy of education. Instead a substantive theory of good teaching is advanced which is supported by a theory of philosophy. In a sense the book follows on from and attempts to cohere with an earlier book of mine which is more theoretical.

Throughout the reader will find case exemplars which are designed to illustrate a particular argument and to provide points of contact between ordinary experience and proposed theories of that experience. I should like to thank Lawrence Ingvarson of Monash University for his help with some of the references that informed these case exemplars. I should also like to thank other colleagues at Monash who welcomed me to their campus recently and provided me with facilities to complete this book. In particular David Aspin was as supportive as he always has been in the fourteen years that I have known him. I also need to thank him in his capacity of editor of *Educational Philosophy and Theory* for permission to reproduce parts of a paper of mine which was published originally in that journal and which forms part of Chapter 8. Finally I want to thank Paul Standish of the University of Dundee for his careful editing of the penultimate draft and for his advice which prevented me from making more mistakes that I otherwise would have made. Naturally despite this assistance any mistakes and omissions that remain are entirely my responsibility.

John Halliday
May 1995

NOTES AND REFERENCES

1. See Tripp (1993), Hargreaves and Fullan (1992), Apple (1986) and (1993), Harris (1994), Rowland (1993).
2. I have been unable to find any evidence to support the view that parents or others actually value teaching of this sort. In a digest of UK surveys and polls on parents', teachers' and pupils' attitudes to school, MacBeath and Weir (1991) explain that there tends to be a high level of consensus that good teaching is the most important constituent of a good school (p. 41). They go on, 'parents and public are more likely to prefer a broad general education to a specifically vocational education' (p. 43).
3. Hoyle and John (1995) pp. 40–42 give a British example of this irony. An example taken from the USA is given by Apple and Jungck, p. 21 in Hargreaves and Fullan (1992).

Introduction

A large body of literature is concerned with the topics of teaching and learning, effective educational institutions and community involvement in such institutions. In academic circles these topics are sometimes discussed and researched as if they were distinct. Yet it is not hard to see that the topics might be closely related in practice. Effective educational institutions employ good teachers and involve members of the local community as partners both in the educational enterprise and in the management of the institution.

There are a number of books that promote this democratic vision of schooling primarily on the basis of moral and ethical concerns.[1] In this book however an account of good teaching is derived from a philosophical concern with the problem of knowledge. Essentially the argument advanced is that unless teaching, community involvement and education systems are conceived and practised in particular ways, we cannot even begin to know how to distinguish good from bad, progress from degeneration, in teaching, schooling or systems. In that way morally informed practice depends upon theoretical and practical engagement with the problem of distinguishing between knowledge and conjecture.[2]

Traditionally the problem of knowledge has not been treated as a practical problem. Claims to know however may be regarded as ways of speaking and writing that are inextricably bound to the ways that people act. Much theoretical work has been directed towards developing a plausible account of the way that knowledge develops and ignorance is decreased.[3] I draw heavily on this work and adapt it to propose a tentative solution to the problem of distinguishing between good and bad practice. We might say that the distinction between good and bad practice is similar to the distinction between knowledge and ignorance. I focus on practices in order to avoid privileging the use of the words 'know' and 'knowledge' above all other uses of words within a practice. A great deal of confusion has been generated by the traditional attempt to isolate the problem of knowledge from the practical contexts in which claims to know have a point. I attempt to relocate knowledge within human practices so that the use of the word 'know' might not be privileged over the use of other words, forms of acting or what I call 'authentic silence'.[4]

It is widely assumed that education is an induction into worthwhile practices that characterize the best features of our way of life.[5] According to this assumption we are working up our ability to take part in various practices from infancy onwards. We learn to take part in some practices with our parents, some with our friends, some with our colleagues and some with our teachers who are located within formally constituted educational institutions. It is also widely assumed that some legally binding arrangements for educating children in some core practices are essential for the proper functioning of democratic societies. In that way all children may come to share a common cultural inheritance which enables them to communicate with each other and come to agree or disagree about how their societal institutions should be run and developed in the future.

It is neither possible nor desirable for all children to be inducted into the same set of practices overall. For example, parents and guardians have different interests and abilities and quite properly they will induct their children into the practices that correspond to those interests and abilities despite what goes on in school. Some parents will teach their children to sail, swim, play the violin, write poetry, read comics, watch television, play sports and other things. The desire of children to please their parents will serve as an entering wedge to further learning of the particular practice in which the parents have an interest. In a similar way the desire to please a particular teacher may serve as an entering wedge into those practices that form part of the school curriculum.

It is obvious that we cannot predict the precise content of the formal curriculum for all children because we cannot predict the practices that they will take part in at home and elsewhere. We can however make reasoned guesses and our reasoned guesses will inform the practice-specialisms of the teachers that we seek to employ. That does not mean of course that the teachers will be incapable of linking a practice in which they have particular expertise with other practices in which students already have some experience. Indeed it would seem to be essential that they are capable of making such links for otherwise it is hard to see how their students could begin to learn what at first sight appears to be a new practice.

The term 'practice' is notoriously difficult to define because it is not clear at what level of abstraction the use of the term is helpful. In this book I use the term to mean some combination of talk, deliberation and action that is most often characterized by the use of a single noun. For example joinery, history, physics, tennis, bricklaying and geography might be taken as examples of practices. I argue that such practices share what might be called a 'family resemblance'.[6] That is to say that while all practices do not have one thing in common they do share overlapping similarities. This degree of overlap is helpful in explaining how people learn a practice that is new to them on the basis of their familiarity with other practices that overlap with the practice to be learnt. The degree of overlap is also helpful in explaining how communication is possible between different sorts of practitioner.

The notion of a family resemblance can be extended into the notion of an 'overlapping consensus'[7] through which it may be assumed that we agree on many things without agreeing on all things. This latter notion may be used to explain how we may come to an agreement of how educational institutions might be run on democratic lines without it also being necessary for everyone to agree on all educational matters. The former notion allows us to understand how practices are not exclusive and how an example taken from one practice can also serve as a useful example in another practice and vice versa.

I refer to an education system as the set of institutions, practical norms and human relationships that are supported by governments formally to provide educational opportunities for citizens. If the idea of education as initiation is accepted and if it is accepted that formal systems of education may be based on this idea[8] then a number of consequences follow: first, it is important to ensure that there is a sufficient number of teachers well-qualified in practices that are unlikely to be learnt outwith formal educational institutions so that students may be provided with equal and sufficient opportunities to learn; second, there is little point in trying to prescribe the formal curriculum in great detail in advance of particular attempts to teach because parents as co-educators may have already taught parts of the prescription; third, there will always be a tension between funding the system on the basis of individual needs and funding the system on the basis of a common minimum requirement for all students to achieve.

Whenever people pay for something, some form of evaluation is implied. The important question however concerns the amount and type of detail of evaluation that is appropriate to a system in which product and process are intertwined with personal commitment and values of a non-monetary kind. Certainly it is important to make some attempt formally to evaluate the system so that educational practices, like other practices, may be based on some criteria for what counts as good practice. This third point really is the nub of the matter for it is argued that sorting out good from bad is the most difficult part of any practice. Those practices which we do not manage to sort in this way, degenerate. It is possible to support degenerating practices by increasing the resources spent on them and in particular by increasing the resources spent trying to convince others that the practice is not degenerating. However I argue that the most successful practices are those that continue to offer results and that by general agreement in the most open and least coercive debate are progressing.

Just as we do not want to induct students into practices such as astrology or pornography so too we do not want to induct them into a social practice of schooling that is itself degenerating. We cannot have a set of rules that can be applied to all practices to distinguish progress from degeneration because the application of those rules will itself constitute a practice that might be degenerating. Nor can we appeal to the authority of a professional group to settle matters for us for that group might also be degenerative. It is true that professionals, as the practitioners themselves, seem best placed to distinguish progress from degeneration. However, their distinctions are not isolated from the concerns of everyone else and it is through what I call the reservoir of common sense[9] that claims to know what is progressing are filtered by those who look at the claim from the vantage point of a different practice or combination of practices than that of the professionals.

It is sometimes asserted that people only really understand something when they come to teach it themselves. At that point they have to convince a sceptical group of students to become committed to a particular way of looking at things and teachers are unlikely to be able to do this unless they are committed themselves to that perspective. Quite rightly students are not prepared to give up easily their prior conceptions that are embedded within the language they use. In a similar way people generally are unwilling to give up their 'prejudices'[10] unless they are persuaded to do so by others who, at the very least, seem committed to a different understanding.

This account of teaching may be likened to the quality forum or critical circles that are constituted as part of modern industrial practice to try to iron out defects in production before these defects occur.[11] Through these circles or forums, the advocates of new ideas subject those ideas to widespread critical scrutiny in an attempt to persuade others to accept them. In that way everyone involved in the production process has a part to play in thinking through the potential problems with a proposal. Policy-makers, managers, theorists and practitioners become committed to the new idea through a shared understanding of the production process and the need for cumbersome *post hoc* evaluation or quality control procedures is avoided. While I argue that the language of production is inappropriate to education, this industrial example is helpful in drawing our attention to the way that successful industrial practice may be seen not to be based on over-burdening control, hierarchy or bureaucratic *post hoc* methods of accountability. This example is also helpful in explaining why many students do not seem to learn well through the completion of workbooks on an individual basis. The context for the demonstration of commitment on the part of the teacher and public scrutiny of that commitment is not available in the use of this method.

Therefore a central argument in this book is that an education system should, above all else, encourage the value of open discursive rationality by ensuring that all students are able to take part in critical yet productive discussions. That means that an education system should encourage students to be as accomplished in as many practices as possible so that they are most able to take part in critical debate and to inform their arguments with examples taken from a wide range of practices. In that way they may illustrate their arguments with examples and analogies that are likely to engage the attention of more people and to enrich the ensuing debate.

It is however of little use having students who can illustrate their arguments with examples from a wide range of practices if they are unable to differentiate right from wrong, better from worse, progress from degeneration. For without the ability to recognize such distinctions, debate is pointless. Therefore I argue that it is important for students to be inducted into at least one practice in sufficient depth that they come to recognize goodness as an intrinsic value and not as a means to some other preferred end. For example, a student may come to learn a practice because she wishes to please a teacher or impress a friend. At some stage however it is important that she comes to value the practice for its own sake and not as the means to something else. It is important to be able to recognize the difference between a job that is completed in which the prime motivation was financial reward and the job in which the prime motivation was to work in such a way that the object itself was the prime focus of attention along with the relationship between the object and the people who are to use the object.

Debate about what to do is pointless unless it is informed by some sense of what is the right thing to do. To lapse into subjectivism is simply to lapse into battles as to who has the most power. Of course the subjectivist tendencies of modern times may be the result of widespread cynicism in which it is claimed that there are no criteria for goodness other than membership of a powerful elite which decides what is in the members' best interests and links this decision in with what is to count as good practice. Deconstructionists of various persuasions seek to unmask these power relations but of course the deconstructionist project is open to the charge that it too is just another cynical attempt to manipulate power relations in its favour.[12]

Against these forms of subjectivism we can argue in favour of certain forms of enquiry that are characterized by more open discursive rationality and that are widely agreed to have been successful. For example certain forms of physical science have led to knowledge that is taken at least provisionally to be correct and which has led to some spectacularly successful technologies. Certain democratic forms of political and managerial systems are widely believed to be more successful than other more autocratic forms. Common sense cannot easily be dismissed as mere superstition. Such an account of educational evaluation does not offer an illusion of mathematical precision but it does offer the possibility of democratic participation in a fairly understandable process in which good reasons can be advanced to support certain sorts of enquiry and systemic organization.

I argue that the promotion and maintenance of a tradition of good teaching is the most important part of any education system. The idea that education need be subject to a constant stream of government initiatives should be rejected. The notion of a practical tradition carries with it the implication that members follow the developments within the tradition without compulsion or control. To try to prescribe those developments from outwith the tradition is actually to run the risk of destroying that tradition.[13] For example we do not need a highly detailed prescription of a national curriculum. If teachers were to regain more control over what they teach, there is no reason to suppose that a revolutionary or de-stabilizing curriculum would result since the selection of teachers is not usually based on their revolutionary or de-stabilizing credentials. Any curriculum that is based on the idea of education as initiation is bound to be conservative otherwise there would not be teachers to teach it. All worthwhile practices must be based on criteria for what is to count as good and bad and those criteria may only be located within already existing social traditions.

We need a rough idea of the sorts of practices that should be included in the curriculum and a rough idea of balance. Short of such general guidelines there is no point over-specifying something that cannot practically be checked. There is ample evidence that teachers value their autonomy in the classroom and that they may modify and subvert those developments that they do not support.[14] There is little point issuing a constant stream of guidelines for teachers to follow. Such guidelines will always need a further set of guidelines to guide the interpretation and so on until we arrive at a form of language that is so abstracted from everyday experience that it is meaningless. When we get to such a state that we end up appointing particular people to control the interpretation essentially by giving them the power to penalize those who do not accept their sometimes arbitrary view.

The point that designers of highly detailed sets of curriculum guidelines seem to miss is that these guidelines only have meaning to those who share a common background or tradition in interpretation that is sustained by common values, customary actions and ways of talking. Teachers are already members of such traditions through their professional knowledge as geographers, physicists and most especially teachers. It is foolish therefore to try to ignore this professionalism which seems to have been the case in some countries. As I described earlier, professionalism cannot be divorced from non-professional concerns.

These arguments have implications for practice which are derived throughout the book and are summarized in the remaining section of this introduction. I argue that programmes of teacher education need to be directed much more towards knowledge of subject and justification of teaching practice in ordinary language rather than knowledge of teaching methods. If students are to be inducted into practices then teachers need to be experts in those practices. Perhaps controversially I go along with those who believe that primary teacher education should be more subject-based than it is at present. For me the notion of child-centredness masks a number of confusions about the nature of the primary curriculum and the nature of the epistemic and pedagogic authority that comes from being knowledgeable in a subject. The more common term 'subject' is used here instead of 'practice' in order to highlight the point that subjects are practical in the sense that they too consist of characteristic ways of speaking and acting. While practices like joinery may appear to involve more non-verbal actions than the practice of theoretical physics, in either case both words and actions are interwoven in ways that characterize the practice.

Teacher education that is based on seemingly endless courses on method, over-emphasis on psychology and in-service days spent being told how to do things should be changed. In their place more time should be spent updating subject knowledge and exploring shifts in educational values through attempts to justify those values. The idea of a democratic consensus requires teachers to be able to explain and justify their practice rather better than they have in the past. The notions of justification and explanation imply theoretical reflection. Such reflection enables teachers to explain a wide range of phenomena in a way that appeals to the particular interests of particular parents and others who have a legitimate claim to take part in educational decision-making.

Recent moves to commodify education and to treat parents and others as consumers completely miss this point about justification in favour of some idea that education can actually be bought. Rather than education being something that people engage in and show commitment to themselves, albeit aided by teachers and others who happen to be paid, there has been the idea that education should be bought at the lowest possible price. Even in a one-to-one learning situation where a tutor is paid for a certain amount of time it is unclear just what is being sold and to whom.

Other recent moves to increase the amount of school-based teacher training may provide an opportunity to explore and test some of the recommendations that are made in this book. It has been argued that such moves may be seen as politically inspired attempts to de-professionalize teachers and further to promote a technicist view of teaching.[15] Such a view is based on the idea that teachers should be managed at local level in order to 'deliver' in the most efficient manner a highly prescribed national curriculum. According to this argument money spent on teachers studying 'barmy theory' as the present British Chancellor of the Exchequer put it, should be saved in favour of technically based training.

School-based teacher education need not serve to de-professionalize teachers however. Indeed it could be argued that previous attempts to train teachers in Institutes of Higher Education served to de-professionalize them. If those so-called mentors or staff development officers located within schools have the time to think through programmes of school-based training with those who have detailed knowledge of educational theory, then there is no reason why school-based teacher training should not be a force to re-professionalize teachers and to be a bulwark against technicism. An alliance between parents, students and teachers is a strong force as many officials and politicians have discovered when they have tried to close popular schools or to promote what are seen to be unfair policies.[16] An alliance between parents, students and teachers may well be the best defence against a technicist view of teaching and against current conceptions of educational policy as something that is immutable. Such conceptions are based on the idea that policy relates to values which are necessarily subjective and not subject to public scrutiny.

It will be seen from the title of this book that I argue for diversity within tradition. That is to encourage diversity both in the type of educational institution and in the practices of the teachers who work within those institutions. It is to reject the superficial security that appears to come from being able to legitimize decisions by claiming that 'the guidelines were being followed'. It is to enter a world of uncertainty with doubts that one has taken the right decision. It would be difficult enough deciding how to go about enabling an individual to learn but of course teachers are usually faced with the problem of how best to enable between thirty and several hundred students to learn in the course of a year's work. Teaching is not just about enabling students to do things that they could not do before but crucially teaching is about enabling students to go on and find things out for themselves. Were it the case that all students were equally motivated then teacher evaluation might not be so difficult. As it is however teachers face some classes where a majority of students, for whatever reason, do not want to learn and in which class discipline becomes a problem. We may wonder how a teacher might ensure an orderly learning environment without destroying the atmosphere necessary for students to question, discuss and develop their own lines of enquiry?

To teach is to be committed both to particular students and also to a practice and the values intrinsic to that practice. There is always a tension between the two sorts of commitment. Good teachers want students to master the greatest challenges that they can without destroying the students' self-esteem. There is a narrow line between challenges successfully overcome and failure. The temptation is to play safe and to set easier tasks. They are also sometimes tempted to tell students that they are nearly right when they are plainly wrong if only to save the student's self-confidence.

At the same time however teachers do students no favours if they compromise rigour of the subject for popularity or even for student satisfaction. In the end the only defence against the scepticism that arises out of an inability to justify diverse practice in the short-term is the authority that comes from knowing subjects well. Good teachers have an accurate idea of how well their students are progressing within their subject. Students too can easily compare their progress with that of their peers. There is however no substitute for the recognition that comes from external assessment of progress made by those who are masters of the subject but have no conflict of loyalty between subject and student. Moreover systems of external assessment may serve as a defence of teachers' integrity against managerial imperatives to maximize performance indicators such as student successes in internally assessed courses.

I argue that a system of assessment should be maintained across all practices so that students can, if they wish, assess themselves externally. There is no reason why such assessment should always take the form of a written examination. Nor is there any reason why that assessment should not be conducted by teachers other than the student's own who are also accomplished practitioners. The time that it takes to prepare a written examination makes it impractical to offer such examinations throughout the year. In the case of other assessments however that involve perhaps one examiner talking with or watching a group of students, the time for assessment could be chosen by the student in conjunction with the examiner. Examination of performance of musical instruments would be an example of this type of assessment.

Readers will notice a number of themes or motifs running through this book. The first of these is a concern with the particular rather than the general in education. For example arguments are offered to challenge the prescription of educational aims and methods in advance of particular attempts to educate. The second is an exploration of elitism in education policy, theory and practice. While we might be able to see the attractions of elitism in such a value-laden activity as formal education, there are nevertheless strong arguments to reject elitism. The third theme is the advantage of bold conjecture in education coupled with the invitation to others to try to refute such conjecture in an open decision-making context. This leads to a fourth theme of the importance of common sense to educational theory. Finally there is the importance of the tacit dimension in human practices. No matter how well a practice is described, there remain certain features of the practice that are not describable but that are internalized by the practitioners themselves. Those features remain the most important part of authentic practice.[17]

The language used to explain goodness in teaching has shifted from commitment and responsibility to efficiency and effectiveness of method. Moral and ethical concerns have been marginalized through the language of quality into a separate curriculum component as if values and facts were unrelated. Teachers have been left somehow to reconcile these shifts with the reality of classroom life in which student needs and interests vary widely and in which human relationships and feelings are all-important and unpredictable. For me it is helpful to regard the promotion and maintenance of good teaching as a kind of moral foundation upon which to build rational decisions about formal education. In that way a crisis may be said to occur when that moral foundation is de-stabilized. I argue that it is a matter of urgency to re-focus attention on a tradition of good teaching because it is only against the background of such a tradition that we can evaluate educational developments. Historically there has been an attempt to promote quality in education systems by trying tightly to prescribe teaching practice as if such practice could become a sort of standard service. I seek to promote quality in education systems through diversity in practice sustained by a tradition of good teaching.

NOTES AND REFERENCES

1. See Aspin and Chapman (1994), Kelly (1995), Ranson (1994) and of course Dewey (1966).
2. In essence we need to know good teaching, and teachers themselves need to know whatever it is they are going to teach.
3. I refer here to work in the post-empiricist philosophy of science. See Chalmers (1978) for an accessible overview. Also see Halliday (1990, Chapters 3 and 4). Here I draw heavily on the work of Popper. See the Bibliography for a list of his main publications.
4. The idea of 'authentic silence' may be seen to be related to Wittgenstein's (1922) distinction between saying and showing. See Kenny (1984) for a discussion of this distinction and for

the idea that philosophy need not be conceived primarily as a response to the problem of knowledge. See also Rorty (1980, Chapter 6) for further discussion of this latter idea.

5. The idea of education as initiation has a long history. For a recent account see Peters (1966). Oakeshott (1959) also writes of an induction into a 'cultural inheritance' as a prerequisite for participation in what he calls the 'conversation of mankind'. The idea accords well with the common-sense idea that a certain amount of training in a practice is necessary before a student can begin to understand, let alone take part in, the future development of the practice. Wittgenstein (1953) seems also to support something like this idea in his discussion of ostensive teaching and training (PI 1-9).

6. The notion of 'family resemblance' is taken from Wittgenstein (1953). Here Wittgenstein invites us to consider what is common to all the proceedings we call games. He concludes that nothing is common and goes on 'we see a complicated network of similarities overlapping and criss-crossing: sometimes overall similarities, sometimes similarities of detail' (PI 67). Therefore, for Wittgenstein, questions of the form 'What is the essence of good teaching?' are pointless because teachers do not share one thing in common but a range of overlapping similarities that may only be understood through what he calls a 'perspicuous representation'.

> A perspicuous representation produces just that understanding which consists in 'seeing connections'. The concept of a perspicuous representation is of fundamental significance for us. It earmarks the form of account we give, the way we look at things. (PI, 122)

7. The notion of an overlapping consensus is taken from Rawls (1993) who develops the notion to elaborate his theory of justice (1972). It is widely believed that liberalism depends upon a separation of public from private values. The notion of an overlapping consensus allows Rawls to explain how a public consensus consists not in a set of common public values but on a series of overlapping values. For example we cannot expect everyone to agree on the way that every public institution should be run but we can expect some people to agree on the way some public institutions are run. The notion helps us to understand why we may simply give up on a particular issue, knowing that there are other issues with which to engage.

8. We need to be careful not to conflate education and schooling automatically in this way. For warnings against such conflation see Carr (1992), Hartley (1991) and Harris (1977). Harris argues that one purpose of schools is to train students in the skills for employment and to differentiate between students in order to legitimize the employment of some of them in awful jobs at low rates of pay. According to Harris, if schools did produce educated people, such people 'would be a menace to the society which created them'.

Even if it were correct that some jobs are plainly awful, it does not follow that schools should collude in the selection of people for such jobs. Nor does it follow that it is not possible to make those jobs more interesting. For example some garbage collectors keep fit by running alongside the cart. Park attendants get a lot of time to think about things as they mow the grass.

9. See Halliday (1990, p. 21).

10. I use the term 'prejudice' here not in the normal sense but in the Gadamerian sense (Gadamer 1975, p. 240) to mean the effect of traditional ways of doing and describing things, which cannot be avoided.

11. See Drucker (1992, p. 243).

12. The term 'postmodern' is used to describe the view that there are no unifying principles with which to distinguish good from bad practice but that all practices have their own criteria for what counts as good and bad and that these criteria are themselves subject to sudden and unforseen changes. The reservoir of common sense, which was referred to earlier, may be seen by some post-modernists to be a convenient myth for those who wish to hang on to a discredited rationalist project. See Chapter 1 for a further discussion of post-modernism. Against this view Gellner (1992) stoutly defends the idea of reason through an excellent account of the relationship between reason and culture. See also Windschuttle (1994) and Derrida (1982).

13. See MacIntyre (1981, p. 23).

14. See Nias (1989), Hoyle and John (1995).
15. Hoyle and John (1995, pp. 132–52).
16. For example the British Government's climbdown over Key Stage 3 Assessments in England and Wales and Primary testing in Scotland. See also the number of proposed school closures that have been successfully resisted by an alliance of teachers and parents.
17. See Polanyi (1958, 1967).

Chapter 1

System, Policy and Empiricism

It is sometimes claimed that we are now living in a postmodern age[1] in which the ideals of the late eighteenth-century Enlightenment are no longer valid. For example many people no longer believe that systems may be founded on rational principles nor that those principles can be founded on some universal theory of goodness. The belief in critical reason, private freedom and progress through the application of natural science have been so seriously challenged, it is claimed, that all forms of foundationalism are untenable and that all we are left with is rival practices or forms of discourse that are based on power differentials. Some post-modernists argue that modern practices do not even share a family resemblance and are not amenable therefore to any sort of meta-theoretical analysis.

While we may accept the general thrust of these claims, we should not give up entirely on the idea that reason can help us to distinguish between progress and degeneration, albeit in a piecemeal and pragmatic way.[2] We may agree with many post-modernists and others that the distinction between a knowing subject and an objective reality which underpins empiricism is untenable. That raises a problem however in accounting for the notion of common sense which seems to embody precisely that distinction.

In this chapter I try to solve that problem and to explain how empiricism has had such an important but harmful influence on educational practice. In particular I argue against the empiricist separation of policy from theory and practice. At the same time I argue that theoretical analysis may help us to find coherence between practices where superficially there appears to be none. It may be going too far to suggest that all progressive practices cohere with some common theory of goodness.[3] It does not seem to be going too far however to argue that we do not generally seek to hurt one another. Nor does it seem to be going too far to argue that life generally is more interesting and enjoyable when people know themselves, have some say over what they do and are able to work authentically in an atmosphere of trust and cooperation.

The idea should be rejected that we must submit to being 'owned' by forms of discourse and deceived by an education system into believing that we actually choose where choice is no longer an option. In this I argue that empiricism led us to believe in a form of certainty. As it became clear that this theory of knowledge was mistaken, the temptation was to assert that everything was relative to interests and power.[4] The challenge now is to retrieve a tradition of practical decision-making within education from the technicist vision that threatens to destroy even the possibility of distinguishing between progress and degeneration without recourse to an analysis of power.[5]

If you have a procedure that appears to offer certainty and that procedure lets you down then you may plunge, on the rebound as it were, into the opposite view that everything is relative and subjective. The problem with this view is that if every statement is relative then so is the statement that 'everything is relative' and so there seems little point in asserting or doing anything. A better view is to struggle with the contingency of systems and the unpredictability of people on an ongoing basis. The struggle may be messy in the sense that it inevitably involves arguments and compromise but that does not mean that people cannot hold on to their principles, disagree strongly with those who hold seemingly opposing principles and yet retain a strong liking for them. It is paradoxical but it should not surprise us that we sometimes prefer those with whom we most disagree to those who seem to share our views.

EMPIRICISM

My book *Markets, Managers and Theory in Education* (1990) is a theoretical discussion of the way that certain currently popular educational practices cohere with a particular philosophical theory broadly termed empiricism. I argue that empiricism coheres with practices that are based on three particular ideas: consumerism is the idea that education is a commodity that can be sold and marketed like any other; vocationalism is the idea that the prime purpose of acquiring the educational commodity is to exchange it for money through work; and managerialism is the idea that the overall exchange of commodities can be managed by those not intimately concerned with the practical realities of teaching.

While many reviewers of that book were supportive both of my philosophical theory and my practical educational suggestions, they were not totally convinced by my attempt to elucidate the relation between educational theory and practice. In particular it was pointed out that even if it can be established that a particular theory is mistaken and that it coheres with a particular set of practices, that does not mean that the proponents of those ideas or the practitioners themselves somehow form a coherent group with shared but mistaken ideas. As one reviewer put it:

> it does not follow that the people who engage in these practices and hold these ideas have
> been influenced by the same mistaken philosophical assumptions . . . [Instead] they [may]
> have failed to give any attention to ideas at the level of epistemology at all.[6]

I accept this point and the suggestion that a deeper analysis of educational and philosophical ideas might not have detained many Anglo-American policy-makers or practitioners for too long. I do, however, still support the argument that empiricism and many of our currently popular educational practices are related. These practices may be related more to a sort of caricature of empiricism rather than to the empiricism of philosophers such as Mill and Russell. Nevertheless I believe that it can be shown that disdain for theoretical analysis is related to this sort of caricature and that we have good reason to challenge policies that are made by people who have no interest in theoretical issues and no interest in examining their own theoretical preconceptions. When I use the terms empiricism and empiricists I refer more to this caricature and people of this persuasion rather than to sophisticated accounts of empiricism and their authors. The relationship between theory and practice may not be entirely clear but that does not make it unimportant. On the contrary, I believe that it is impossible for educators at all levels to avoid some sort of theoretical analysis because it is precisely the search for theoretical coherence that may be taken as an important part of any practical attempt to educate. For example teachers who are incapable of locating the particular practices in which they have some expertise within a wider set of practices in which students might have an interest, are unlikely to be able to convince students to join them in the educative endeavour.

Empiricism is a theory of knowledge or epistemology. According to this epistemology there is a world external to us that can be known through our senses. The better we know this world, the more efficiently we can move around within it. What we can never know, according to this epistemology, is what we ought to do in the world. Thus we get the idea that values are essentially subjective preferences and that there will always be value conflicts which logically are not resolvable according to epistemic criteria. Practically however conflicts of value might be resolved in two ways for empiricists although I argue that the second way is in fact dependent on the first. An élite might be appointed that is supposed to have superior insight into what others prefer and that elite might be given sufficient power to enforce its decisions. The second way that empiricists might attempt to settle value conflicts is by instituting the idea of an educational market. The market provides the ultimate test for empiricists in that observable preferences are used to settle conflicts of value.[7]

Many problems with current educational practice in the English-speaking world may be traced to a sort of empiricist ethos within education. Let us set out some of the main features of this ethos. First, there is the idea that *theory guides practice*. If theories are conceived as maps of the world then our practice will be more efficient if we follow the maps. Natural science has been spectacularly successful at describing the world and natural scientific theory has been applied to provide us with very useful technologies. If educational theories could be modelled on natural science then, according to empiricists, those theories may be applied to education systems to derive great benefits. Second, there is the idea that *facts and values, means and ends, theories and policies are distinct*. Thus we get the idea that *policy* – as a statement that is designed to bring about some desired change in the world – guides *theory* – as a statement providing guidance of how best to achieve that change – which guides *practice* – as action on the world. Hence we arrive at the idea that practices within systems at work no longer should consist in the interweaving of considerations of means and ends. Instead these practices are conceived as techniques for the achievement of ends set for practitioners by others. In contrast practices that are primarily located elsewhere may well be authentic in the sense that means and ends are interwoven into some notion of self-development. Third, there is a *fear of disagreement on fundamental issues* and a tendency not to open up to democratic scrutiny the most fundamental evaluative issues. Values are excluded from rational debate. Disagreement and discussion in which there are no conclusions are discouraged. For example, socially acceptable ways of engaging in difficult debates involve the use of phrases such as 'let me play devil's advocate for a minute' or 'it's always good to listen to a different point of view'. It is as if discussion always ends in consensus and serious disagreement with accepted wisdom should be patronized as different but not challenging enough to consider doing things differently.

Thus educational policies are interpreted for teachers and others practically concerned with the educative endeavour. These practitioners attempt to implement the policy according to guidelines given to them by the interpreters. That implementation is checked by a series of inspections and managerial controls. Where minor problems arise, individuals are held accountable for not following the guidelines. When major problems arise, the policy is changed. What seems never to be changed is the overall system of formulating and implementing policy which is based on empiricism.

We may wonder however how we can ever know whether a part of a system or the system itself is in need of reform. This is of course one of the central problems for those trying to implement schemes of teacher appraisal and a major issue for all teachers. At a personal level it is never clear whether failure with a particular class or student is due to the failings of an individual or the failings of a system. Poor management, lack of a disciplinary framework and a number of other factors may be more in need of reform than the performance of an individual.

It is a difficult philosophical problem to work out how evaluation of an individual can be carried out within a system. It is not clear how an epistemological perspective can be established from which criticism of the individual or the system can be made. That is because any criticism of a system or an individual must itself be located within some alternative systematic perspective on education. It is logically possible that the critical perspective may be as defective as the system or person that has been the subject of criticism. There is the possibility of an infinite regress of critical perspectives arising here.

Unfortunately it is not possible to halt that regress in the idea of a value-neutral foundation upon which all satisfactory justifications and evaluations may be erected. It has not been possible to excavate such a foundation. Of course empiricism was meant to provide for its supporters the most secure foundation for policy-evaluation in the form of objective observation of the effects of particular policies. Not only are there good theoretical reasons for rejecting empiricism as I argue, but in the case of education there are practical reasons too. For example the effects of particular education policies may only be felt in the longer term. Particular governments are likely to have left office long before many of the effects of their education policies are apparent. Hence there is both a lack of accountability for policy and a lack of urgency in tackling the issue of educational evaluation at the level of policy. It is easy to come up with a superficially plausible idea. It is much more difficult to implement that idea successfully over a period of time and even more difficult to establish satisfactory criteria for determining success.

The failure of empiricism to provide a secure foundation for educational evaluation led to the idea that policy-making and evaluation are determined by the *preferences* of the makers and evaluators. Hence it has been argued that there is a need for further or meta analysis of the prior commitments and evaluative norms that guided those preferences.[8] However it is not clear just whose preferences are important. Educational policy is not made by members of governments in abstraction from officials within education departments and institutions. It is not easy to separate party political influences on policy from the professional influences of a semi-permanent policy-making group. Given the influence of the latter there is the logical possibility that the same mistaken assumptions may lie behind numerous failed policies.

Empiricism is entirely unhelpful to us here because we cannot come to know the world except through the use of language. While there are rival accounts of the way the world is, there is no extra-linguistic reality to which appeal can be made to determine which account is to be preferred. When things seem to be going badly according to one form of discourse the temptation for some empiricists is to institute yet another form of discourse to counter the claim. Yet once it is accepted that facts are just other forms of discourse that are supposed to describe the world, the relativistic conclusion seems inevitable. Consider the following case.

CASE EXEMPLAR

THE LEAKING SCHOOL ROOF

The Inspection Team reported that Rathbridge High School provided a good quality education for all pupils. Facilities were good for a school of its size and the management structure within the school was highly satisfactory. Teaching was also of a generally high standard with only a few exceptions. The report continued in a fairly positive way . . .

Talk in the staff-room however was focused on the leaking school roof and the dilapidated conditions in the science block. Staff had to teach in their overcoats whenever a strong wind blew and lessons were often interrupted during storms by the need to empty the buckets that were placed strategically around the block. Many staff were annoyed at the decision taken by the Senior Management Team to spend more money on management and assertiveness training rather than repairing the leaking roof

---

These accounts may be described as rival forms of discourse and, as I argued above, empiricism does not help us to determine which account is to be preferred. Let us assume that no one would deny that the roof was leaking and that the windows in the science block were rotten. We might say that those statements do indeed correspond to a state of affairs in the school and we might agree that empiricism has something going for it in that there is no disagreement about those facts. They are embedded within common sense as the residual wisdom of traditions and normal ways of speaking and acting that have been validated over many generations. So that for example just as we do not choose to work in damp and draughty buildings, so too we do not try to walk through walls, nor teach people to try to walk through walls. We do not do this because of a deep-rooted desire not to hurt ourselves or other people that is based on a recognition of certain characteristic gestures of pain and pleasure that ground forms of discourse in human reality.[9]

Educational claims however are not so obviously grounded in characteristic ways of speaking and talking. In this exemplar the rival accounts of educational management and teaching quality do not match. It is not possible to appeal to the facts of the matter because there are no facts. Recently there have been a number of instances where the ordinary use of words like 'quality', 'partnership' and 'enterprise' have been commodified in order to suggest that things are better than they might otherwise seem to be. Yet in this exemplar it does not seem plausible to talk of quality where the fabric of the school is so dilapidated. People cannot speak just how they like without there being some inter-subjective checks on what they say. The claims of the Inspection team seem inauthentic in the sense that they seem to contradict common sense. We are unlikely to take the report seriously because the Inspectors appear to have misinterpreted a situation. Something is not quite right about their response. We are led to believe that they speak as they do because they are less concerned with the practice in which they are supposedly participants than on the basis of the extrinsic rewards that speaking in a preferred way brings. Such speech may, however, lead to human misery as the speech attempts to legitimize a situation in which people may become sick. Let us take this case further.

CASE EXEMPLAR

REACHING AGREEMENT

We return to Rathbridge High and a meeting that is being held between the teachers and inspectors. The teachers are attempting to persuade the inspectors that mending the roof is a greater resource priority than assertiveness training. The teachers would like to appeal to the foundational premise that the fabric of the school should be in a good state of repair before anything else is attempted. Ideally they would like to claim that all reasonable people would agree with this premise. The inspectors point out, however, that refurbishing the buildings could consume the entire development budget and that such refurbishment will not contribute to the maintenance of teaching quality.

The teachers must look elsewhere for a premise that will serve as a 'touchstone'[10] for agreement. Let us suppose that inspectors and teachers agree that the maintenance of teaching morale will serve as a touchstone in this dispute. The teachers argue that morale is bound to suffer if the roof leaks for much longer. The inspectors argue that assertiveness training will improve morale. Now I dare say that many readers' sympathies will lie with the teachers. As described earlier, even without witnessing the dispute, the inspectors' argument seems inauthentic. There is something faintly ridiculous about teachers wearing overcoats in class in order to save money to go on assertiveness training courses.

We should notice that empiricism has not helped directly to resolve this dispute. We should also notice that it is rare that disputes are settled by appealing to the facts of the matter. Instead most disputes are evaluative and the foundations for values are based in human concerns with safety and health. Those concerns are mediated rather than underpinned by agreed ways of describing and acting in the world that are embedded within common sense.

We may view empiricism then as a pragmatically useful way of minimizing harm by describing the world of inanimate objects in particular terms. That pragmatism is embedded within common and well-established ways of acting and speaking that enable us to recognize inauthenticity. Now the notions of authenticity and common sense need rather more unpacking than they have received so far. However it should be clear the direction in which the argument is going. We are moving away from the idea of permanent foundations[11] upon which to build satisfactory claims to know towards the idea of rival forms of discourse that are meditated by common sense and authenticity. We do not have to agree once and for all on particular forms of discourse in advance of a problem for which we seek a solution. Instead we can appeal to the idea that we have an interest in coming to an agreement in order not to harm one another.

When it comes to describing people and designing education systems however, empiricism can be harmful. By promoting the idea that values can be detached from practices, empiricists have led us to accept that educational evaluation may only be carried out by an élite whose members must simply share common values with which to appraise practice. That is because empiricism can provide no basis for knowing which values are to be preferred both in the matter of policy-formation and the matter of educational evaluation generally.

Yet the problem of educational evaluation is central. Without some sort of convincing idea of how this problem can be solved it seems hardly worthwhile if not actually damaging to continue to present new policy initiatives either at government, institution or individual levels. To continue with a seemingly endless stream of initiatives without the means adequately to evaluate them may be likened to digging holes without knowing where to dig and how deep to go. We need to stop looking for either/or type solutions to this central problem. It is not helpful to alternate between the idea that there is an objective method of evaluating educational development and the idea that educational development is guided by personal preference. After all at the individual level we often make rational decisions without recourse to either of the alternatives mentioned above. For example we recognize problems, debate possible solutions to these problems and proceed sometimes by continuing to reformulate the problems and solutions as we go along in consultation with others.

All of this begs a number of important questions central to moral philosophy concerned with objectivity, rationality and values.[12] The way that we see things affects what we come to regard as problems. Moreover we do not see things in exactly the same way and so our perception of a problem is itself value-laden and not amenable to identification within the empiricist notion of value-neutrality. Theoretical reflection about purpose and rationality is not part of the empiricist tradition that sustains current arrangements for policy-making. It is always possible therefore for policy-makers and evaluators to deny that a problem exists. Political advantage may be gained by such denial. After all it is never comfortable and may be politically disastrous to have one's prior assumptions and policy mistakes open to public scrutiny and debate. As long as things seem to be going reasonably well then there may be few reasons for policy-makers to reflect that they could be mistaken.

Those people who presently control and manage education systems might argue that the objectivity of their judgements and hence the rationality of their decisions is based on their experience of listening to differing opinions, weighing up various alternatives and estimating the likely consequences of implementation. No paradox of objectivity is apparent in this claim. Educational development is located within the system and is based on experience of the system. There might however be the suspicion of subjectivity and complacency. For example, we may wonder how many instances of anomalies and problems there has to be in the system before those who control and manage it begin to take seriously the view that radical reform might be necessary. After all, one of the causes of the putative crisis might be the attitude and values of the controllers and managers themselves.

It is not just managers and controllers who might be concerned to maintain the *status quo*. Everyone who is professionally concerned with the education system is unlikely to be inclined to criticize it for to do so could be interpreted as a form of self-denigration.[13] Unless scepticism is accepted as a normal part of the ethos within which educational professionals work, then they are unlikely to engage openly in the kind of theoretical reflection that might lead them continually to review not only their own procedures but also the procedures that are embedded within the system for distinguishing between development and regression. However the language of educational development is dominated by positive rather than reflective metaphors. Scepticism does not cohere easily with phrases like 'coping with change', 'meeting challenges' and 'forming action plans'. There is not much room in any of this for the idea that the system is in need of radical reform.

On the other hand it seems to be politically convenient sometimes to find evidence to support the claim that education systems across the so-called liberal capitalist democracies are in crisis. Some politicians and industrialists assert that their national system is not promoting economic development and that basic standards are in decline.[14] For example some members of the British Government of the early 1980s argued that the British education system was in need of radical reform. Educational professionals were demonized as either harmful or ineffective and the market-led reforms were set in motion. It was supposed that the market would introduce a much-needed dose of objectivity to educational decision-making as educational professionals were forced to respond to the demands of those who they were meant to serve. In that way the supposed self-interest of the professional would be balanced against the supposed objectivity of the market. The educational system would be regulated by a combination of élitism and consumerism.

The introduction of consumerism to education systems has not led, however, to a decrease in the tensions that are straining the integrity of those systems. These strains and tensions are often apparent at the receiving end as it were. Here the sharp effects of policies made in abstraction from practical realities are felt most clearly. The attempt to institute a national curriculum in England and Wales provides a good example of such a tension. Initial proposals for highly complex arrangements have been the subject of extensive modification in the face of concerted protests from those who have tried to implement these arrangements.[15]

More generally there is a growing realization that many students are still badly served by present arrangements to educate them. For example in many countries there has been a continuing stream of initiatives designed to offer the so called 'less academically gifted' students what is termed a vocational education. Such an education is supposed to contribute to national economic prosperity, social harmony and individual satisfaction. However parts of these countries are characterized by high rates of unemployment, lawlessness and individual dissatisfaction. There is a deep irony and considerable risk of harm involved in the promotion of vocational education in these circumstances. Moreover while tensions and difficulties such as these are plainly undesirable and generally recognized as such that does not mean that the education system is most in need of radical reform. Instead these tensions and difficulties may be the results of a failure in social policy generally.

All political systems reflect or sustain some balance between an individual's freedom and a limitation on that freedom in favour of a notion of a common good. The so-called mixed economies reflect that balance in a form of economic liberalism within which individuals should be free within the law to pursue private profits by providing goods and services which people want. On this view the market is the fairest and most efficient means of distributing many goods and services. Some politicians of the political right go further than this however in claiming that the common good is served best by minimum government interference with market mechanisms.[16]

According to the balance outlined above education systems may be viewed as services that are purchased by parents, students, industrialists and others and that these consumers should expect to have similar rights and relations to each other as consumers of any other type of service. By now we might expect to see a proliferation of different types of educational institutions offering differing provisions with little in common other than success in providing what people want at an economic rate. Yet this has not happened. In many countries there is a statutory common curriculum. There are roughly similar working conditions within educational institutions. There is a statutory school leaving age and a limited range of examinations on offer. In short so-called consumers may be seen to have a very limited choice that is controlled tightly by government.

What has happened is that the logic of individual consumerism has become tangled with the logic of securing the common good through collective economic development. The tangle began when governments in the capitalist democracies challenged the idea that the education budget was well-spent. It ought not to have surprised educational theorists of the liberal persuasion that that challenge would be met by framing educational accountability in ways that resemble those that are in operation in business and commerce. After all, many people earn their living in business and commerce and are familiar with this form of accounting. In some ways those liberal theorists might have welcomed the move to an increase in consumer choice. Ironically the logic of individual consumerism is not that incompatible with liberalism. Moreover the notion of an educational consumer satisfies the demand for accountability. However, the product on offer was defined in terms of its contribution to national economic prosperity rather than individual needs and the drive to vocationalism and managerialism in curriculum gained momentum at the expense of some liberal ideals.

The reasons for these shifts in educational debate and the resulting entanglement may be easy to understand. However, the reasons for the inertia of educational practices to keep pace with the debate and the reluctance of governments to disentangle two logics in education policy are not at all clear. Those changes that have taken place seem concerned more with an increase in the management and administration of existing institutions rather than the creation of innovatory new practices designed to meet the needs of an emerging educational market. It is as if debate and action, theory and practice are somehow passing each other by.

Perhaps there has been a political loss of nerve to follow through the logic of securing the common good through market-led policies. Instead we seem to have been left with an extreme form of subjectivism in which radical rhetoric is combined with institutional conservatism. When theory and practice become detached in this way the educational conversation begins to close down. Somehow market-driven reforms have left many of the features of the older liberal rhetoric in place. Thus we find talk of needs mixed with talk of wants – values mixed with prices – evaluation mixed with quality. We find teachers viewed as deliverers of an educational product, the cumulative effect of which is meant to secure economic development. However we also find people who believe that they and their children will have a more fulfilling life if they are educated in the traditional liberal way. These people believe that they have educational needs that are best satisfied if they are taught by teachers who have a broad but systematic view of things. They despair at the amount of documentation that is available to prescribe the activity of teachers and they believe that while the educative endeavour is immensely complex, the documentation associated with it need not be. Finally they recognize that there is an urgent need for rational agreement upon a range of issues so that reform of the education system might not preclude them from contributing to the public conversation about education.

Lest it be thought that all this has little or nothing to do with the practical realities of teaching and learning it is worth contextualizing the notions of élitism, consumerism, accountability and an overlapping consensus in an imaginary example of a parent's evening. During the course of such an evening parents as consumers may believe that they have an opportunity to ensure that teachers are accountable for the way that a certain part of the taxpayer's money is spent on the education of their children. Teachers may explain that they are attempting to follow the guidelines that have been prepared for them by an elite group that has been charged with the responsibility for interpreting Government Policy. They may point out that as consumers, parents may choose to send their children elsewhere if they are unhappy with the service that they have received.

Were teachers and parents to follow the logic of educational consumerism then the above scenario might be played out many times. Yet few parents have exercised their choice as consumers in this way and this fact should not surprise us. In the first case the educational product is defined in a standard way by a professional group so there is little point in parents moving their children elsewhere – the product should remain the same. The method of delivery or service however might differ from teacher to teacher. However parents do not have a choice of preferred teacher, merely preferred school. Hence choice becomes a lottery between unknown teachers who happen to work in different schools.

In the second case many parents recognize that teaching is not best characterized as someone doing something to a collection of individuals but that teaching is a communal activity in which interpersonal relationships are complex and important. If there is a perception that a particular student could do better that does not mean that it is the sole responsibility of the teacher to ensure improvement. Finally many parents recognize that it is not necessarily helpful to anyone if they engage in what might turn out to be an ill-informed and one-sided critique of a particular teacher.

The logic of consumerism and elitism are largely irrelevant to the conversation that takes place as part of many parents' evenings. Instead it seems to be more helpful to view such occasions as an opportunity to learn from people who have a different perspective on a particular student. The logic of an overlapping consensus allows the participants to engage in dialogue and to debate difference between them based on an idea of what the participants share in the way of educational values. Now it seems reasonable for parents generally to expect teachers to be rather more able to articulate a range of educational options than themselves. Therefore it seems reasonable for teachers as part of their training and in-service development to practise such articulation. In particular it seems reasonable for teachers to have some grasp of the issues that are discussed in books such as this so that when they are asked to justify their actions they can offer better responses than 'I am just following the system' or 'it was just a matter of personal preference'.

There is now an increasing realization that consumerism is the most appropriate regulatory mechanism where the point of contact between consumer and supplier is least in need of regulation. That is why the privatization of the water and electricity industries in the UK have been less well regarded than the privatization of the steel and shipbuilding industries. (Some of course would argue that none of the privatizations have been successful.) The point is however that in the former case it is not clear that there is any market operating at all where customers have no choice as to who supplies them with water and electricity. In the latter case customers do have a genuine choice between suppliers even if some of those suppliers might be seen to be subsidized more heavily than their competitors.

Now if it makes sense to refer to the point of contact between customers and suppliers in an educational context, then plainly the point of contact is between teacher and student. Yet students have very little choice over who should teach them. Even where they choose to attend a school in which there is a particularly good group of teachers that does not guarantee that their choice will be realized. Teachers may move, students have little say in the classes they take. Moreover unless governments are prepared to give up entirely on the idea of equality of opportunity then some form of regulation is inevitable if only to ensure that there is some equity in resource allocation.

Of course both the collection and distribution of resources and the broad formulation of education policy are essentially matters for government. However it is important for any government to be able to justify its decisions on the basis of argument that goes beyond the appeal to majority voting. It is not as if a procedure for rational decision-making can be devised that somehow determines all decisions in abstraction from individual and collective human interests. In particular politicians will always have an interest in educational policies which promote their particular political persuasion.

POLICY

According to empiricism, policy may be described as the statement designed to bring about a desired state of affairs – a statement of values in the form of desired ends. As we have seen an empiricist ethos does not help us to determine what these ends might be other than through a combination of elitism or consumerism. Whereas the logic of consumerism depends upon market-research into individual wants, the logic of elitism depends upon justifications of decisions about collective needs. The notion of wanting something is quite straightforward. People are supposed to know what they want and they are not obliged to justify those wants. On the other hand there is something more urgent about a need. Moreover people may not necessarily know what they need. The notion of needs implies that there is someone or some group that has superior knowledge and insight that enables them to determine another's need and to justify that determination.

When educational policy-makers attempt to justify their decisions, they often appeal to the idea that societal needs can be satisfied by developments in the education system. These people use phrases like 'the changing needs of contemporary society' and not unreasonably they argue that educational development should relate to changes in society generally. However to attempt to justify a particular educational development on the basis of a response to changing needs presupposes a number of assumptions: first, that education in general and education systems in particular are the same thing; second, that an education system should be primarily reactive in its relation to society – students should fit in to an existing collective order rather than help to shape the way that that collective order develops; third, that the needs of society are, have been and will be identifiable; and finally, that there are means of checking whether the development actually does satisfy the perceived needs or whether the development simply creates more problems which in time become interpreted as some other needs of the then contemporary society.

These needs are not of equal value however nor are all societal needs readily translatable into educational needs. It seems that there is a further political need to prioritize societal needs and to determine the kind of development that will lead to their satisfaction. Government might be easy were it not for the fact that this apparently limitless number of societal needs have to be satisfied by a finite number of resources. It is relatively easy to direct resources towards a large number of initiatives. It is much more difficult to ensure that sufficient resources are available to sustain those initiatives in the longer term. In the case of education there is always a danger that the education system will be overloaded with initiatives that are not sustainable. The problem is that presently those who control the system and those who prioritize its responses have no mechanism for detecting when this overload might occur.

A seemingly endless stream of initiatives may lead to a deterioration in the set of human relations that once sustained certain parts of certain educational institutions. This deterioration occurs simply because people overloaded with work begin to look to their colleagues to check to see that the overload is evenly distributed. The notion of even distribution of workload is notoriously problematic however particularly in a hierarchical management structure where people are paid at different rates. There will always be the temptation therefore to reward those institutions and those individuals that best demonstrate that a politically sensitive and therefore fashionable societal need has been met.

It is recognized that the quality of teaching and student learning deteriorates beneath this welter of new initiatives. Were the system to be regulated exclusively by consumerism, then we might have expected market-research to have indicated that no-one actually wants this deterioration and we might have expected market-mechanisms to have ensured that the deterioration did not take place. As it is however a good deal of elitism coupled with an inadequate methodology for determining priorities has led us into a crisis in educational policy development and a consequent overloading of the curriculum.

CASE EXEMPLAR

CURRICULUM OVERLOAD

In an interesting study Broadfoot and Osborn (1988) compared the professional responsibilities of teachers in France to those of teachers in England and Wales. In France they found a system that is similar to the one that is described in this book. Teaching is seen as an induction into a cultural inheritance through a traditional pedagogy. Assessment of achievement and teacher accountability is relatively unproblematic because French teachers accept responsibility for academic not social outcomes and they are selected for employment on the basis of a thorough knowledge of subjects.

In contrast British teachers are expected to keep up to date with a continuing stream of developments in curriculum, management and assessment. They are expected to become familiar with information technology, personal and social development often involving liaison with social services. They are expected to combat racism and sexism, to implement schemes of European awareness, health education and supposed developments in pedagogy such as cooperative teaching and differentiated learning. In all these cases British teachers not only have to try to understand what these supposed developments mean and to implement particular schemes but also simply to accept that things will improve if they spend more time on the developments than on their day-to-day teaching.

They may wonder for example whether the French are disadvantaged by their lack of such 'exciting new initiatives' or whether systems that rely on strong traditions in which there is a reluctance to impose new initiatives do not have something going for them. (See the case exemplar about the Irish Education System p. 42.) Again we return to the central difficulty that needs to be taken most seriously by educational practitioners and that is to recognize that not all developments may be progressive, however progressive they sound. For example, we may not best combat racism by the production and use of anti-racist teaching packs, however plausible the use of these packs might seem. There is something superficial about the view that a problem as complex as racism can usefully be tackled by the issuing of packs. Instead such a problem is embedded within a range of practices and the way that those practices have developed over long periods of time. Only teachers who are knowledgeable within those practices are able to analyse practice with students to enable a deeper understanding of how the problem might be tackled at both a personal and social level.

To return to the French comparison, it is not as if French teachers are unaware of racism, nor that they would wish to condone it. Indeed it is hard to see for example how certain novels or periods in history could usefully be discussed without some discussion of racism. A similar argument could be applied to many of the other problems for which the British response has been the production of yet more guidelines, policies and packages whereas the French response seems to have been to trust teachers and not to try to make schools cover everything!

PRACTICE

Even though consumerism does not seem to have helped us to distinguish between development and regression in education policy, it is widely believed that market-led educational practice is desirable. In many countries legislation has been introduced with the aim of shifting power away from the producers of education to its consumers, from the professionals to non-professionals. Systems of devolved school management, devolved management of resources and grant-maintained schools have proliferated across the world.

The supporters of market-led educational practice might draw an analogy between a factory that makes televisions and the present public education system. According to this analogy, presently there is only one factory available which makes a very limited range of televisions. Few televisions can be relied upon to work correctly. The work force complain bitterly about conditions in the factory while their representatives or advisors attempt to assure consumers about the quality of the televisions. Consumers are supposed to recognize the virtue of equality of opportunity when it comes to acquiring a television at a state-subsidized price.

The market-led remedy for this state of affairs is to privatize the factory – not into a private monopoly, nor into a series of private enterprises constrained by legislation to produce a standard product. Instead state subsidy should be directed towards setting up several new television factories, the products of which will be judged in the market place. If consumers want them, then the new factory flourishes while the old one declines. Thus consumers should have a range of products on offer. Comparisons may be made between products on the basis of well understood criteria like reliability and picture clarity. In addition for the first time producers should have comparable enterprises against which to judge their own performance.

This remedy seems to have much to commend it, appealing as it does to our deep-rooted ideas of fair play in competition and to the idea that measurement depends upon the possibility of comparison. Put simply we need alternative products on offer which share an overlapping range of similarities in order to make comparisons and have real choices. The supporters of this remedy might claim that just as the running of a television factory is not thought to be much of a political issue, so too an education system might be run on politically neutral lines by managers dedicated to meet the demands of the market.

It is worth rehearsing the reasons why the market-driven analogy is limited. First it is not clear how fair competition is to be assured. If people are considered to be the raw materials for the education system then it should be noted that we do not have (nor may we want) any reliable ways of measuring their potential educational quality. Even if a material state subsidy could be fairly divided among the competing subsystems, it is not clear how quality in raw material could be fairly divided. The same problem arises at the output stage: if people are to be considered to be part of the output, then again we do not have any reliable ways of comparing their quality. The most important limitation arises however because it is not possible to ensure a uniform interpretation of education policy nor a uniform interpretation of quality in education. To return to the analogy it may not be possible to produce a standardized television set or any sort of television set if the production workers do not interpret the plans in a standard way. Neither the plans themselves nor statements purporting to guarantee quality are of any interest to consumers of television sets. Their interest is in the set itself.

In the case of education it is not possible to isolate an educational product as it were. Policies and quality statements are of little long-term value in themselves. The nearest that we get to the idea of an educational product which consumers want is through the notion of good teaching. However good teaching is located within a system that is both reactive and proactive in its relationship with other aspects of society. Development does not take place in a linear continuous manner towards some pre-determined goal. Moreover in many cases people do not have any clear idea of the nature of the society they want. Instead people value different things at different times and their language is not especially suited to the clear expression of those values.

CASE EXEMPLAR

MARKETS LIMIT CHOICE IN EDUCATION[17]

It is widely believed that a market in biscuit production is a good thing because it enables consumers to have a wider choice of biscuits which they actually want rather than a standard biscuit that is produced for them by a state factory. Why should the same logic not apply in the case of schools? Quite simply because a customer cannot add or contribute anything to a biscuit whereas educational customers, whoever they might be, will necessarily add and contribute something. Those customers who have more to add and contribute in terms of both money and expertise will make the collective product more attractive to other customers and thus the school will become bigger. At the same time less popular schools which may be only marginally worse than the perceived best schools will be threatened and may close. What we end up with therefore is a small number of large schools which are perceived to be good and which will tend to be located in the prosperous areas and other schools which are perceived to be 'sink' schools located in areas in which housing is cheap. If the State intervenes to support the 'sink schools' then it distorts the market so that there becomes little or no incentive for other schools to strive to improve. A greater subsidy will be seen to result from being perceived to be poor.

A period of apparent choice for some leads to a diminution of choice not only for the poor but ultimately for everybody. The same logic may be seen to apply in the case of Universities where the removal of the so-called binary divide has led to the emergence of a top group of 'Ivy League' type Universities and the rest. It is hard to imagine why anyone would wish to pursue policies that so obviously lead to a diminution of choice and opportunity for some people from birth as it were. There may have been many problems with the so-called liberal consensus but educational consumerism does not seem to help solve many of those problems. To imagine that attempts to standardize teaching practice within a market would ensure equality of opportunity as if such practice could ever be standardized independent of the people involved in the attempt seems foolish and wrong.

Certainly the way that they speak reflects those things that they value and they are not precluded from expressing principled preferences. However, it is foolish to suppose that people could somehow choose from a range of long-term forms of nirvana. It seems to be even more foolish to suppose that an education system could be set up as the primary means of achieving one of those forms. On the other hand, some people think that they know exactly what they want society to be like and they are far from reticent in expressing their views.

SUMMARY

In this chapter we have seen how an empiricist ethos pervades many education systems at the present time and how empiricism leads to a combination of elitism and consumerism as a methodology for educational evaluation. This methodology is increasingly regarded with suspicion by educational professionals and non-professionals alike despite its use in the evaluation of many other aspects of our communal life. In these cases a group is responsible for taking decisions on behalf of everyone else and if the group consistently makes mistakes then the political system allows for its replacement.

In the case of the education system, not only have all people had first-hand experience of the system as students themselves but also the results of decisions affecting the education system take far longer to assess than other areas of public endeavour. Moreover the 'results' are not so easily separable from the effects of social policy generally. So in many cases the membership of an elite has changed before the result of its policies can be detected. Hence a consumerist check on the decisions of the elite is virtually impossible and an important means of legitimizing educational development is lost.

It is hardly surprising therefore that education professionals are particularly susceptible to the charge that they are self-serving. Not only are they necessarily concerned with a plurality of strongly held educational beliefs but also they must look to each other to provide the means of support for the actions that they have taken. Consumerism was meant to provide a counterbalance to elitism and to shift power away from the suppliers to the consumers. However this shift in power takes place only when the consumers feel sufficiently detached from the suppliers to criticize without fear of retribution. In the case of education not only is this detachment practically impossible but also detachment is undesirable. For example it is desirable that parents work with teachers in the education of their children rather than as critics of their children's teachers. Moreover teachers may try to defer criticism by adopting a defensive attitude to their work.

Commitment to particular educational institutions works against the consumerist ethic as does the practical difficulty of assembling a range of educational 'products' for the consumer to choose from. Moreover the supplier in education is able to influence the consumer because complaints procedures are not straightforward. To use an analogy taken from the health service, patients are not going to complain about the nurse if they are dependent on that nurse for care in the future. Similarly students are not likely to complain about the teacher if their examination results depend upon that teacher's reference. In short we can explain why the present combination of elitism and consumerism cannot function effectively in the case of education and why in this fundamental respect the system should be reformed if we are to have any means rationally of choosing the best course of educational action. That is not to preclude some form of leadership or management. Nor is it to deny that both educational policy and practice must pay some regard to what people want. While neither the idea of consumerism nor elitism is sufficient in the regulation of an education system, it seems that these ideas must form some part of any improved attempt to regulate the system. In the next chapter we begin to work out an alternative educational theory that puts teaching and learning at the centre of the system and that includes a democratic discursive methodology for educational evaluation.

NOTES AND REFERENCES

1. See Usher and Edwards (1994) for an account of the impact of post-modernist thinking on the theory and practice of education. See also the *Journal of Philosophy of Education*, 29(1) March 1995 for four papers on postmodernism.
2. According to Popper (1945), it is not possible to proceed by way of formulating a grand vision of what ought to be and devising methods to achieve that vision. Instead we must confront the problems that face us now and try to solve these problems in a piecemeal manner.
3. See Murdoch (1970, 1992).
4. See Bernstein (1983) for a discussion of the objectivism/relativism dichotomy.
5. Much of Gadamer's work may be seen to be concerned with such retrieval. See also Taylor (1989).
6. See Haydon (1991).
7. See Halliday (1990, Chapters 1 and 2) for a more comprehensive account of the theory-practice relationship.
8. See Humes (1986).
9. Wittgenstein (1953, PI 241) writes:

   'So you are saying that human agreement decides what is true and what is false?' – It is what human beings *say* that is true and false: and they agree in the *language* they use. That is not agreement in opinions but in form of life. (italics in original)

   Wittgenstein draws our attention to the way that language is grounded in a form of life not in a 'picture' of reality. Despite cultural differences, humans share a basic form of life which includes certain characteristic ways of responding to and recognizing pain and suffering. We build up our 'common sense' ways of doing and describing things on the basis of a shared form of life.
10. The term 'touchstone' is used by Lakatos (1976). See also Aspin and Chapman (1994, p. 29), for a further discussion of 'touchstone' and its application in the solution of educational problems.
11. Evers and Lakomski (1991) provide a comprehensive critique of all forms of foundationalism.
12. See D. Carr (1993) for a useful overview of some of these questions. See also Carr (1991).
13. Taylor (1985b, p. 49) writes:

   The structures of this civilisation, interdependent work, bargaining, mutual adjustment of individual ends, are beginning to change their meaning for many, and are beginning to be felt not as normal and best suited to man, but as hateful or empty. And yet we are all caught in these inter-subjective meanings in so far as we live in this society, and in a sense more and more all-pervasively as it progresses. Hence the virulence and tension of the critique of our society which is always in some real sense a self-rejection.

14. In the USA, 'A Nation at Risk' (in Gross and Gross (eds) 1985) was followed by the *Carnegie Forum on Education and the Economy* (1986) and a number of other reports with a similar theme. In the UK the *National Commission on Education* (1993) has recently made a number of suggestions for fundamental changes to be made to the British system of education. Callaghan's Ruskin College Speech (1976) is widely credited as a significant acknowledgement of a lack of international competitiveness in the UK and an anti-industrial bias in the education system.

15. I refer here to the 'Dearing Review' (Dearing, 1994).

16. See Hayek (1960, 1976). See also Gray (1993) for an account of the moral foundations of market institutions. Chubb and Moe (1990) has also been very influential.

17. For a more detailed account of how markets limit choice in education, see Ranson (1994), especially pp. 97–8 on a 'prisoners dilemma'. See also Jonathan (1990).

Chapter 2

Tradition, Theory and Authenticity

As we saw in the previous chapter the dominance of empiricism in education leads to the separation of policy from theory and from practice. Policy-makers determine the ends, theorists determine the means and practitioners do the work. It is argued in this chapter that this dominance leads to inauthentic practice at all levels as authentic practice is characterized by an interweaving of ends and means, thought and action.[1] It is also argued that teaching is the most important educational practice and that teachers necessarily are committed to certain enmeshed accounts of means and ends that might be said to constitute practical theories on which they base their actions and according to which they define themselves.

In the first part of this chapter we examine some theories of learning and outline an interpretive account of learning that helps us to consider afresh the relationship between policy, theory and practice in education. This examination is meant to suggest that many problems that beset education systems presently are not so much problems with inadequate theories of pedagogy, inadequate teachers or inadequate guidance for teachers but systemic problems that may be solved by reforming educational institutions on more democratic lines. We then go on to consider the implications of these reforms for attempts to distinguish between good and bad practice.

LEARNING THEORY

According to empiricism, educational theory is concerned principally with how people learn and how institutions may best be managed to facilitate learning. This emphasis on theories of learning and management has led to the dominance of psychology as the theoretical practice most concerned with educational theory.[2] For a while the psychology of education was concerned principally with behaviourism – the theory that learning is a change in observable behaviour. Based on experiments with animals and birds some influential behaviourists suggested that people would learn the correct responses to stimuli if those responses were reinforced in some way perhaps by praising the learner or giving them some materials that they wanted.

Thus it became fashionable for teachers to praise children whenever they got something right.

Perhaps the most trenchant criticism of behaviourism is that people learn many things without there being any change in their behaviour. Moreover behaviourism seems to suggest that learning may only be motivated by extrinsic means and that learnt behaviour will be extinguished unless the necessary reinforcers continue. In that case we may wonder whether behaviourism describes learning at all since the possibility of people going on to learn on their own seems essential to any adequate account of learning.

For these reasons and others many psychologists have turned to cognition as the key concept in understanding learning. As is the case with behaviourism there are many different types of cognitive psychology. For example gestalt theorists argue that learning is a process of gaining or changing insights, expectations or thought patterns. They share with other cognitive psychologists the idea that there is some internal cognitive structure that is somehow modified when people learn. That cognitive structure is supposed to affect bodily movement in some way and so while learning does not necessarily result in an immediate change in behaviour, the disposition to behave differently may be traced to a change in cognitive structure.

We may wonder however just what cognitive structure might be other than material states of the brain. If learning is to be interpreted as a change in brain state then the obvious research programme for psychologists to follow is to try to identify which brain states correlate with learning particular practices. At the present time such a research programme is pursued often using computer models of neural networks in order to try to show how such networks are based on known physiological aspects of the brain. In that way it is assumed that algorithms of learning might be discovered.[3] Such research may well lead to interesting theory. To date however it is not clear that teachers and others practically involved in education can draw much from this research to illuminate their practice.

It has always struck me as odd that a supposed scientific approach to educational theory that has had so few unproblematic applications should have dominated teacher training for so long. As one of the authors of a popular introductory text in the psychology of education points out:

> Before students adopt the orientation of one family of psychology or the other, they should recognise that objections may be made to any position one takes in psychology and to any currently available theory of learning ... there is wide divergence on how a given interpretation should be applied to the solution of a concrete learning problem ... A psychologist's philosophical leaning may ... influence the conclusion he draws from the evidence that is secured through experimentation.[4]

This admission further casts doubt on empiricism and highlights the importance of philosophy to educational theory.

Many philosophers argue that the cognitive science research programme is bound to fail because it conflates brains with minds in an attempt to pass by the problems of human agency and the social nature of learning. One of the central points they make is that words like 'belief', 'know' and 'mind' are meaningful because of the role that they play in social practices and that those practices make it possible to check whether these words are used correctly. When an attempt is made to correlate these words with particular configurations in the brain then the problem arises as to how this identification is to be checked. If the identification is to be checked by experiment then it is hard to see how the knowledge itself (whatever that might be) for example is to be distinguished from the use of the word 'knowledge'. The same problem seems to arise in the case of other words that are commonly used to conceptualize learning.[5]

For the time being therefore it looks as if teachers will have to make do with the best stories that they can collect about learning from whatever source those stories emanate including philosophy and common sense. According to common sense and Aristotelian philosophy we learn a practice by working with those who are accomplished in that practice as an apprentice as it were. We are shown what to do and encouraged to try things out for ourselves. Our attempts are corrected and the teacher encourages us to make further progress. We are socialized into practices from birth onwards and we learn to extend the range of practices in which we can engage by looking for connections between a new practice and a practice with which we are familiar. For example, from being accomplished tennis players we may move on to play badminton through the use of similar tools such as rackets, familiar terms such as courts and familiar procedures such as rule-following. To take another example we may learn about a new country by looking for similarities with features of a country with which we are familiar.

We do not have to know exactly how these moves are made in order to encourage them. Teachers may develop a range of techniques to help people to 'cotton on' as it were. What is important and somehow mysterious is why some people seem to want to learn whereas others seem content not to try to extend the range of practices in which they have an interest. Again teachers develop a range of techniques to encourage learners to go on on their own – they appeal to their authority, to extrinsic rewards, to peer pressure and to punishments. They try to encourage learners to work things out for themselves and throw away, as it were, the 'ladder'[6] that was provided by motivational techniques such as personal liking of the teacher that were used to try to engage the learner's imagination and interest.

Readers will recognize that the above account of learning theory is merely the briefest of sketches of a vast range of connected topics. For example, there is a massive literature in the philosophy of education that is concerned with the idea of personal autonomy as a main aim of a liberal education.[7] According to that idea education should be liberating in the sense that educated people are able to interpret their predicament within practices in which they have become familiar and imagine new ways of thinking and acting without being constrained by the norms and values of the familiar. That is in contrast to the idea of indoctrination, the main function of which is to induct learners into practices with the intention that learners should not see beyond those practices.

There is a sense of course in which all people are autonomous in that they choose what they want to do and education could hardly be said to be concerned with this weak sense of the term. There is a stronger sense of the term however that is much more educationally interesting. Used in this way a person may be said to be autonomous if they act according to reason rather than inclination and if their reasoning is sufficiently developed to enable them to consider possibilities that go beyond what they have achieved to date. Those possibilities would need to be achievable however. We would not consider someone to be autonomous if they always tried to do things that were entirely fanciful. Nor would we consider them autonomous if their reasoning was

CASE EXEMPLAR

MORAL EDUCATION IN THE CURRICULUM

Moral education tends to be thought of as an education that is concerned with dilemmas of a particular type that are most obviously contentious and evaluative. This tendency may be seen to be related to the fact-value distinction which is a feature of empiricism as well as other philosophical theories. If it is accepted that the fact-value distinction is not sharp, as I argue, then a more extensive conception of moral education is possible which is explored in this exemplar.

It is widely believed that study of the humanities is an important part of a moral education. Indeed the traditional liberal arts or grammar school curriculum may be seen to be closely related to the idea that moral awareness depends upon an understanding of intrinsic values which study of the humanities is best placed to encourage. However one of the reasons for what has been described as the breakdown in the post-war liberal consensus[8] about education was that a majority of students were not engaged by the humanities curriculum as it was instituted.[9] If students could not be motivated intrinsically in this way then it was assumed that some extrinsic motivation in the form of a vocational education would be appropriate. On the face of it vocational education conceived in this way as an instrumental activity is disastrous as moral education. Students are hardly likely to come to see some things as intrinsically worthwhile if they are led to believe that practices are worthwhile only in so far as they lead to some materialistic rewards.

It is a mistake to distinguish between the liberal and the vocational in this way.[10] All practices can be described as both vocational and liberal. Moreover it is not easy to distinguish between extrinsic and intrinsic motivations, moral and instrumental concerns. For example joiners may install doors because it is technically correct to do so but also because they do not want anyone to be hurt by a dangerous installation. An artist may be intrinsically motivated to paint a picture even though the picture has been commissioned. Moreover teachers can recall students who at one time were uninterested in a practice only to become enthusiast practitioners at a later stage.

Now the upshot of this discussion is that moral education may not only be encouraged through induction into the humanities, nor even through any practice known as moral education or moral practice. Instead moral education may be encouraged through induction into any practice that is moral and in which students come to do something for its own sake and not for extrinsic rewards or to avoid punishment. If proof were needed of this then we only need consider those joiners, hairdressers and builders who were not engaged at school and who missed out on an early induction into the humanities but who nevertheless lead decent and interesting lives and come to enjoy novels and music later in life.[11]

purely technical and they were incapable of re-thinking their inclinations and desires in the light of experience.

The notion of autonomy seems to refer to an ideal that pays little attention to the practical nature of experience and the interplay between reason, experience and inclination. For example, it is not clear how the virtues of spontaneity and humility relate to the supposed educational ideal of autonomy. That is not to say that inclinations to act spontaneously and an inability to go on justifying courses of action might not themselves be rational in the sense that they embody justifiable values. Instead it is to argue that it is not possible to justify every course of action even if it were desirable to do so. Wittgenstein[12] reminds us that justifications must end somewhere. We may suggest that justifications end in the unreflective behaviour that is constitutive of and understandable within a practical tradition. Within such traditions, people sometimes just act and trust others to act in morally correct ways. This argument has implications for courses in moral education.

Let us consider the problem of trying to teach students who, for one reason or another, have little sense of self-worth and have never recognized excellence in anything. Instead of imagining that there must be a way of solving this problem through a curriculum component called moral education, we may simply have to accept that any one teacher, however good, may never engage the interest of students of this sort. The best we can do is to provide as many opportunities as possible within schools for students to choose practices in which they might become engaged. It is a mistake to continue to try to prescribe all aspects of the curriculum as if the interests of students could be ignored and as if certain practices were essential components of a moral education for all students. Even if students do not come to be excellent themselves in a practice, they may come to recognize a good from a bad performance as an essential part of a moral education and an essential prerequisite for rational debate. If they do not come to recognize those things at school then they may still come to recognize them elsewhere.

The idea that a liberal education may be achieved only through an induction into just six or seven forms of knowledge has led us badly astray in our formal attempts to educate. We have not been helped either by an over-emphasis on the ideal of autonomy as if educated people were knowledgeable so that they could act *on* the world and as if all moral actions were based on knowledge. We may be inclined to say that if morally educated people are the ones we would most like to spend our time with then we prefer those who accept that they act *in* the world often by remaining silent when they do not know what to do and by simply going along with practical tradition. In that way moral education consists in being initiated in some worthwhile practice as an essential prerequisite for developing a breadth of understanding sufficient to respond appropriately to circumstances which life presents.

These sorts of consideration lead me to draw on the idea of authenticity[13] both as an educational aim and as an essential concept in educational evaluation. We have already touched on this idea and it is developed further throughout this book. However it may be helpful to say a little more about the idea at this stage. It is usual to define authenticity as that which is achieved when people take hold of the direction of their own lives without the direction being determined for them by external factors. To take hold of one's own life seems to imply both an examination of one's capacities for taking stock of what one is *and* of what one might become. But of course the two sorts of examination are interconnected. Tradition enables authenticity by providing a stable background against which to frame possibilites and to distinguish self-interests from those interests that are distorted by ends imposed on people from without the tradition.

The possibility of authenticity depends both on individual reflection and a community that is sufficiently open to enable its members to distinguish between ends that are imposed on them from ends that are considered to be intrinsically good. That is not however to imply that all forms of professional communities must be inauthentic because their members are paid. Nor is it to imply that authentic practices are only those practices that are characterized by a great deal of talk. Rather it is to say that authentic communities preserve what is intrinsically worthwhile from the tendency for extrinsic considerations to dominate. Farming communities can be just as authentic as academic discussion groups!

We may recognize authenticity in teaching as a balance between a commitment to goodness that informs particular actions and an openness to the possibility that one might have made a mistake. That balance is demonstrated in a respect for the views of others combined with a scepticism about forms of directives. In that way it is appropriate simply to act in some circumstances, sometimes to deliberate, sometimes to hesitate and sometimes to listen. It follows therefore that it can only be on the basis of a sort of apprenticeship into an authentic community that one comes to act authentically.

We have seen that the idea of going beyond the immediate practice in which students have an interest needs to be tempered with the idea of going along with practical tradition. How might this balance be achieved? According to a discursive hermeneutic account of learning,[14] learning may be regarded as a series of conversations between people or a series of interactions between people and situations that may be imagined to be a sort of conversation. Everybody is inducted into some practices from birth and that induction serves as an entry to other practices through conversations with experienced practitioners whom we call teachers. Certain features of all practices are sufficiently routine and well-established for learners simply to copy their teachers without the need for much correction or encouragement. Such copying is a preliminary to learners being encouraged to try things out for themselves and to work out the best way of doing things. Conversation between learner and teacher may be characterized by attempts to check that the learner is on the right lines. At some point this questioning leads to the teacher's admission that she too is unsure. She exhibits an openness to the learner and a willingness to look both within herself and beyond the practice to try to decide what to do. The learner comes to see this kind of openness as characterizing the practice in some way and comes to accept it as normal. No one is giving or taking anything on this account of learning. Heidegger puts this very well when he writes:

> If the student only takes over something which is offered he does not learn. He comes to learn only when he experiences what he takes as something he himself already has. True learning only occurs where the taking of what one already has is a self-giving and is experienced as such. Teaching, therefore, does not mean anything else than to let the others learn, i.e., to bring one another to learning. Learning is more difficult than teaching; for only he who can truly learn – and only as long as he can do it – can truly teach. The genuine teacher differs from the pupil only in that he can learn better and that he more genuinely wants to learn. In all teaching, the teacher learns the most.[15]

When it comes to an interaction between learner and situation the matter is not so easy to understand because an empiricist ethos tends to lead us to imagine that a situation is something extra-linguistic and fixed. We should remember however that situations do not exist apart from people who describe and act in characteristic ways and that we cannot distinguish the situation from the social practices in which the situation has a point and relevance. So just as the background assumptions that people make or their 'prejudices'[16] may change in the course of a conversation with a partner who makes different assumptions, so too the prejudices of tradition that embody characteristic ways of describing the situation may challenge the person's prior assumptions about themselves and their inclinations.

Perhaps the best example of the way that prejudices are embodied within situations comes from our attempts to understand a work of art.[17] Plainly the artist does not speak to us directly but through a representation that somehow engages our interest. If it were the case that we were only ever engaged by works of art and not by people in actual conversations then it is not clear that our artistic interest could be sustained. That is because it is only in the course of normal conversations that we are able to check our interpretation of the work of art even though such checks are oblique in the sense that there is not some final correct interpretation to which we can appeal. Instead we are bound up in what is sometimes called a circle of interpretation in which interpretations may be checked against one another but not against something outside the circle.[18]

CASE EXEMPLAR

TEACH YOURSELF BRIDGE

'Teach yourself books' are common enough. They consist of a text that is used in a context that is not normally part of the practice on which the book is titled. In this case the learner is asked to imagine that they are playing bridge and an appeal is made to their previous experience as a whist player. They are asked to imagine what the other three players' hands might contain and are given conventional rules to guide their imaginary bidding. They try these conventions out in imaginary examples and after turning the page are given an indication of whether they are on the right lines. They might be encouraged to purchase a bridge simulator that enables them to play against pre-programmed players that are represented on a computer screen. After some time they may come to beat the machine on all occasions. We may wonder whether they may be said then to be an expert bridge player.

I suspect not. The only way that they can check their understanding of bridge is to engage in the social practice itself. Certainly we can imagine a community that only plays bridge against each other on the internet or by telephone. Perhaps the practice of bridge may develop in this way in the future. The point is that 'teach yourself' books only work if there is some established social practice against which the learner can check their interpretation of a situation. The book therefore is parasitic upon the actual practice of playing bridge and not a substitute for it.

Notice that prejudices are continually being discarded and refined as a result of reinterpretations and so induction into a practice, as the quote from Heidegger was meant to illustrate, *necessarily* involves the notion of going on on one's own. We may wonder then what is going wrong in schools where some students fail to go anywhere on their own. I suggest that such students are not being inducted into practices at all. They are being taught set routines as if school was primarily a preparation for later life in which they apply these routines in a job or something else. They are taught abstractions of practice that are inauthentic precisely because they are abstractions and have no immediate point or interest either to teachers or students. (Neither may they have any long-term point as the number of jobs that are routine diminishes, if there ever were such jobs.)

This account of learning may be extended in two ways. First it may be extended to explain how linguistic practices develop generally and second it may be extended to explain how policy, theory and practice may be re-conceptualized as strands in an ongoing conversation between different sorts of practitioner. First let us recall that practices are not self contained – they overlap. People are members of different sorts of practical communities to different degrees. All people share certain common responses to human suffering and pain that enables them to communicate with each other however wide their cultural differences. Within cultures, people share rather more than common reactions to human suffering. We call this shared way of interpreting situations, speaking and acting 'common sense'. All practices change as people develop both themselves and the institutions that support the practice. Development occurs as people talk with others who have different practical backgrounds. As we have seen, authentic practices are those where the practitioners are open to possibilities from within the practice but resistant to the imposition of ends from outside the practice.

Let us now consider how policy, theory and practice may be re-conceptualized along the lines of the learning theory advanced above. Educational institutions are collective organizations which have to be managed in some way. We should not imagine however that management is synonymous with control nor that all policies need to be highly specific as if correct interpretations were more likely if more documentation was made available. The opposite may be the case and a broad statement of values may be a much more effective means of communicating intent than highly specific guidelines. All documents have to be interpreted.[19] Rather than imagining that a correct interpretation is one that somehow corresponds to a state of affairs that was in the mind of the writer of the document, we may recognize that interpretation necessarily involves a 'fusion' between the prejudices of the interpreter and the prejudices that are presented by the text. We find it difficult to accept that something new is created in the process of interpretation because our empiricist ethos leads us to believe that the text is an object in the world that is unchanging. We need to accept the idea that textual interpretation cannot be precise and that a state of affairs cannot somehow be pictured accurately once and for all.

When we accept this then we see that there is no point trying to tie down policy as if we could control the future in some way. Instead we start to see the relationship between policy and practice in terms of a conversation between people charged with different but not unrelated tasks. Of course some texts may help that conversation develop. Moreover some theoretical accounts of the prejudices of policy and practice may also help and it may be useful to employ people to theorize in that way. According to this discursive hermeneutic educational theory, policy, theory and practice are merged within practices and conceptualized as strands in an on-going conversation. Just as a division of labour is helpful within some practices, so too in educational practices may a division of labour between policy-makers, theorists and practitioners be helpful. That does not mean that the educational labour force need be organized hierarchically nor that workers of different types need not talk to one another.

We may regard a successful interpretation as one in which the participants come to use the language in which the policy or theory was formed – to make the values on which the policy or theory was based their own. They may be persuaded by arguments and through a process of open debate and discussion and come to incorporate those values and that language into their common sense way of practising. That is to say they come to accept those values and that language as part of the tacit background that informs future practice. Just as a new and superior scientific theory comes to be accepted as part of the tacit background of the practice of scientific research, so too that background often becomes part of a general common sense way of describing the world. For example we know that sticks do not bend when immersed in water but that the light coming off them is refracted through the water. Eskimos hunting for fish with a spear simply act as if they know the laws of refraction although those laws have no place in their practice of fishing.

We go on talking and acting the same way until we are shown some better way of talking and acting. We do not so much decide to accept a new theory as come to talk and act in ways that reflect our acceptance of it.[20] As I argued earlier however even though many criteria for determining good from bad practice are internal to the practice, that does not mean that all criteria are internal or that outsiders cannot have a valid opinion of the practice. There are occasions when the practitioners themselves may believe that the practice is progressing when everyone else believes the opposite. The most obvious and horrific recent example of this was provided by the Nazis during the Second World War. At that time many people learnt to behave in ways that were and are widely regarded as degenerative.

This example may serve as a useful reminder to those who wish to separate ends from means in educational practice. No doubt some Nazis were very efficient killers and efficient teachers of killing but we would not want to suggest that they were engaged in an educational enterprise. We expect educated people to be able to work out for themselves what good practice involves and not to isolate means from ends. That is why the Judges at the Nuremberg Tribunals refused to accept the excuse that the executioners were merely doing their job. It is also why many teachers refuse to accept that their job is a technical matter of achieving ends that they regard as harmful or of little benefit. To be sure people may try to copy prescribed behaviour in an attempt to appear authentic. Yet somehow the nuances are not quite right, they seem too easily to take certain actions and too easily to agree with the *status quo*. They do not display the hesitancy of the authentic practitioner who is never quite sure that they have interpreted the situation correctly. It should be obvious why an empiricist ethos leads to inauthenticity in teaching practice. The idea that interpretation is unproblematic and that, given clear guidelines, people may always achieve set ends leads to the kind of certainty in disposition that does not characterize best teaching practice.

EXISTENTIALISM

We have drawn on the notion of authenticity to develop a better account of educational theory to empiricism. This notion is drawn from existentialist philosophy which is broadly the theory that the fact of human existence precedes the essence of human existence. In other words we are something before we can consider who we are. Existentialists argue against inauthenticity. Sartre for example, uses the term 'bad faith'[21] in place of inauthenticity and describes in a series of novels and theoretical texts the ways that we are more free than we like to suppose we are. He suggests that the 'angst' that comes from realizing this freedom is sufficient to cause us to act in bad faith by denying to ourselves that we have so much freedom.

For example some people may be dissatisfied with their work as professional teachers, but rarely will they face up to the essential freedom that they have to teach as they want or indeed to give up as professional educators all together. Instead they tend to find excuses for constraining their actions. They like guidelines because guidelines seem to limit their freedom and legitimize a decision to do nothing about their unhappy predicament. They rationalize what amounts to an unwillingness to face up to their predicament through acting in bad faith. Empiricism may be seen to offer the ultimate support for this bad faith because all practice for empiricists is directed for us through the supposed superior view of our predicament that is provided by science.

CASE EXEMPLAR

SARTRE'S WAITER[22]

In a famous passage, Sartre describes a café waiter who is a little too attentive and assiduous in performing his tasks: Sartre explains that the waiter is 'playing at being a waiter'. The point of this explanation is that the waiter's being a waiter is always in question because he himself defines who he is and he may define himself as he wishes. Yet he acts as if his role as a waiter were defined for him. The realization of his own freedom to define himself as he likes is alarming and uncomfortable. Since our existence precedes our essence we are continually defining ourselves anew in terms of the practices into which we have been inducted. We cannot appeal to any higher authority than our choice to determine the story that we tell ourselves about ourselves. Sartre insists that we face the anguish of existence without the comforts of self-deception.

From this example we can see that authenticity cannot be decided from outside the person. Authenticity is an issue for the existing individual alone. The authentic individual has faced up to the existential dilemma and the contingency of self.[23] Authenticity is something that can be described however as in the above example. We can sense that there is something inauthentic about the waiter and we can talk about that presumed inauthenticity with others.

CASE EXEMPLAR

THE CAREER TEACHER

They describe themselves as educators. They conform to all the social norms that might be expected of a good teacher yet somehow their behaviour is not quite right. They always describe students in positive terms . . . They are familiar with all the recent policy documents. They never appear tired on a Friday afternoon and are always available for any extra-curricular activity for which a volunteer is needed. Sometimes recognizing that colleagues might think of them as a 'goody goody' they attempt to appear angry at some decision taken by the Head of Department, but they never follow their anger with any action. Their comments are made in private.

Colleagues come to see such a teacher as inauthentic in the sense that this person's life seems to be driven only by ambition and the pursuit of a better *curriculum vitae*. Colleagues recognize something of themselves in this but somehow they do not seem to go to the same lengths. They are ambitious and of course their work is partly directed towards the achievement of financial rewards to support their material existence. Yet these extrinsic concerns do not dominate their practice and they display in their dealings with colleagues and students an uncertainty about themselves that seems somehow appropriate for the context in which they work.

It is not as if authentic teachers are obsessed with explorations of themselves or the existential problem of 'angst'.[24] Instead authenticity is meant to pick out those individuals, practices and moments when for reasons that cannot be set out in advance things seem genuine, honest or simply 'just right'.

ELITES OR TRADITIONS?

It will be seen that élites and traditions have much in common. In both cases there is the idea that communities determine what is to count as good and bad practice on the basis of criteria that are internal to the elite or members of a tradition. Yet we have implied that traditions are good because they are authentic whereas elites are bad because they are inauthentic. In the case of members of élites inauthenticity is characterized by the belief in the efficacy and possibility of separating means from ends. Inauthenticity is also characterized by closure of discourse rather than attempts to open up decision-making to widespread scrutiny. There is more emphasis on bringing about changes rather than going along with things. It is as if bringing about continuous changes in the world is obviously good but that attempts to look beyond those changes to a view of human flourishing and the notion of self within that view, is pointless.[25]

I have argued that the idea of authentic community is essential to the idea of educational development. We have seen that this illusive notion can be useful in enabling us to explain not only how people learn but also how a stable tradition is important for educational evaluation. We have seen how consumerism amounts to a red herring in determining good from bad practice. Consumerism is important in education not as the means to promote choice but as a signal of the importance of democratic participation in educational decision-making. The idea that education professionals could continue without taking people along with a practice in which they all have had some experience as students themselves was a mistake that these professionals made to the cost of the integrity of their traditions. The task now is to regain that integrity through participative dialogue.

Let us examine in detail some of the practical and theoretical difficulties that such reinstatement might involve. We note the suspicion that groups of people charged with making difficult decisions that affect the lives of others may become self-serving and divorced from the realities of practical life. In order to counter this suspicion it has been suggested that the membership of these elites should be extended to include non-professionals. In this way it is supposed that the policemen would no longer police themselves as it were. Instead an independent body of industrialists or an interested body of parents or a supposed disinterested body of respected people might perform this policing of professional educators. However it is not entirely clear that any new composition of an elite does not in the longer term become just as self-serving as its predecessor. Notice the controversy in Britain that has surrounded some of the Enterprise Companies and Councils (LECs and TECs) which were set up to promote training and enterprise generally, not to promote the enterprise of particular board members.[26]

I have argued that we should prefer genuine openness in educational dialogue rather than a less restricted form of elitism. However it is not clear how to unpack what is said about education now by a wide range of people who choose to express their aspirations for the future and perceptions of the past in different ways with differing degrees of commitment. Their expressions would seem to need to be synthesized into some form of guidance for those who work within the system. Anyone who has tried to seek agreement among a large group of people about a detailed matter knows how hard and time-consuming this process can be. Moreover it is generally accepted that if all matters of legitimate public interest were debated in full by all those concerned then decision-making would become unwieldy and very expensive. Finally it is generally accepted that however well-intentioned a group of people are to encourage genuine participation, that there is always the tendency for sub-groups and alliances to form which serve to exclude the genuinely novel and interesting contributions.

It is easy to see why elitism is popular. Whether we like it or not schools are public institutions, mainly bureaucratic and routine. Perhaps they should be run on instrumental lines. Elitism avoids the practical difficulty of taking into account a wide range of views and ideas. Moreover elites are more easily controlled by governments that have an interest in bringing about change in a short period of time. The disadvantages of elitism are also clear: in order to perform their function the members of elites need to become knowledgeable about particular procedures. This knowledge enables members to exploit the system for their own self-interest. While that is not to imply that all members of elites behave in this way, it does mean that there will always be the suspicion that members might behave in that way. Moreover since elites are charged with the responsibility to take decisions that affect others, they enjoy considerable power which arouses suspicion on the part of those who do not enjoy the same degree of power. There is always the tendency for elites to establish norms that relate more to the interests of the members rather than to the interests of the wider community that they are meant to serve.

We have already considered and dismissed the idea that there might be a sort of meta-tradition to which we might appeal to adjudicate between competing solutions to moral dilemmas. Instead we have considered the idea that there is a variety of groups with a variety of different interests that nevertheless share what might be called an overlapping consensus about what is valuable. That is to say that while these groups might not all agree on a core of values, one group shares a set of values with another. Some but not all of these values are shared with another group along with some other different values into an overlapping consensus. Of course the degree and nature of that consensus changes over time. For example changing one's mind about something depends upon there being a possibility of understanding an alternative and coming to accept that alternative while at the same time coming to reject a previous commitment. If this were not the case then there would simply be groups of people unable to see

---

CASE EXEMPLAR

RELIGIOUS EDUCATION[27]

I believe that I can illustrate this notion of an overlapping consensus as it might operate in the case of religious education. This case is notoriously problematic and has led to calls for more sectarian schooling for Muslims and others. No doubt there are all kinds of pragmatic reasons concerned with power, status and convenience in favour of sectarian schooling. In this exemplar however let us consider the theoretical reasons for continuing sectarian schooling. Religious education is not conceived by many people as an induction into the practice of a particular religion as if religious practice was of the same status as tennis for example. Nor is religious education conceived by many people as an induction into religious practices generally as if religions of the world should be compared in some way. People who favour sectarian schools tend to argue that religious practice transcends all other practices to such an extent that the school is bound together by values of a religious kind.

In contrast to that view, people who are in favour of non-sectarian schools might argue that schools are bound together by values of an educational kind which overlap rather than transcend practices. According to this view, students should be encouraged to challenge the values that they hold by openly debating issues with fellow students who do not agree. In that way schools promote the value of open discursive rationality above all other values. Proponents of multicultural education might argue in this way. Instead of the idea that the curriculum should be based exclusively on the dominant perspective of Western imperialism, some multiculturalists might argue that education should be informed by a variety of perspectives that are brought to the school by people of different ethnic and racial backgrounds.

beyond their prior evaluative commitments and ultimately unable to communicate with the members of other groups. They would have no means of interpreting each other's actions in a common language. So while individuals and groups may value different things there is sufficient overlap between their values to enable them to interpret each other's actions in ways that are mutually understandable. In the case of an education system people may reach a consensus on the ways that that system should develop without agreeing on every aspect of their personal educational development or that of their children. There is room in this notion for individual choice and communal agreement.

In the next case exemplar the Irish education system is considered as one in which there is a strong religious tradition that may be seen, perhaps paradoxically, to promote and enable open discursive rationality even though the tradition seems to be based on a set of values that are tacit and not challenged.

CASE EXEMPLAR

THE IRISH SYSTEM OF EDUCATION[28]

Ireland may well be unique in having a system of formal education that is not enshrined in legislation and that is not characterized by highly prescriptive sets of guidelines on teaching method. As such the Irish system may serve as a paradigmatic example of diversity of practice within a strong tradition that is provided by a stable set of values that are anchored by the Catholic Church. As Brown and Fairley report[29] this lack of educational legislation may be explained in part by the hostility of the church to increased state interference in education. This reminds us of the deformation of traditions by institutions that MacIntyre[30] charts. However, while there may be a degree of self-interest on the part of the Church in preserving certain traditions, any attempt to modify these traditions may be seen to originate not so much from the Irish Government but from the international community in the form of the Organisation for Economic Co-operation and Development (OECD).[31] Two reports from that organization suggest that the system is in need of reform and in 1992, partly as a response to the OECD report, a Green Paper was published which has been the subject of widespread debate.

It might be imagined that the publication of a consultative document such as the Green Paper was simply a preliminary indication of the White Paper or policy that was to follow and that debate about the Green Paper was pointless since the outcome had already been decided. British and American readers might well imagine that this would be the case. Yet it is paradoxical that even though Ireland has a centralized bureaucracy that is neither open nor accountable, there has been a genuine debate about the Green Paper and a genuine sense of partnership in policy formation. As Coolahan (1994) reports:

> Ireland has a complex and deeply rooted education system. Part of the complexity resides in the historical depth of the educational tradition . . . education has always been valued by the generality of the people even those who have benefited little from formal education.[32]

Coolahan goes on to report how the debate was wide-ranging and diverse and how it led to a 'National Convention' planned by a Secretariat that was independent of Government to try to achieve as much consensus as possible. This debate was coordinated and a report was prepared to assist in the policy-making process. All of this signifies a strong commitment to democratic involvement in the policy-making process and a willingness on the part of Ministers not to take the easy option and to grapple with the complex evaluative issues that such a wide-ranging debate was bound to raise.

In Ireland, it seems that tacit agreement on a set of fundamental religious values might actually enable discussion of policy at a fundamental level because there is always a set of agreed values or a touchstone to which the Irish can appeal to settle matters without having to articulate that touchstone. So tradition actually enables fundamental discussion and seems to avoid the need for constant directives perhaps because those values that characterize the tradition are not open to question.

From these exemplars we may conclude that while the notion of an overlapping consensus appears to underpin the idea of a liberal society generally, that notion is itself in need of the underpinning that may only be provided by tacit acceptance of democratic liberalism as a more fundamental value. That does not mean that traditional values remain static. Nor does it mean that we can set out those values as a touchstone in any operationally effective way. Fundamental traditional values are useful to us only in so far as there is no need to set them out. In other words we may know good teaching better if our social institutions are based on democratic discursive liberalism as a matter of fundamental importance. Our social institutions generally may only come to be based on this fundamental value if our educational institutions and traditions embody this value. That does not mean that we should base all our schools on one model. Rather it means that we should encourage a variety of schools of different types to flourish. It is not possible to stand outside a system to scrutinize it. Nor is it possible for everyone to agree on every aspect of the system. That does not preclude them from agreeing upon how particular institutions should be run and comparing those institutions against others that are run on different lines. The evaluation of particular institutions and particular teachers depends upon the possibility of learning from others who practise in diverse ways while sharing some practical traditions with us.

An ability to justify a decision as widely and openly as possible may be taken to be the nearest that we get to the idea of moral truth. From a basic question about whether a particular course of action is good we have moved on to the further question about why it is good. The basic question is elucidated by a consideration of the practical ability and obligation to justify decisions that are taken on behalf of others. People may not know that the best is being done in education but certainly they want to know that all reasonable options have been taken into account and one option selected on the basis of acceptable reasons. For example, some parents will be able to recall their attempts to balance a desire to protect their children with a desire to let their children learn experientially. Normally the need to justify a particular decision arises only when something has gone wrong. Sometimes the justification itself is essentially private – the child has fallen out of the tree and the parent ponders the wisdom of their earlier decision in favour of experience! In the case of those employed in the public education service however, the justification needs to withstand scrutiny and may be required even where things seem to be going well.

SUMMARY

In this chapter we have examined the paradox that is involved in the notion of diversity within tradition. We have come to the view that educational development should be based on a balance between practical traditions and democratic scrutiny of those traditions in order to distinguish between good and bad practice. The best guide that we have to the nature of an appropriate balance has been through a consideration of the notion of authenticity. We have seen that policy-making in Britain and North America may be governed more by the values that are shared by an elite than by the value of open discursive rationality that underpins the liberal notion of an overlapping consensus. Whether the system is regressing or progressing becomes more a matter of the immediate interests of those who have the power to shout loudest than a matter for rational debate. Hence educational developments tend to be introduced and sustained by means of narrow elitism and public relations rather than democratic persuasion.

In contrast a genuine attempt to persuade would be accompanied by attempts to engage people in conversation with the aim of determining what their genuine feelings towards the development might be. Coercion is sustained by manipulative human relationships and there is a danger that students come to see this sort of relationship as the norm. Increasingly therefore it becomes more difficult to appeal to the idea of a common good as for example in the case of the legitimation of ordinary commercial enterprise.

Commercial enterprise is accepted by most people as the best way of regulating the supply of many goods and services. However, as we have seen, educational goods and services cannot be regulated entirely in this way. There cannot be any certainty about the effects of particular developments and that is why Popper, among others, recommends piecemeal development rather than Utopian planning.[33] The more people are involved with and support a development the more likely it is that the development will be successful. To try to impose developments is unlikely to lead to commitment – just the opposite as people seek to undermine developments in which they have played no part and which run counter to their deeply held beliefs and values. We may never be confident that today's decision about an educational development will not turn out to be the cause of tomorrow's problem within the education system, but we can at least ensure that we all have a stake in trying to make the system work.

While it will never be possible to solve all these problems and difficulties and while we may never know that we have the best solutions, we may derive better ones in a pragmatic way. That is not to deny the importance of ideals; it is simply to suggest that education systems are best developed pragmatically by making systematic improvements in a piecemeal manner. We should not imagine however that by doing more we are necessarily improving matters. Nor should we imagine that problems are only solvable at the operational end of the system – policy-making and policy-makers may also be improved. If we conceptualize education as a moral rather than a technical endeavour and centralize the notion of justification within that conception then democratic scrutiny of educational policy and practice may follow. When all justifications seem equally balanced, we should favour those courses of action that are supported by the maximum opportunity to prove that they are mistaken. Rather than supporting those courses of action that are shielded from widespread and regular scrutiny, we should favour those that are most open to sceptical review and those that include the most opportunities for people to act in an authentic way.[34]

In this chapter we have considered educational theory in general and have set out broad principles to enable us to distinguish between development and regression. In the following chapters I elucidate further these principles by trying to apply them to some important practical problems that face us. It is common to distinguish between three sorts of educational development: curriculum development is concerned with what is to be learnt; staff development is concerned with the continuing education of the professional educators themselves; administrative development is concerned with administration, management and control of the education system. While these distinctions are not important to my developing account of educational practice I refer to them in the following chapters simply because presently they are widely used and generally established.

NOTES AND REFERENCES

1. Authenticity may also be achieved when the members of a community reflect upon their immediate self-interests and distinguish between those interests that are distorted by ends imposed on them by members of other communites and those that are not. In this way immediate self-interests are transcended in the reflective-discursive process so that people may identify their 'real' interests and act in 'solidarity with one another'. See Rorty (1989) for further discussion along these lines.
2. There is a large number of books about the psychology of education. I find Bigge (1982) and Child (1994) to be helpful.
3. See the work of the Churchlands, especially 1986 and 1989.
4. Bigge (1982, pp. 49–50).
5. See Malcolm (1972, Chapter 18) for the case against a materialist research programme such as this. Evers (1993) makes the case in favour of such a programme. For Evers, the use of terms like belief, desire, intention and meaning is characteristic of 'folk theory' which may be expected to be superseded by more 'scientific' theory. He writes:

   > Despite its formidable practical, everyday utility and predictive power, folk psychology . . . has a provisional status, with the expectation that deeper accounts of language, thought, learning, knowledge and purposeful behaviour will need to mesh with the developing neurosciences.

6. The metaphor of a ladder is taken from Wittgenstein (1922) who writes:

   > My propositions serve as elucidations in the following way: anyone who understands me eventually recognises them as nonsensical, when he has used them – as steps – to climb beyond them. (He must, so to speak, throw away the ladder after he has climbed up it.)
   > He must transcend these propositions, and then he will see the world aright.

   I refer to a ladder of technique and the point of my reference is to suggest that good teaching is not a matter of technical expertise, but a matter of seeing situations in particular ways. Techniques may help that orientation but they are not a substitute for that orientation.
7. See Standish (1992, Chapter 5) for an overview.
8. See Ranson (1994).

9. See Kelly (1995).
10. See Pring (1994).
11. O'Dea (1993) gives an account of '*phronesis*' in musical performance. She argues that learning to play a musical instrument contributes to the development of practical wisdom. This argument is highly generalizable to the learning of other practices and to the idea that such learning can be a form of values or moral education.
12. Wittgenstein (1953, PI 217).
13. Cooper (1983) is excellent. He gives an account of authenticity through consideration of Nietzsche's educational philosophy. See also Grimmett and Neufeld (1994) for an account of teaching and authenticity.
14. I use this term to refer to the account of learning that is advanced in this book.
15. Heidegger (1967, p. 73).
16. Gadamer (1975, pp. 269–77) explains that the use of the term 'prejudice' has become distorted by the 'modernist' project so that it only functions in a perjorative way. He seeks to restore its pre-Enlightenment meaning as the effect of tradition that is manifest in ordinary linguistic use.
17. Again see Gadamer (1975, Part 1, Chapter 3). For an overview, see Halliday (1990, Chapter 5).
18. See Taylor (1985b, Chapter 1) for an account of the 'hermeneutic circle'. For an account of textual interpretation, see also Gadamer (1975).
19. Gadamer (1975).
20. Kuhn (1977) gives an account of scientific development that is based on interpretation.
21. Sartre (1957).
22. Sartre (1957, p. 59).
23. I am indebted to Robin Small for bringing this to my attention through his 1981 paper. See also his entry in the second edition of the *International Encyclopaedia of Education*, pp. 4429–33.
24. '*Angst*' or 'terrible freedom' may be seen to arise when one realizes that choice is no longer contained within certain pre-defined options but that the choice of option itself is a matter for the individual alone.
25. See Standish (1992, pp. 209–21).
26. As for example was reported in the *Glasgow Herald* 23 November 1993, p. 12.
27. The Education Reform Act of 1988 has raised interest in this form of education in Britain. For some contraversial views, see Watson (1992).
28. I am grateful to Tom O'Donoghue for bringing this exemplar to my attention.
29. Brown and Fairley (1993, pp. 34–45).
30. MacIntyre (1981).
31. OECD (1991).
32. Coolahan (1994) gives an overview of the debate.
33. Popper (1945). See note 2, Chapter 1.
34. Popper (1968) gives an account of scientific discovery which stresses the importance of bold conjectures that are most open to falsification. Successive bold conjectures are made with the knowledge that some of them will turn out to be false. By a sort of negative implication, some conjectures asymptotically approach the truth though they may never reach it. Truth functions as a regulative ideal. For Popper, the more that conjectures are tried, the more they seem to 'work', the better they are.

Chapter 3

Teacher Development

It is often claimed that trainee teachers are more interested in advice about teaching method rather than material which might challenge their prior assumptions about educational values. Experienced teachers too, it is claimed, are more interested in material of the 'how to do it' variety than material of the 'why should we do this at all?' variety. It seems that there must be something in these claims because there are a number of publications with titles such as 'Teaching Business Studies in the Secondary School' or 'Discipline and the Teacher' and so on. There are also a number of curricular materials that are designed for teachers to use.[1]

I have often wondered however whether publications such as these meet a genuine need – genuine in the sense that educational practice is enhanced after teachers have read them or used them – or whether some of these publications and materials merely appear to offer easy solutions to perennial and difficult problems. My scepticism is based partly on conversations with many teachers over the years – teachers like me who find some of these methodological studies to be limited in usefulness and interest. My scepticism is also based on fairly simple logical considerations.

Put simply the particularities of teaching practice are such that general prescription of best practice is not possible. Material which purports to offer such general prescription may be little other than a restatement of the author's or someone else's prior evaluative commitments. Instead I argue that the only hope for better practice is through teachers examining their own evaluative commitments in the light both of current educational policies and previous attempts to theorize. In that way good teachers tend to make better decisions in the particular circumstances that they and only they can interpret. The same tendency may be apposite to forms of practice other than teaching: good practical decisions are made by good practitioners who crucially *recognize the futility of attempts to offer, follow or apply generalized prescriptions for action.*

EMPIRICAL RESEARCH INTO TEACHING

The conclusion reached above would seem to imply that empirical research into the nature of teaching is a waste of effort. There seems little point trying to derive generalized prescriptions for action if their application is necessarily futile. Yet this conclusion itself is a generalized prescription for action albeit of a negative kind and so we seem to arrive at a paradox. The paradox arises because of the way that the terms 'particular' and 'general' function within the dominant empiricist practice/theory relationship. The idea that general statements should guide particular practice is so pervasive that we find it difficult to accept an alternative idea that a theory is just an interesting story which refers both to a particular attempt to describe coherence between practices and to the practice of theorizing itself.[2]

We cannot assume however that a story that purports to bring coherence to a seemingly disparate group of practices is necessarily of interest and value to those whose practices it seeks to describe. People are encouraged to act differently in different ways. A description of coherence between practices is not necessarily seen to be valuable. Moreover encouragement does not obviously lead to changes in behaviour. What are seen to be improvements within a particular practice may not be the result of any effort whatsoever on the part of other sorts of practitioner. Indeed such efforts that are made may do more harm than good.

On this view empirical research into teaching is as likely as any other form of research to tell a story that will interest teachers. Many empirical researchers want to claim more for their stories than this. They want to claim that their stories are about best practice and many policy-makers would like to appeal to such stories as a means of legitimizing their proposals. There is nothing wrong with these desires of course. Things begin to go wrong however when over-ambitious claims are made for research and teachers are coerced into behaving in particular ways in order to conform to some stereotype that is supposed to be based on empirical research.

For example, what was once a popular empirical research programme involves a comparison of the use of different teaching methods in an attempt to prescribe the best methods for teachers to use. Another programme attempts to describe the best of what actually goes on in classrooms. Various schedules of classroom observation have been devised in order to guide such research.[3] Something of both of these programmes may still be seen to inform some courses of teacher education. Yet both research programmes have largely been superseded by research into the way that teachers think.[4]

The 'teacher thinking' research programme is discussed as four related programmes.[5] First a programme is derived from cognitive psychology involving concepts such as schemata, cognitive skills and strategies which were discussed in the last chapter. Second a highly influential programme is derived from the concept of a reflective practitioner.[6] Schon argues that teachers engage in at least two types of reflection: reflection whilst acting and reflection about actions. The latter sort of reflection is the more easy to understand. This appeals to the common sense idea that on reflection we could have done it better. By reviewing our actions in the light of different practices with which we are familiar and which we now have time to consider, we come to the view that we would act differently in similar circumstances in the future. Using the language of interpretation, we may describe this as having the time to confront our own prejudices by recalling the prejudices that were presented to us through our experience.

The former notion of reflection in action is much more problematic and has been the subject of some criticism on the grounds that it is not clear how we can reflect while acting.[7] This notion may be seen to be related to the idea of tacit knowledge which guides courses of action but which cannot be explained either at the time or after the event. The third research programme was first articulated by Shulman[8] and is based on his idea of pedagogical content knowledge. This type of knowledge is to be distinguished from content or subject knowledge and is knowledge of how to make the subject interesting and how to enable students to cotton on to ideas within the subject.

A fourth research programme is based on Aristotle's concept of a practical argument and may be seen to be related to the action research movement where researchers do not try to investigate how teachers think. Rather researchers work with teachers to try to get them to change their preconceptions on the basis of an encounter with the findings of research.[9] The extent to which the preconceptions of the researchers should also change in this encounter may be a valid consideration for those who work within this research programme. The action research movement may be located rather more suitably within the reflective practitioner programme or seen as a practical means of realizing the aims of a critical theory which will be discussed later.[10]

I should also mention some other types of empirical research into teaching. Berliner (1986) found that good teachers tended to interpret situations in similar ways, thus lending support to the practical interpretive account of learning that was discussed in the last chapter. In effect this research supports the view that members of traditions tend to share similar prejudices. Also Brown and MacIntyre's (1993) work on teacher craft knowledge tends to support the account of learning as apprenticeship that has been outlined in this book. Brophy's (1991) work on the importance of subject knowledge to good teaching also provides support for the general thesis that is presented in this book. Finally there is the research into teachers' lives[11] that tends to emphasize the interweaving of teacher's professional responsibilities and the type of people they are.

From this latter research programme it is a short step to describing teaching as a social practice and recognizing that the kinds of relationships that teachers have with their colleagues and friends have an enormous effect on their teaching. The research into teacher development[12] may be seen as a reaction against the idea that teachers are static resources just waiting to be developed to implement the next curriculum development. Instead the teacher development research programme may be seen to support the idea of teachers being given the opportunity to develop themselves. Researchers of this type are more interested in the practical and political contexts in which teachers locate themselves than in the derivation of new tricks for teachers to learn. For example teachers' personal outlooks, the stage in their professional development, whether or not they have been promoted and how well they get on with their colleagues all have a major effect on their classroom teaching.

From this brief survey of empirical research into teaching it is possible to highlight several important dimensions of good teaching that support the thesis advanced in this book. These dimensions have also been highlighted by the OECD (1994) in its research on *Quality in Teaching* in the following terms:

- Knowledge of substantive curriculum areas or practices that are taught. Authority is derived from this knowledge.
- Ability to reflect. A sceptical disposition is related to this ability.

- Empathy and commitment. An ability to relate to people and to understand their difficulties. Commitment which comes from enjoyment in teaching practice and a belief that the practice is worthwhile.
- Collegiality. A feeling of genuine solidarity with colleagues which supports the open discussion of future possibilities and past errors.

THE ALLOCATION OF RESOURCES

While the research evidence about good teaching seems clear enough, it is not clear that institutional and systemic developments have kept pace with the research. Perhaps it is felt that such developments would be too expensive to implement. In many places the empiricist conception of teaching remains firmly in place: teaching is a technical practice which should be controlled by managers who are supposed to respond both to the market and a policy-making élite with limited resources to disburse. According to this conception it is possible to evaluate the work of teachers and managers but not the work of policy-makers and the interpreters of policies. As a result of the implementation of this conception, most teachers now accept that there is no way that they can influence the direction of educational policy. Depressing though it is, they conclude that they might as well get hold of the latest book on problem-solving, records of achievement or whatever and do their best.

While this pessimism may be understandable, it is highly undesirable. Not only do we run the risk of losing from our education system the liberal notions of expanding students' horizons and broadening their experience – but also we tend to lose the vocational impetus for students to show initiative, to be flexible and to be able to react to changing circumstances. If we do not expect teachers to be genuinely enthusiastic, flexible and innovative then it is not clear how we can expect students to develop these characteristics. In the longer term we run the risk of losing a tradition of teaching conceived as initiating others into the most worthwhile practices constitutive of our form of life. Instead we develop teaching as a form of marketing in which appearance and image are everything and honest endeavour counts for little.

Of course not everyone agrees with this pessimistic view. It would be surprising for example to find policy-makers, curriculum developers and educational managers arguing publicly that the education system is in crisis because many teachers have become demoralized within it. Instead we find most formal attempts at policy evaluation containing assertions that the system is basically sound and that those problems that have arisen may be solved by redirecting public funds away from the maintenance of a tradition of good teaching towards developments that have a high profile within the existing system.

Good teaching is expensive and it is perfectly reasonable for governments to want to minimize this expense. It is also perfectly understandable that politicians will want to be seen to be doing something and there is nothing particularly glamorous about directing public funds towards the maintenance of something that sounds as obscure and obsolete as a tradition. Yet most teachers spend most of their time trying to interest students in practices in which the teacher has some expertise. Good teachers know that this specific induction into practices is only part of the educational enterprise. They know that the notion of the school as a community is important and that they need to involve the community and be involved themselves in the development of the school as a focus for educational activities.

If teachers feel cut out of that involvement, if they feel unsympathetic towards the way things seem to be developing and if the school is managed so that they have few opportunities to reflect on their practice and keep up to date with developments elsewhere, then it should not surprise us that many teachers become demoralized. A sense of solidarity with colleagues, students and members of their community generally gets lost as teachers are encouraged to take individual responsibility for duties that are devolved to them by management under pressure to *show* that something is being done about the latest initiative. If this is true of teachers then we should not imagine that things are much better for managers. Certainly managers tend to be paid more than teachers and they tend not to have the same amount of routine teaching to do. Nevertheless most managers are sufficiently in touch with teachers to know that something important is threatened when the continuing pressure upon schools is to respond to changes that are imposed from outwith the school and its community rather than to agree from within, as it were, those moves that are most important.[13]

CASE EXEMPLAR

'HARD-UP POLICE FORCE SPLASH OUT ON HARMONY CRUSADE'[14]

This recent headline attempts to draw the reader's attention to the lack of authenticity in much of the public relations output that now characterizes the public services generally. In this case the author explains that a police force that is making 800 officers redundant because of government cash curbs is spending £45,000 on a politically correct 'Year of Harmony'. This money is to be used to pay for a musical setting of Abraham Lincoln's Gettysburg address, a black cartoon figure called 'Joe' to present a positive image to children on road safety, a 'conscious cafe' drama group to promote 'all aspects of integration' and so on.

No doubt many of these projects will be worthwhile in themselves without any need for the instrumental justification of anti-racism. The implication of the article is clear however. We should not mind about a deterioration in day to day policing, so long as public relations on anti-racism is itself high profile. We can imagine the headline adapted to describe aspects of the public education service and no doubt teachers can think of many examples similar to the one presented in the previous chapter about the leaking school roof. For example, expensive systems of school inspection often lead to reports that are bland in tone and seem to miss the most obvious aspects of school improvement and development. At the same time teachers struggle to buy textbooks and collect funds to support the library and a computer resource.

The above exemplar is not meant primarily as a warning that schools are often under-resourced (though no doubt many of them are). Instead the exemplar is meant to highlight the tendency of modern systems not to direct resources towards support for the tacit but most important aspects of practice. Instead the tendency is to direct them towards appearance however irrelevant to the supposed problem that direction might be. The exemplar also serves to highlight the way that resource allocation becomes fragmented in an attempt to rationalize educational decision-making. Fairly obviously the money that is collected from taxation needs to be divided in some way between different government departments that have a reasonable claim on some of that money. In turn different departments within departments present claims for a share in the money down to departmental level within schools. At that level a very small sum is typically left for teachers to spend – perhaps £20 on this textbook, £700 on that computer, £500 on replacement equipment might be involved. Teacher salaries, fixed costs like heating and electricity and budgets for in-service work are not usually included in departmental budgets. Nor are the costs of employing teams of inspectors, curriculum developers or system managers included. Instead these costs are determined at a higher level.

It is usual for all the money to be spent during a financial year or else the residue is clawed back to central funds. The situation often occurs therefore where there is a rush at the end of the financial year to spend whatever money is left on whatever plausible idea can be dreamed up. Now there is nothing rational about this situation yet we seem not to have moved much beyond it despite the introduction of consumerism and devolved systems of educational management. This irrationality may be seen as a further consequence of the attempt to separate means from ends in education. The usual procedure is for managers to submit plans and bids for resource allocation to a group which decides, supposedly on the basis of objective criteria, how the resources should be divided. Managers are then left with determining the most efficient means of achieving their planned targets within their allocation of resources.

All of this might be rational if it were possible to separate means and ends and if objective criteria could be interpreted in a value-free way. As we have seen however this separation and value-free interpretation are not possible. In the previous chapter it was argued that practical decisions should be taken within the most democratic forum possible. We may now add that resource allocation should be determined *along with* the practice in a similar way. In other words, however we want to describe the interweaving of policies, theories and practices, any educational proposals have implications for resource allocation and it is pointless to imagine that a practical development can be determined in abstraction from a decision about the resources involved.

Lest it be thought that this holistic approach to resource allocation is entirely impractical, I am not arguing for an ideal state of committees in constant session always checking up on what other committees were doing and allocating resources on a second-by-second basis. Instead I am arguing that resource allocation and hence educational development can be improved if we give up our empiricist predilections for the application of objective criteria and the belief in the effectiveness of trying to write documents as if statements of fact could be distinguished easily from statements of value. By linking resource allocation in more tightly with educational discussions, educational development may be more rational than it currently is.

The idea that a problem within an education system may be identified without some idea of what an education should consist in is as foolish as the idea that a solution to that problem can be found without some idea of what other problems might be created by the solution. When resources are re-directed towards solving the perceived problem, another problem might be created. For example there may be a problem in many of our schools with the education of the 10–14 age group. Solutions to the problem may be debated in the abstract, as it were, on what are termed educational grounds. Not only does such debate consume resources itself however, but any proposals that come out of the debate also have resource implications. Inevitably there is a trade-off between solving one problem and creating another by starving some other part of the education system of resources.

The empiricist separation of theory from practice leads to the separation of educational from financial matters. A problem that appears to be shared by a number of schools is not necessarily best solved by taking money away from each school and giving it to a central body to produce a series of documents for distribution to each

---

CASE EXEMPLAR

THE PARADOX OF CONTROL[15]

Across the liberal capitalist democracies headlines such as the following are common enough: 'Young people are unable to find employment'; 'There is a sense of moral decay'; 'The nation is not economically competitive'. The diagnosis of the cause of these putative problems is also familiar – something is wrong with the education system. But what is wrong precisely? Is it the policy-making process and the conception of system that is embedded within it? The answer given to this question is usually an emphatic no. Instead it is alleged that teachers and teacher trainers (the educational establishment as they are sometimes called) are to blame. It is claimed that many of them are ineffective and inefficient at meeting the needs of industry and society generally. The remedy to this alleged state of affairs would appear to be clear: decide how to distinguish good from bad practitioners and get rid of the bad. The practical and theoretical difficulties of making such a distinction are perceived to be so large however that the decision is usually avoided. Instead the proposed solution to the problem of poor teaching has been to conceptualize theory as the production of guidelines and curriculum materials by supposedly expert teachers for all teachers to follow and use. Hence it is assumed that a series of bureaucratic controls will ensure effective and efficient teaching towards prescribed targets.

But of course the problem has not been nor could be solved in this way. If there is a problem with the performance of particular teachers, the solution is not to demoralize the good ones by demeaning their practice, starving them of resources and making it more difficult for them to work effectively. Nor is the solution to support the weak ones as if following a worksheet and ticking off completed tasks were the epitome of good teaching. The net effect of these attempts to control teaching practice is not to control teaching practice at all but to destroy a tradition of good teaching so that ultimately nothing is controlled except the behaviour of certain individuals at certain times when they are due for inspection.

school. The problem may be compounded when even more money is taken away from each school to check whether or not the issuing of documents has improved matters. Instead many problems may best be solved by devolving the decision and the resources down to the people who are actually responsible for solving the problem – in this case, the teachers.[16] That is not to deny the importance of deep theoretical analysis to such decision-making. Such analysis is essential. The criteria for successful theorizing and hence rational decision-making, however, may never be located entirely within one practice in abstraction from other considerations.

The decentralization of management and administration and the institution of programmes of teacher preparation within schools and colleges may be seen to be moves in the right direction.[17] These moves ought to result in more money being spent directly on teaching, learning and associated theoretical practices. On the other hand these moves may be seen as the result of diminishing public sector resources for education and an attempt by governments to control education systems and to hold those working within them responsible when things seem to be going wrong. There is no way that in the present circumstances we can determine which of these alternative interpretations is correct. The decision-making process is not sufficiently open to scrutiny to allow us to judge whether those concerned are acting with cynical indifference or with a concerned and tactical awareness of just how far it is possible go towards opening up the system at the present time.

It is obviously tempting for those who work within the public sector to argue against all moves that appear to be based on financial restraints, particularly when colleagues' jobs are threatened by those moves. Ironically moves to decentralize in favour of school-based training need not necessarily be a bad thing. As I argue in the next section, college-based programmes of teacher education are not without their problems.

TEACHER EDUCATION

During the 1960s and early 1970s there was an expansion in the number of teachers undergoing initial training. Many new colleges of education were built to cope with demand and during these boom years the curriculum for the initial training of teachers became established. Most trainees attended an institution of higher education on a full-time basis where they studied a mixture of theoretical subjects, such as philosophy, psychology, history, sociology, and practical studies in teaching method. These practical studies would often consist in writing lesson plans, presenting those plans to the trainee's peers and receiving constructive criticism from the teacher trainer or tutor. This simulated practice was then followed by a period of teaching in a school or college of further education during which tutors would visit, assess and advise trainees on their progress.

The relationship between this practical preparation and theoretical studies was always problematic and a massive literature built up around the theory-practice issue.[18] Very often trainees did not make any connection between theory and practice and theoretical studies was held by many trainees to be a boring irrelevance. Later in their careers some former trainees would return to colleges or university departments of education to follow up a theoretical interest that had developed in the course of their experience as teachers. Masters and Diploma courses were offered to satisfy this interest and also, on occasions, to serve as a sort of career marker for ambitious teachers.

The pattern of initial and post-initial training was thus established and this pattern continued in more or less the same form until recent reforms introduced the idea of school-based teacher training and teacher development. As is often the case moves to reform parts of the education system may be seen to be underpinned by a number of quite different and sometimes conflicting values. In the case of the teacher education curriculum there was a concern that the old system of higher education-based teacher education was expensive and a luxury that could no longer be afforded. (It remains to be seen whether school-based systems work out any cheaper! There have been some suggestions that such systems may not be cheaper at all.)

At a time in which there has been an expansion in the numbers of institutions of higher education and a general blurring of the boundaries between the various sectors of education there seems less of a case for locating all teacher training within institutions of higher education. This concern may be seen to be underpinned both by an interest in status but also by a form of egalitarianism in which class distinctions based on the vocational-academic distinction are to be discouraged. Indeed the ascendancy of utilitarian values generally may have served to downgrade anything that might count as theory so that teacher training, both at the initial and post-initial levels becomes dominated by institutionally determined practical priorities. Hence the idea that theory (based in institutions of higher education) somehow guides practice in all other sectors of education (and indeed industry) has been attacked from a wide range of perspectives including the perspective that was described in the previous chapter.

The success of those attacks in weakening the dominance of higher education in the teacher education curriculum does not mean that educational theory has somehow become irrelevant. On the contrary what is required is a different conception of educational theory that is based on the idea of a constant critical reinterpretation of theory into practice and practice into theory. Theoretically informed teaching practice, wherever that practice is located, is directly opposed to the currently fashionable and impoverished conception of teaching as a technical activity. I believe that many teachers despair at what often passes as their in-service education or staff development that is based on the latter conception.

As we have seen there is a great deal of dissatisfaction with the idea that educational theory should guide teaching practice and there have been moves to re-conceptualize theory as the production of curriculum support materials. The supposed primacy of practice over theory may be seen to be instituted in school-based programmes of teacher education[19] to the extent that we may wonder what role educational theory should have within these programmes. For example if trainee teachers are expected to 'learn from Nelly' by copying experienced teachers then educational theory seems to drop out of teacher education altogether. It is doubtful however if anyone would want to take the primacy of practice argument so far. It is argued that teachers not only are knowledgeable in their subject but also have a form of pedagogical knowledge[20] which they acquire through experience and through reflection on experience. According to this argument their practice is theoretically informed through successive refinement that is based on reflection on and in practice.

Whole programmes of teacher education have been based on the reflective practitioner model and programmes of action research have been built up around the idea
that teachers themselves are best placed to identify and solve their problems through
systematic analysis of practice. The recording of critical incidents, diaries and
perceived problems may form part of such programmes and research. Often it is
argued that reflection is a sort of therapy in which an experienced partner aids the
inexperienced teacher to come to see where they might have gone wrong and how they
might change in the future.

It is not hard to see that reflection might lead teachers to consider the kind of
people that they are and not just the kind of knowledge that they have. The notion of
self and the kinds of stories that teachers tell about themselves will in some way affect
their practice. In contrast to the idea that teaching is a technical activity, reflective
practice tends to suggest that teaching is a moral activity in which it is important
constantly to reflect upon the type of people that teachers are and the kinds of theories
and beliefs that they hold. That is why programmes of research based on reflective
practice may be seen to have led to research into teachers' lives and the relationships
that teachers have with their colleagues. For example it is now accepted that those
schools in which there is a genuine collaborative ethos are more successful than those
schools in which collaboration is contrived.[21]

Programmes of teacher education based on reflective practice seem particularly
suited to school-based initiatives. What better place could there be for the trainee
teacher to reflect on and in practice under the supervision of experienced colleagues
who, it might be assumed, see the world aright. We may wonder however how this
assumption might be validated. It could be argued for example that anyone who
believes that teacher education can consist only in a limited form of reflection cannot
possibly see the world aright. In order to even begin to have any idea of whether one is
a good practitioner it is necessary to appeal to the authority that comes from
membership of a community with an established tradition of distinguishing good from
bad practice.

For that reason school-based programmes have been organized on a consortium
basis so that trainees may come to see a range of alternative practices and come into
contact with a range of 'therapists'. Even then it has been recognized that there is a
number of established disciplines in education to which appeal can be made in order to
ground reflections in practices. I am thinking of the traditional practices of philosophy,
history, psychology and sociology of education as well as subject disciplines. While it
is not fashionable to admit to being a member of one of these communities at the
moment and even less fashionable to suggest that educational theory might be based
on such communities, membership does allow one to appeal to the authority of
tradition that comes from a continuing engagement with problems of a meta-
theoretical kind such as the distinction between good and bad. Hence we may favour
those programmes of teacher education in which there is a partnership between
teachers working across a range of practices including the theoretical practices of
history, philosophy, psychology and sociology.

Even when school-based programmes of teacher education are based on broad
experience between consortia of schools and universities, reflection on practice may
lead to conflicts both within and between schools for which the teachers concerned are
little prepared. For example reflection may lead trainees to realize that a structural

feature of the school such as time-tabling or methods of communication should be changed. All problems are not necessarily best solved by trainees changing themselves in some way. Instead reflection may lead trainees to come to the view that just as they improve by reflecting on their theoretical prior conceptions, so other members of the school or policy-making community too would benefit from such reflection. At this point in the trainee's reflective development, the reflective enterprise may appear to lead to a dead end and a collapse of confidence in the value of this enterprise. Some writers argue that the next step in the process of enlightenment is for teachers to become 'transformative intellectuals'[22] working politically to change the way that the education system is conceived and run.

CASE EXEMPLAR

CONTRIVED COLLEGIALITY[23]

We have seen that our membership of communities that have practical traditions allows us to distinguish between good and bad practice. We have also seen that empirical research into teaching suggests that teaching is improved when teachers are not only members of communities associated with their subjects, but also members of a community of teachers. It is not clear however just how this latter sort of community might be realized in practice. Of course teaching practice might be conceived along the same lines as any other practice and the notion of community associated with it might be centred on the university department of education.

In the situation where more and more pre- and in-service teacher education is carried out in schools, the staff-room might appear to be the obvious site for the teaching community within a school to meet and share ideas. As teachers know however and as researchers have documented,[24] staff-room talk is seldom concerned with teaching. Instead such talk often centres on the least contentious issues that are least related to teaching and learning. Perhaps we should not be surprised at this. After a morning of explaining things and correcting students, it is unlikely that teachers would want to spend their lunch-times trying to correct their colleagues and explain concerns to them.

In some places teachers do form groups to discuss educational issues but these groups tend to be small and they tend to be based on shared values often surrounding a subject or a group of subjects. For example, in many secondary schools, teachers of technical subjects may be seen to group together in the workshops and feel themselves to be somehow different from the teachers of English and history. We may speculate that the fragmentation of the teaching staff in this way is based simply on the way that rooms are often located or the way that chairs in the staff-room are arranged. Alternatively teachers may simply find it more relaxing to talk without fear of serious disagreement.

We may also speculate that teachers tend to form small groups in order to preserve an authentic view of themselves. For example if they perceive their job in the kind of negative way that I outlined earlier in this chapter, then they may look to a small group of similar minded individuals to share their mutual discomfort and to act in bad faith by rationalizing their thoughts and actions through an appeal to the idea that others are acting in a similar way. There is a sense in which these groups are trying to preserve a sense of authenticity that is based on a mutual recognition of inauthenticity outside their group. It is worth noting that these small groups are likely to resist strongly any inauthentic or contrived attempt to get them to share their ideas and confront differences in values between their colleagues in other parts of the school. This likelihood provides as strong a basis as any for the argument that teacher education should be concerned to go beyond the contingencies of the particular into a theoretical awareness of possibilities.

In some schools there is what Hargreaves calls a 'culture of collaboration' in which the personal and the professional are mixed. Failure and uncertainty are not protected but opened up to wide scrutiny. There is no covering of backs. Teachers act as curriculum consultants for their colleagues by having specific subject knowledge with which to promote the integration of learning. They act as therapists for their colleagues to work out better ways of doing things and they genuinely like their colleagues even though, and possibly because, they can disagree with them in a non-threatening way.

Hargreaves notes however that such collegiality is rare. There is a number of systemic constraints that work against a culture of collaboration. First, teachers are often under contractual obligations to teach a fixed number of hours and there is rarely any slack in the system for teachers to develop a sense of collegiality. Secondly, opportunities for promotion are essentially competitive and these may be used to destroy a sense of collegiality though the idea of 'divide and rule'. Thirdly, the guidelines approach to teaching tends to lead to the cynical view that if everything is decided in advance of the teaching enterprise then there is little point teachers bothering to debate matters. Few teachers are inspired by conversations about methods and techniques alone.

Yet it is easy to see that managers would want to encourage a culture of collegiality. Hargreaves uses the term 'contrived collegiality' as a warning against the idea that collegiality can be manufactured, as it were, by a series of management techniques. The manufacture typically consists in rewarding those who most appear to work well with their colleagues, to make set times available for joint planning in set rooms specially designated as 'consultancy' or 'cooperation' suites and to organizing social events for staff to 'let their hair down' and 'really get to know one another'. In other words the manufacture of contrived collegiality uses sticks to try to beat teachers into eating the carrots of collegiality.

The problem with this manufacture is that it is not likely even to be a preliminary to a more authentic notion of collegiality. Instead the manufacture may be a barrier against there ever being an authentic sense of collegiality. Not only may teachers get fed up with unwanted and contrived meetings but they also may get fed up with what they see as contrived behaviour on the part of their colleagues, ever anxious to please. Once the sense of trust is broken through the suspicion that people are trying to achieve extrinsic rewards through a kind of pastiche of good practice, it is very difficult to regain that trust.

Not all teachers want to become transformative in this way particularly at the early stage of their career, and informed reflection may lead them to become disillusioned and unenthusiastic as they come up against structural constraints. Yet enthusiasm is one of the main features of good teaching and so paradoxically rather than reflective practice promoting good teaching the opposite may be the case. That takes us back to the view that some form of theoretical analysis of the education system is an important part of any programme of initial teacher education. Without some understanding of why the system is the way that it is, how the structural constraints apply, what possibilities there are for changes, trainees would seem to have little to prepare them when they come up against structural constraints.

In the end school-based programmes of teacher education may not differ that much from their university-based counterparts. It matters little where teachers meet to reflect upon their practice in a collaborative atmosphere that is brought about by successful tutors who can guide the reflective enterprise. Bringing the site of such meetings nearer to the schools however is bound to lead to discussion of particular difficulties within particular schools. Heads of schools offering such programmes will come to recognize that reflective practice cannot be limited to pedagogy but that it is likely to involve reflections on management. Reflection can be uncomfortable. No one likes to have their prior conceptions continually under scrutiny yet reflective practice seems to imply this degree of scepticism and accompanying discomfort.[25]

The rewards of instituting good programmes of teacher education are potentially high since the whole school community may become involved in a programme of self-monitoring and improvement. Such programmes are unlikely to be easily limited to schoo's however since the promotion and maintenance of a tradition of good teaching is central to education policy generally. Successful programmes may come to challenge the whole basis on which education systems are currently conceived.

APPRAISAL, EVALUATION AND ACCOUNTABILITY[26]

These terms are often used interchangeably to refer to formally constituted ways of distinguishing between degrees of goodness in teaching. There is of course a prior question of whether formally we should attempt to make such distinctions at all. It is worth remembering that people learnt to do all kinds of things before there were formal systems of education and before the idea of teacher appraisal was considered. In the same way people learn to do things well outwith formal educational institutions – so good teaching may develop informally as a result of watching and working with other teachers, copying what seem to be good ideas, trying those ideas out, discussing the results with others similarly engaged and coming to a broad consensus on what counts as good practice and who is a good practitioner.

Perhaps the recognition from one's peers that one is a good teacher is recognition enough and such collegiality should not be destroyed by the imposition, formally as it were, of extrinsic rewards for good teaching based on publicly observable criteria. The use of extrinsic rewards may destroy the sense of collegiality that was essential for the recognition of good teaching in the first place. There is something in this argument when it is applied to teaching outwith the formal education system. Within the system however teachers do receive extrinsic as well as intrinsic rewards for their work and so in a sense their tradition is already affected by other forms of discourse associated with general employment and their conditions of service. That is why people are quite rightly suspicious of a form of professionalism that looks like self-interest. Like every other practice, teaching does not exist in a vacuum and teachers, like everyone else, may choose not to teach if the extrinsic rewards that they receive are perceived to be inadequate. Unless teaching is perceived to be an attractive occupation both in terms of extrinsic and intrinsic rewards, the only entrants to the profession will be those who are unable to gain useful employment elsewhere. In order to avoid this prospect, it is important to offer teachers a career progression that is comparable with other careers to which entrants might be attracted.

The question now arises as to how that career ladder is to be structured. If my arguments in favour of good teaching are correct then it is essential that the ladder is based on progress as a teacher and not as an administrator, manager, developer or any other practitioner ancillary to teaching. It seems obvious that the best people to determine what counts as good teaching are good teachers themselves. Not that those determinations can be divorced from the views of everyone else who comes into contact with teachers. Nevertheless the prime responsibility for appraisal, evaluation or accountability must lie with the profession itself. For the reasons advanced earlier it is only from within a tradition that criteria are meaningful.

It is in the interests of the profession to take into account the views of parents, school principals and others involved with teachers (in fact it is impossible not to). The profession is also obliged to justify its decisions to those who legitimately have an interest in good teaching. To be sure non-professionals have criteria for what counts as good teaching and it is in the course of conversation with professionals that the prior commitments of both parties are modified. That is not to suggest that both parties have equal authority in these matters. Nor is it to suggest that a consensus is always reached. Plainly someone who has taught for many years and is able to justify their practice is more authoritative than another who has perhaps only an immediate interest in a particular student. Moreover they may not agree on the particular student. If it were the case that a teacher hardly ever agreed with anyone then we should have good reason to doubt that they were authoritative in the way suggested.

Before we get carried away with the idea of a career ladder with many rungs that are linked with some sort of appraisal of performance, it is worth noting that we can reduce the rungs by insisting upon high entry standards to training programmes based on good knowledge of subject. We can trust teachers to develop their practice on the basis of their intelligence, enthusiasm and willingness to learn from colleagues. Teachers' pedagogical knowledge is important but very difficult and expensive to assess. We can reduce the need to assess this type of knowledge if we are prepared to trust teachers on the basis of their expertise in the practices into which we want to induct students.[27]

In the UK, USA and Australia the issue of teacher appraisal, evaluation and accountability has been high on the political agenda for some time. Methods of dealing with the issue have differed in each country and it is disappointing to note that this central issue is far from even a preliminary resolution. In the UK it is common to find 'top-down' schemes of appraisal in which teachers are appraised by their line-managers, line managers by principals, principals by chairs of boards.[28]

CASE EXEMPLAR

STAGES IN TEACHER DEVELOPMENT[29]

The following list of stages in teacher development have been discussed by several groups of teachers as a preliminary basis for discussion about teacher development.

Levels of teaching ability

0   Administratively incompetent, has fixed ideas, is often prejudiced, acts first then thinks, uses one or two methods only, needs to be told exactly what to do, has a poor knowledge of subject.

1   Administratively competent, has fixed ideas, can be prejudiced, uses a limited range of methods, likes to be told what to teach. Has a reasonable knowledge of subject but not much knowledge of other subjects.

2   As level 1 but takes the trouble to make lessons enjoyable as well, often by telling amusing stories to break up what is seen as 'boring' material. Often talks of 'getting through the material', is fairly obsessed with assessment and worries excessively that standards are too variable.

3   Uses a wide range of methods, does not like to be told what to teach, has devised a strategy for self-evaluation based on both 'hard' and 'soft' indicators, is interested in the idea of the school or college as a community with shared values and recognizes that progress depends upon a sense of community.

4   As level 3 but has also devised a strategy for personal development based both on regular up-dating of subject knowledge and developments in educational theory.

5   Personal development is based also on a rigorous examination of self, believes that teaching is a moral activity and is able to make space within a crowded scheme of work to try to achieve those aims that are not easily expressed and that are highly sophisticated. Tries to work with colleagues at the same level. Has worked out a way of reconciling the ideas of authority and scepticism, struggles for authenticity at the personal and social levels.

This list is not meant to imply that all teachers must move through these levels. Nor is it meant to suggest that a final list of such levels could ever be compiled. Instead the list is meant to illustrate the way that professional teachers might talk about teacher development in ways that are not necessarily all that meaningful to non-professionals, but that nevertheless can be used as part of a justification for schemes of teacher appraisal.

These schemes have in the main been resisted by the teacher unions on the grounds that the schemes are likely to lead to performance-related pay, local bargaining of conditions of service and a destruction of a collegiate ethos by the imposition of standards of performance that are managerial rather than professional. Little has depended upon these systems of appraisal and in many cases appraisal interviews have been viewed by both parties as a waste of time that detracted from other activities. If staff development needs were identified in the course of appraisal, rarely have there been sufficient resources set aside to satisfy those needs. Matters of promotion and remuneration have been excluded from the appraisal process. Weak teachers had already been identified prior to the appraisal interview and such teachers have been unlikely to use the occasion to admit their weakness even assuming that they knew that they were weak. It is a paradox that the worst teachers are often the ones who appear to have little doubt about their ability. Scepticism does not form part of their sense of self. In the UK therefore while it has been the Government's intention to introduce a system of teacher appraisal, little other than token acceptance of systems has been achieved so far.[30]

A more vigorous and some would say successful attempt has been made in Australia where in some states an 'advanced skills teacher classification scheme' has been introduced.[31] This scheme appears to offer teachers a professional career path as a recognition of their work as good teachers. In practice however it seems that the

---

CASE EXEMPLAR

GOOD TEACHERS

We may summarize the discussion so far by describing good teachers as people who are accomplished in one practice and able to participate in a wide range of other practices so that they can induct others into those practices. They show their commitment to the values of justice, honesty, fairness, democracy in the ways that they organize their teaching and talk to each other, parents and students. They are enthusiastic about the possibilities for their students and about their practice. They are learners themselves. They try to influence policy so that the values which they hold may be encouraged. They are collegial in the sense that they recognize that the widest possible scrutiny of practice is to be preferred. They recognize that teaching involves a number of dilemmas and they manage to be innovative at the same time as dedicated to the rigour of their practice. They cope with dilemmas such as the tension between practice and student, between the authority that comes from that practice and doubt that one has taken the correct decisions, the thin borderline between tasks that stretch students just far enough without destroying their confidence. Finally they know that accounts of good teaching such as this are limited and misleading because these teachers do not share any one thing in common other than a sceptical disposition and the ability to practice in diverse ways within a tradition. Accounts of good teaching are therefore inevitably limited in use and attempts to prescribe good teaching in detail are impossible.

scheme has become tied to managerial rather than professional requirements. Most teachers seem to attain the advanced status provided that they are prepared to meet certain managerial requirements like contributing to out of school activities and taking on extra administrative responsibility. Incidentally the Scottish Senior Teacher Scheme met a similar fate to the Australian scheme. An attempt to reward excellence in teaching became in many cases just another promotion given for taking on extra administrative responsibility.

In the USA the situation appears more hopeful. The National Board for Professional Teaching Standards provides a valuable list of tasks that good teachers should be able to perform well – lists that are compiled by teachers themselves. Teachers pay $1000 to be assessed against these standards by other teachers (who do not know the candidate) in the course of a rigorous two-day process of interviews, presentations and case studies. In that way assessment is carried out by professionals on professionals according to professionally defined standards. Some states are sufficiently convinced of the value of this development that they pay the fees for successful teachers and in some states employers are beginning to recognize professional teaching standards as criteria for promotion within teaching.

In that way it is hoped to encourage a collegiate ethos within school in which a joint commitment to get as many teachers as possible recognized as good teachers is taken as a mark of recognition of excellence within the school. The scheme is expensive. The Americans estimate that it will take well over $50 million dollars and 10 to 15 years to implement fully. At the present time this scheme seems to be the most promising scheme of teacher appraisal available. Of course the scheme will only meet the criterion of accountability if the teachers that are recognized by the scheme equate by and large with those teachers that most other informed people think display the attributes of goodness. If that equation does not happen then it seems likely that there will be further pressure to consumerize the education system possibly by rewarding the most popular teachers. For all the reasons advanced earlier, we should hope that the value of open discursive rationality based on professional standards succeeds.

SUMMARY

In this chapter we have examined an empirical programme of research into teaching and have shown how that research has informed courses of teacher education. We have also seen how that research programme has broadened into a consideration of the social and institutional contexts within which teachers work. That consideration led us to look at the allocation of resources in education systems and the way that such allocation tends to be directed towards easily demonstrable outcomes rather than maintenance of the tacit elements of teaching. We saw that moves to school-based programmes of teacher education could be helpful in countering that trend. That is because such moves may enable a holistic approach to resource allocation, teacher development and parental involvement. Finally we looked at the structuring of a career ladder for teachers that might encourage teaching rather than management and administration.

CASE EXEMPLAR

MIKE ABBOTT: SCIENCE TEACHER[32]

Mike has read the above account of good teaching and agrees with most of it. The problem for Mike is that he has been teaching for ten years without any opportunities for continuing professional development and does not really see that his style of teaching is going to change much now. 'After ten years you know how you teach'. He would like promotion but has not yet managed it. 'I suppose I've got a few chips on my shoulder about this' he complains. He goes along to group meetings but does not really think that they amount to very much.

When asked what would most improve his teaching quality, Mike replies that he would like smaller class sizes and more equipment for experiments. Mike has minimal contact with 'the real world of science'. He has only occasional and informal contact with scientists. He has however been sent on some in-service activities based on the latest curricular developments. He explains that he sees the main advantage of these to be that he gets to meet teachers from other schools and to find out 'how they are coping with the latest changes' and 'what it's like in other schools'.

Mike is sceptical about any attempt to evaluate teaching. He wonders who is going to do the evaluating. He knows that experience should have a lot to do with improved practice but he also knows a lot of older teachers who have just switched off whereas new members of staff often get on really well with the students. In any case, he complains, 'when are we going to get the time really to get to know what other teachers are doing?'

At present Mike does not feel engaged with school development planning. His only contact with parents comes at parents' evenings which he sees as 'pretty contrived affairs anyway, five minutes with one lot, five minutes with another'. He reckons that most parents don't value teachers anyway and that if you try to involve parents in school, you just get 'the pushy ones'.

Mike spends his lunch-times with the technical teachers. He feels comfortable with them. They talk about the improvements that they have recently made to their houses and cars while they eat their sandwiches. Mike's attitude to teaching appears to have evolved from a phase of initial enthusiasm to increasing frustration with what he regards as petty administrative procedures and the lack of prospects. He reflects that sometimes he gets satisfaction when his students seem to have understood. He concedes too that most students are fine, but somehow that is not enough.

The contrast between the last two case exemplars is an indication of the challenges that face us. Somehow in the midst of recent educational reforms the importance of teaching and learning has become obscured. Whatever notion of educational evaluation is developed presumably no one could reasonably claim that teaching and learning are unimportant to it. In order to stress the importance of teaching and learning, the last four chapter headings are organized in ways that correspond to the headings that are often used by teachers as they plan for learning. It is my conjecture that the educational decision-making process should be opened up to non-professional scrutiny and these chapters are meant to support that conjecture and to offer material that might be of use to those involved in school- or college-based teacher education.

NOTES AND REFERENCES

1. A perusal of the catalogues of major educational publishers would confirm these claims.
2. This view may be attributed to Rorty (1980, 1982, 1989) who argues that we tell such stories in the 'ungrounded hope' that things improve if we tell them.
3. Brophy and Good (1986).
4. Clark and Peterson (1986), Shavelson and Stern (1981), Marland (1975).
5. Brown and MacIntyre (1993).
6. Especially important here is Schon (1983, 1987).
7. See Eraut (1994, pp. 142–9).
8. Shulman (1991).
9. Fenstermacher (1986).
10. Carr and Kemmis (1986) has been especially influential. See also Carr (1995). John Elliott and his colleagues at the Centre for Applied Research in Education, University of East Anglia, are also heavily involved in the 'teacher as researcher' movement. See Elliott (1993b) for several accounts of 'action research' projects and their relation to teacher development.
11. Ball and Goodson (1985), Fullan and Hargreaves (1992).
12. Hargreaves and Fullan (1992).
13. See Bottery (1992, 1994) for accounts of the interface between education and industrial systems of management.
14. *Sunday Times*, 23 April 1995, p. 9.
15. McNeil (1986).
16. Of course much legislation has been concerned with the devolution of resources and the creation of a number of 'cost centres' within educational institutions. Very often however such devolution has taken place at the same time as the centralization of other educational functions.
17. See Hoyle and John (1995, Chapter 2).
18. See note 7, Chapter 1.
19. For a series of international vignettes, see Wideen and Grimmett (1994) and for a British perspective Williams (1994).
20. See Shulman (1991).
21. See Hargreaves and Fullan (1992, Chapter 12).
22. Arnowitz and Giroux (1986).
23. See Hargreaves and Fullan (1992, Chapter 12).
24. Nias (1989).
25. As MacBeath (1994) points out in connection with reflection about performance indicators:

   The indicators should be seen less as barometers than as tin openers, that is not giving us definitive measures of a school's quality but as opening a can of worms. Of course no school likes cans of worms and will only expose them to sunlight if there is some faith that they can be found a less slithery lifestyle. (p. 121).

26. See Ingvarson (1994) for a detailed account of the distinctions between these terms.
27. Compare this with the situation in France and Germany in which high entry standards to the profession of teaching seem to go a long way towards satisfying the need for detailed schemes of appraisal. In Germany for example, student teachers have to have degree level passes in two subjects before they can even begin to learn about educational theory and classroom practice (reported in the *Glasgow Herald*, 23 May 1995, p .16).

28. See Turner and Clift (1988).
29. Dreyfus and Dreyfus (1986) present a model of skills acquisition which is summarized by Eraut (1994, p. 123) as follows:

Level 1   Novice
- Rigid adherence to taught rules or plans
- Little situational perception
- No discretionary judgement

Level 2   Advanced Beginner
- Guidelines for action based in attributes or aspects (aspects are global characteristics of situations recognizable only after some prior experience)
- Situational perspective still limited
- All attributes and aspects are treated separately and given equal importance

Level 3   Competent
- Coping with crowdedness
- Now sees actions at least partially in terms of longer-term goals
- Conscious deliberate planning
- Standardized and routine procedures

Level 4   Proficient
- Sees situations holistically rather than in terms of aspects
- Sees what is most important in a situation
- Perceives deviations from the normal pattern
- Decision-making less laboured
- Uses maxims for guidance, whose meaning varies according to the situation

Level 5   Expert
- No longer relies on rules, guidelines or maxims
- Intuitive grasp of situations based on deep tacit understanding
- Analytic approaches used only in novel situation or when problems occur
- Vision of what is possible

Compare this model which seems to depend entirely on learning from experience with my model presented in the main text.
30. See McMahon (1993).
31. Ingvarson (1994) explains this scheme. He also provides an introduction to the work of Shulman (1991) and Scriven (1994) and his 'duties-based' approach to evaluation.
32. This exemplar is based on an actual case study reported by Ingvarson (1992).

Chapter 4

Curriculum Development

The term curriculum development is sometimes used to refer to any sort of educational development. When used in this way, just about any book on teaching, learning, assessment or evaluation could be described as a book on curriculum development. Moreover if curriculum is taken to be that which is taught in educational institutions, then curriculum development is bound to occur as people who work within these institutions develop. More usually however curriculum is defined along the following lines; 'an attempt to communicate the essential principles and features of an educational proposal in such a form that it is open to critical scrutiny and capable of effective translation into practice.[1] Recently curriculum development has come to mean the attempt to bring about changes in what is taught and how it is taught by producing documents that attempt to guide teaching practice.

While details vary between countries and between states within countries, the general idea behind curriculum development remains the same: an administrative authority seeks to retain some control over what is taught and how it is taught so that in the minimum case, students may transfer easily between teachers and institutions and gross educational inequalities may be avoided. From this minimum case however it has become fashionable to try to set out what teachers should do and when they should do it as if such prescription obviously results in standard practice.

Any attempt to control what others should do involves the specification of intention and some form of inspection to see whether the intention has been realized. It is possible to discern two broad approaches to the specification of curriculum intention: product and process. In general, educational products can be taken to refer to those educational *outcomes* that are easily specified and measurable. Processes can be taken to refer to the *activities* in which students engage, the outcomes of which are more uncertain. Fairly obviously the terms are not mutually exclusive. People engage in educational activities in order to achieve educational outcomes. The difference is more one of emphasis. At one extreme there is the idea that the most worthwhile educational outcomes are not easily stated or measured and so it makes little sense to try in advance to specify these outcomes. At the other extreme there is the idea that the activities in which students engage are irrelevant so long as certain desirable products or outcomes are attained – these may relate to individuals or groups.

On the face of it, the process idea seems attractive. Before formal systems of education were instituted, something like this idea might be seen to underpin an individual's educational development, if it informed their development at all. However once systems of education were instituted and financed through some form of collective taxation, then those who controlled the education system on everyone else's behalf began to demand some accountability from the system – in effect they demanded to know what the products of the system were and how much they cost. The emphasis shifted towards the product approach and hence towards an exploration of suitable aims for the education system. As with many other simple slogans or summaries of ideas however the product-process distinction masks a number of conceptual confusions about the nature of education which have quite different practical implications. This chapter is an exploration of the distinction, the confusions that are masked by it and the role that the notions of value and interest play in determining an appropriate balance between two extremes.

PRODUCT

For some time, and particularly in the 1960s, the aims of education was a topic that was given much attention by teacher-trainers and educational theorists – it was widely believed that if only the aims of education could be got right then efficient methods could be selected to achieve those aims, students could be assessed to see whether and to what extent the aims had been achieved and overall educational provision could be evaluated on the basis of the numbers of people who achieved those aims and the ease and enjoyment with which they achieved them. In many cases it was suggested that the success of the education system could be evaluated with reference to some notion of societal harmony and national economic success. A model of this form of means-ends curriculum planning is given in Figure 4.1. The model is in use today and is taken by some to be the only or main means of curriculum planning.[2]

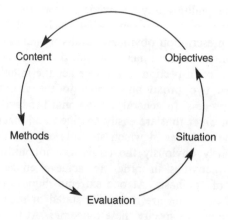

Figure 4.1

The use of this model gives rise to many problems which are discussed in later chapters. For now, I confine my attention to three issues that relate to the formulation of aims. First, it has not been possible to agree upon the precise formulation of the aims and objectives of the education system. Second, even where there is limited agreement upon those aims then it is not clear just how to make these aims operational in the sense that they specify identifiable learning outcomes. Moreover the list of learning outcomes may become so large as to be administratively inconvenient. Finally, and most importantly, even where it is possible to specify identifiable learning outcomes, there remains the problem of how to prioritize their desirability.

CASE EXEMPLAR

THE SPECIFIC OBJECTIVE

The following example may illustrate these problems further: an ability to communicate effectively may be regarded as a suitable aim for students. This aim may be broken down into what might be called general objectives, one of which might be an ability to write clear unambiguous sentences. In turn this general objective might be broken down into more specific objectives. However in order to achieve this specificity, it is necessary to determine the complexity of the sentence that is to be written, the context in which it is written, and the time allowed for composition. Clear unambiguous sentences are found in the tabloid newspapers but they are of a different quality to sentences that are found in the novels of Charles Dickens. An attempt may be made to qualify the specific objective with a list of conditions, but each list may require another list of criteria of interpretation until the list becomes administratively unwieldy and sometimes trivial. Even if this qualification were not seen to be necessary there remains the problem of deciding whether for an individual it is more important that they write clear unambiguous sentences of a high quality rather than performing simple arithmetic calculations. At some stage someone may decide that it is more important for the individual to be able both to write clearly at a low level and perform simple calculations rather than to concentrate only upon improving their literary output. Alternatively an individual may not exactly take a decision to this effect so much as simply let it happen by following their own immediate interest.

Yet this is but one example of the complexity of formulating an educational objective. There are many other objectives that an education system should promote. When this example is supplemented with others taken from a wide range of curricular areas then it is possible to see the enormity of the problems that face administrators trying to implement a product approach to curriculum development. Appreciation of science, geography, history, languages and so on may be thought to be legitimate inclusions of any sort of curriculum let alone a national curriculum. Moreover since educational products are not objects, the only proof that there could be of their acquisition is some form of documentation. (Although such documentation may not in fact prove anything.) Hence the product approach to curriculum development tends to

CASE EXEMPLAR

THE 5–14 DEVELOPMENT PROGRAMME IN SCOTLAND[3]

This programme was implemented after the familiar process described in the previous chapter of:

- identifying a problem with current practice.
- setting up official committees.
- gathering evidence that there is a problem.
- producing a report with recommendations.
- a consultation period.
- producing a development plan.
- appointing development officers from senior staff in schools and elsewhere.
- implementing the programme (this is the stage where teachers become involved).
- evaluating the programme by educational researchers.[4]

As is normal, most stages in the development process were completed by policy-makers and their officials. Two quotes will suffice to illustrate the importance of hierarchical surveillance of teachers to the programme: first as the Consultation Paper made clear 'If there was evidence that education authorities were failing to ensure that schools fully observed national guidelines [the Minister] would not rule out introducing legislation to ensure the proper implementation of national policy'[5]; and at a local level 'Each head teacher should monitor the overall balance of attention to each area of the curriculum throughout the child's primary education; and each class teacher should maintain an appropriate balance throughout the year'.[6]

In this case the curriculum for teachers to follow was divided into five areas and balance was to be assured by specifying the amount of time that a teacher should spend on each area as set out below:

Curricular Areas	Language	Mathematics	Environmental Studies*	Expressive Arts**	Religious & Moral Education
Minimum Time Allocations	20% Flexibility Factor				
	15%	15%	25%	15%	10%

* Environmental Studies includes science, technology, history, geography, health education and home economics.
** Expressive Arts includes drama, music, art and aspects of physical education.

lead to administrative profusion both in the specification of products and in proving that the products have been attained.

The problems with the product approach to curriculum development do not end there however because not all products are of equal value. As we have seen the curriculum may be overloaded and curricular guidelines often include an apportionment of time that should be spent on each curricular area. These guidelines may be written in great detail but that detail does not guarantee uniform interpretation. Nor is it clear what a uniform interpretation of guidelines might mean in an educational context. This is because interpretation is as value-loaded as policy formation or curricular selection. Sometimes it is suggested that interpretation should be guided by what are termed local needs but this suggestion simply pushes the problem of interpreting needs further down the line towards the teacher. In the end teachers simply interpret whatever guidelines are handed to them on the basis of their perception of student needs. That is not to say that curricular guidelines are always useless. For example such guidelines are essential to the appointment of teachers with appropriate specialisms in secondary education. In the case of primary education, teachers may use such guidelines as a means of justifying their teaching strategies to parents and others. In both cases there is a direct appeal to the authority of the curricular group that has issued the guidelines.

While guidelines may attempt to prescribe a curricular balance, that balance will always be upset by the enthusiasm and commitment of teachers and students. Enthusiasm is infectious and skews the attention of students in particular directions. An exciting five minutes may be more effective than a boring day. Those who seek to promote a particular curricular balance might do better to attempt to engender enthusiasm for that balance rather than to produce ever more detailed sets of guidelines. The promotion of values like enthusiasm is not something to which the product approach is particularly suited. Even though that approach appears to offer a systematic development of the curriculum which takes account of values at the first stage when aims are formulated, the approach fails. Let us see how the problem of curricular balance is handled within a national development.

PROCESS

An alternative method of curriculum development is often characterized by the idea that education is a process, either with no predetermined aims or the vaguest aims that are to serve as guides to progress. Hence education is supposed to be a process within which students are encouraged to formulate their own objectives, to discover things for themselves and to evaluate their own success. In the extreme case teachers are seen as facilitators in this process, 'catalysts' who do not affect the direction of the learning.

The child-centred educators who draw their inspiration from reports and publications that were fashionable in the 1960s seem to be the most obvious examples of supporters of the process approach to curriculum development. For these teachers it is the needs and interests of students that are important, not the subject-specialisms of teachers. Followers of Dewey may also be seen to support the process approach to curriculum development in that they see schools not simply as institutions for passing on an existing culture but also as institutions for improving and contributing to culture.[7]

Notice that child centredness and the idea of education as initiation do not necessarily conflict in the same way that process and product may be seen to conflict.[8] The child no more creates the world afresh than a subject teacher reproduces the world as it is. While the process approach does not depend upon the general prescription of educational objectives, that does not mean that teachers have no idea at all about what they are trying to achieve. In the same way, while subject teaching might seem more suitable for the product approach to curriculum development, that does not mean that subject teachers have no regard for their students' interests and abilities, nor their own desire to improve cultural understandings.

The description of one's self as child or subject centred might not amount to much in practice. The way in which teaching practice is controlled however through the specification of curriculum intention may amount to a great deal. On the face of it, the process approach to curriculum development has many attractions – it appears anti-authoritarian, flexible, need not lead to administrative proliferation, puts learning at the centre of curriculum development rather than the periphery, may promote generic skills that are useful across the curriculum like the ability to solve problems and transfer those skills to future contexts including the context of work. This trans-ferability is supposed to arise as students are encouraged to look for their own solutions to problems rather than to rehearse some predetermined objective. Adherents of the process approach might argue that there is little point teaching towards predetermined outcomes that are quite specifically formulated in the past when students have to face a future that is open. There is little point, they may argue, in being able to satisfy many trivial objectives, however clear and unambiguous, when the problems that students face are inevitably complex and do not necessarily resemble problems that they have encountered earlier.

They may go on to argue that the whole is always greater than the parts and that it is pointless to try to break down a complex task into simpler sub tasks in advance of a problem to be solved. Instead they argue that the way in which a complex is broken into simples is very much the key to the solution of the problem and that the more ingenious students become at looking for ways of breaking down problems the more successful they will become. Supporters of the product approach to curriculum development do not grasp the essential point that whatever way is used to express a desirable objective, that way is necessarily framed in the past, whereas students have to cope with a contingent future. Creativity would be impossible if experience were completely described in product terms.

It is not hard to see that the applicability of both approaches to education can be extended to the way that people choose to conduct their lives. On the one hand, readers will be able to recognize themselves and others sometimes formulating lists of jobs, ticking them off as completed, making new lists and so on until paradoxically they achieve the only objective that was ever certain – death. In an attempt to avoid confronting this certainty some people tend to be single-minded in pursuit of one aim. For them all other objectives are fulfilled as a means to achieving the aim. For example some people become obsessive about their children getting better jobs than themselves. For other people the line in the John Lennon song seems apposite. 'Life is what happens while you're busy making other plans'.

This line seems to highlight the futility of lists, pursuing aims single mindedly, and contributing to administrative profusion. People of this more liberal persuasion find it unacceptable for one group to set objectives for others to achieve. They see that the institutionalization of this idea leads people to check up on others to see that they are working towards the institutionally sanctioned objectives. They worry that expressions of doubt may be viewed as subversion and punished. They are concerned that progress is determined according to one set of institutionally sanctioned objectives rather than notions of individual progress and freedom.

It is also not difficult to see a variety of polarities lurking beneath product and process approaches – the politics of right and left, a subject-based and topic-based approach to teaching, examinations and projects, telling someone that they are wrong and telling them that they might be right in certain circumstances, the idea that intelligence is hereditary and the idea that intelligence is socially conditioned, hierarchy and democracy, punishment and prevention, behaviourism and cognition, objectivism and relativism, liberalism and authoritarianism. Of course these polarities do not fall neatly under the two headings product and process, nor under any other two headings. Similarly the way that people think and their behaviour do not fall under two headings either. It is not difficult therefore to accept that both approaches might inform the work of professional educators. For example at times it may be helpful actually to write down an objective that seems non-trivial and assessable simply on the basis that

---

CASE EXEMPLAR

MULTIMEDIA AND THE HUMANITIES

Computerized learning packages are now available which use a variety of media to engage and sustain the interest of students. These packages may be seen to be based on the product approach to curriculum development consisting, as they do, of a product that is completely described in its software. At the other extreme of the product/process spectrum, there is the idea that the development of a new sense of community among teachers encourages the sharing of certain values, norms and procedures to the extent that curriculum development may be seen as a practice in itself with a distinctive tradition.

The Humanities Curriculum Project[9] which was directed by Stenhouse in the 1970s is a good example of such a project. Within the project, policy-making, theorizing, researching, evaluating, teaching and learning were seen to be integral to the curriculum development process. This project was not characterized so much by its documentation, nor by the identification of stages as by the meetings that teachers held to try to engender a shared understanding of the new practice of 'developing an understanding of social situations and human acts and of the controversial value issues which they raise'.

It is not hard to see that some of the latest multimedia packages could be used effectively in projects of the latter sort and conversely that video recordings of discussions that took place as parts of projects of the latter sort could be used in packages of the former sort. Even though these examples of curriculum development may be seen to be at opposite ends of the product/process spectrum, they may nevertheless be combined as part of a worthwhile educational experience.

the meaning is clear to everyone. The following is an example of such an objective: students should be able to add up to 3 two-digit numbers without the aid of a calculator but with the aid of paper and pencil.

At other times it seems appropriate just to take part in a process for the sake of that process only – for example engaging in a game or painting a picture. If qualities such as leadership, creativity, sensitivity are promoted by these sorts of activity, then that is a bonus but the prime motivation for engaging in them is simply the intrinsic value of the activity. Of course teachers may encourage people to engage in a process on the basis of their experience that such engagement does in fact promote other things. It is important to note that the two do not form opposites as if a process never resulted in a product and vice versa. The difference between the two is more a matter of emphasis that is reflected in the way that curriculum intention is written. The important practical decision is the extent to which teachers are to be trusted to select appropriate activities for students and the extent to which attempts should be made to prescribe those choices.

VALUES

For some time, in Britain at any rate, philosophy of education and a concern for values in education have not been popular. No doubt the nature of the work that some philosophers of education were doing led to a general dissatisfaction with the idea that much could be gained from analyses of terms like 'the aims of education' and 'indoctrination'. Moreover the market reforms of the 1980s led to the idea that values and wants were the same thing. In these circumstances, philosophy of education generally and debate about values and education in particular was seen by many commentators to be otiose. After all, it was argued, if market demand can determine the aims of the educational enterprise then there seems little point in debating the matter further let alone paying people to carry on this debate!

Yet despite the dominance and attractions of market-led public policy and the political hegemony that is alleged to have arisen as a result of this dominance and attraction, I suspect that a general shift in emphasis is now taking place: the market is beginning to be seen more as just one informative and useful tool in the determination of desirable ends rather than as the only or main tool. There seems to be a growing recognition of the importance of informed debate about the aims of public institutions to take account of long-term purposes and interrelationships.

There is no logical once and for all solution to this problem of selecting an appropriate balance between short- and long-term consideration. Instead this problem may be treated as a practical problem, the solution to which is based on the best account of the way things are at any particular instance. It is foolish therefore to assume that aim and method can be distinguished once and for all and that the means may always be justified on the basis of the end. In retrospect it will often be possible to see that some people have suffered in the interests of others. However at the time it is hard to justify prolonging someone's disadvantage if only for the reason that there is no guarantee that the desired objective will be achieved. Instead both means and ends are modified in an ongoing way in which the notion of individual practical judgement is central. Hence method and aim necessarily merge in education – people are likely to be as interested in the quality of the experience on offer as in the achievement of some predetermined aim.

We need to take far more seriously the idea that people are attracted to and enthusiastic about those things that they value. Such interest and enthusiasm is not prescribable nor controllable by systems of inspection and appraisal which may be circumvented by getting to know the criteria of inspection and appraisal and learning to play the game as it were. People are persuaded to do things differently when they are shown a better way of doing something and their evaluative assumptions are successfully challenged. Yet the language of persuasion and the ethics of demonstration are not generally included in educational policy and practice. Instead policies are presented as if they were a definitive statement of the way things must turn out and as if it were obvious how to implement those policies.

CASE EXEMPLAR

THE MISSION STATEMENT

If curriculum development is about producing documents to bring about change, then the question arises as to what length of document is most effective. A similar problem faces policy-makers generally. If the document is too long, no one reads it. If it is too short it appears as if the authors have not taken the need to change seriously enough. In recognition of the former warning, many industrial and public sector organizations have taken to forming a 'mission statement' as a statement of the values that underpin the organization. It is believed by many people that the values that people hold have the most effect on how they behave and so short statements of values are seen to be an important means of communication. Yet, typically, mission statements have a similar inauthentic ring to them. There is often mention of quality outcomes, national and international excellence and customer delight. As Harvey-Jones remarks, 'most of these statements show more sign of careful drafting by groups of people than by deeply held emotional beliefs'.[10]

In other cases however a few jottings on a piece of paper have a more authentic appeal. In the OECD study on quality teaching[11] the importance of shared values is stressed many times. The US case study writer describes a 'hand written yellowing sheet that is pinned up in a school and that has been used to good effect for five years. The paper reads

Good Instructional Practices
- Variety of learning experiences
- Reasons for activities
- Frequent checks for understanding
- Risk Taking

The point of this example is to emphasize that detailed documents do not necessarily bring about desired change. As I argued earlier, good stories, no written work at all and pictures may all be useful in curriculum development. As we have seen there seems no alternative to examining personal values indirectly through the kind of open debates and attempts at persuasion that characterize some of the best educational endeavours. Of course such examination and engagement is not easy. Open argument and persuasion are often associated with personal rancour. Therefore the kind of changes that have been advocated in this book depend upon disagreements not being interpreted as personal dislikes. In public and in private clarity, scepticism, criticism and disagreement may come to be viewed as indications of a genuine concern and liking for someone rather than as indications of hostility or threat.

In this way we may argue passionately in favour of our point of view but at the same time recognize the contingency of our passion. The ensuing discussion is informed by a climate of respect for the views of others and a discursive ethos. Empiricism leads us not to value argument and persuasion but instead to value hierarchy as a substitute for the authority that was supposed to be supplied by the idea of an objective reality. It is hard to make sense of the idea of an objective reality against which to judge curriculum development. Instead the contestability of values seems logically essential to any attempts to educate. I believe that we would do better therefore to acknowledge this contestability head-on as it were in particular attempts to persuade rather than to try to disguise this contestability by professional elitism and bureaucratic proliferation. I suspect that something like the former acknowledgement characterizes the best teachers whereas the latter disguise is characteristic of the worst.

It might be objected that my arguments in favour of a discursive ethos amount to little more than a reshuffle of power relations in favour of those best able to justify, argue and debate (the chattering classes, as they are sometimes known). However I am not arguing for some immutable self-perpetuating power structure. The ability to argue well in one area of discourse does not necessarily coincide with recognition of an ability to argue well in all areas. The low esteem in which some academics are held is an example of this. It is said that academics have no common sense, are unable to relate to the ordinary world and that they are in an ivory tower. Nor do I argue that within an organization there should not be some form of executive which takes decisions on behalf of others. Instead precisely the opposite of this could apply. It is economical to devolve executive functions and the possibility of justifying decisions does not mean that every decision has to be justified. Trust is based on a recognition of a person's authority in certain areas. The authority is not imposed on others but recognized by them. Moreover that recognition may be temporary. We need to get used to the idea that positions of power should be dynamic and this dynamism should be institutionalized.

Now if flatter management structures, collegiality and discursive methods of decision-making are best for some businesses then we might imagine that these features would be essential within educational institutions. Open discussion incorporating argument, persuasion and justification enables us to resolve the issue of what we ought to do for the best where there is collective disagreement. Therefore whatever else an education system might achieve, to enable people to take part in such discussions is central. The question arises then as to how this enabling is to be achieved? Part of the answer appears to be that those who work within educational institutions should practise in such a way that they demonstrate their commitment to a discursive ethos.[12]

I dare say that such a demonstration would involve changes in the management

CASE EXEMPLAR

MANAGEMENT AND DEMOCRACY: A SOLUTION FROM
BUSINESS[13]

There is now a great deal of evidence that organizations are more effective and
efficient if 'flatter' management structures are introduced. A range of management theorists make the obvious point that the emphasis in modern business on
rapid response times and changing market conditions points towards the introduction of flexible project teams rather than fixed deep hierarchical structures.

These theorists argue that no one can predict the future and the organizational
risk is reduced if everyone has a say about what should be done. The dangers of
hierarchy are clear. There only needs to be one less than adequate individual at
the top and the organization is finished. In any case as Harvey-Jones[14] points out
hierarchical structures are very costly to maintain. People spend too much time
protecting their position and status and not enough time contributing to the team
effort. He cites, as do many others, the Japanese Kaizen systems which emphasize single status dress, canteens and working hours. He argues that power as
well as responsibility needs to be shared out and decisions taken at the
appropriate time.

It is usually assumed that no one likes to give up power and that managers
might be most opposed to the introduction of flatter hierarchical structures.
Harvey-Jones points out however that within a flatter management structure
there is no hiding place for incompetents at any level. It is less easy to blame
others if one is given the responsibility and the power to act. It seems clear that
competent people respond to trust, scope for initiative and collegiality and that
their performance is impaired by attempts to control them. A business solution
to the problem of management seems to echo the theme of diversity within a
tradition that, in the case of some businesses, is maintained by collegial ways of
working.

structure of many educational institutions to facilitate the culture of collegiality that
was described in the previous chapter. Further changes beyond such institutions would
seem also to be necessary however. In many places the idea of discourse and a
discursive ethos are not common and accepted ways for contesting values; discussing
possibilities and challenging prejudices are not the norm. For example, some contexts
for argument are too aggressive and immediate for many people. Party-political
debates commonly have this quality. On the other hand the context in which scholars
argue in print over the merits of a particular point of view may be considered too
abstruse and lacking in immediacy. It seems to me that a discursive context should be
closely related to what we might call ordinary conventions for the reasons advanced
earlier in connection with the discussion of common sense.

Many people are suspicious of the context in which some formal discussions
presently take place. In many ways the formal public enquiry in which everyone is

supposed to be able to contribute, is the epitome of rational discussion. Yet many people are deeply suspicious of this form of enquiry. Their suspicion arises partly because they feel intimidated by the formality of the context, but also because they imagine that there is a much more open and honest discussion taking place somewhere else at which the real decisions are actually being taken. That is not to suggest a conspiratorial thesis. Rather it is to suggest that it is difficult to explain genuine concerns in a context drained of emotion and normal human reactions.

In the second case there is the issue of the choice of language to be used in discussions. Anyone who has attended a Planning Enquiry will suspect that a familiarity with specialist terms from planning is an advantage to those who wish to gain support for their proposals. Planning consultants are hired so that such an advantage may be gained. So long as the context for a discourse is always constituted in such a way that someone is appointed to take an ultimate decision as in the case of a Planning Enquiry then it will always be prudent to address remarks for their benefit and in a language that they understand easily. In those cases the idea of openness and freedom in discourse is disadvantaged.

A further obstacle to open discourse arises from the fact that language is already loaded with evaluative presuppositions which can distort communication in favour of particular groups. An obvious example of this is provided by some feminists who argue that language itself is loaded against the interests of women. Hence it is now customary to avoid using masculine nouns and pronouns to avoid the exclusion of girls and women. Paradoxically this notion of distorted communication may support a realization of the importance of discourse. This is because the recognition of the notion is only possible because we can subject our evaluative preconceptions to critical scrutiny and that includes those conceptions that are embedded within our language. The notion of an ideal language blinds us into thinking that we must have access to purity in language in order to recognize distortions. However we may expose our evaluative preconceptions one by one as it were against a background of common linguistic use and may come to recognize instances of distorted communication in that way. Theoretical discourse often has this edifying function.

Even if it is accepted that theoretical difficulties with the notion of a discourse can be overcome, the practical difficulties of sustaining such discourse in an educational context that is dominated by an empiricist ethos remain. So long as we continue to conceptualize decision-making as a potential dispute that can only be settled by appeal to some sort of final arbiter then the practical difficulties of appointing such an arbiter and of establishing a context for arbitration seem unsolvable. However we need to keep reminding ourselves that we often come to an agreement without such an arbiter. It may be convenient to have a referee on some occasions where the nature of the game is such that winning is the only point worth considering, where the participants are necessarily partisan and where practically it is not possible to debate the wisdom of a decision. However even in these cases it is possible to evaluate a decision in retrospect as in the case of an action replay for example or in the case of an appeal in a court of law.

In all these latter cases, the issue of an appropriate context for a discussion is central. In some cases the game being played or the activity engaged in determines its own context for arbitration. In other cases like ones connected with the functioning of educational institutions, the prescription and limiting of a context is not possible if

CASE EXEMPLAR

TRUTH AND IDEAL CONSENSUS

It is common to distinguish between three types of theories of truth[15] and it is possible to argue that different types of curriculum development are based on those theories. Correspondence theories are based on the empiricist idea that there is a world external to us and that statements are true if they correspond to the way the world is. Hence it is true to say that it is raining if indeed it is in fact raining. Coherence theories of truth are based on the idea that statements are true if they cohere with other statements that are known to be true. Hence if all the theories of natural science are held to be true and a new statement is held to be scientific in the same way, then we may take it to be true. The third type of theories of truth are called consensus theories of truth. According to these theories, a statement is true if a group agrees that the statement is true. Readers will notice that a consensus theory of truth has been implied in this book. I have however tried to explain how truth and authenticity are interrelated. For me, not just any sort of agreement guarantees the truth of a statement. Rather the more authentic the context is within which agreement is reached, the more likely it is that the discussion will be oriented towards discovering the truth.

As we have seen, authenticity is an opaque concept that is more likely to be realized in the most open and critical discussions that are guided by the ideal speech situation. This ideal is discussed by Habermas[16] in order to indicate that truth claims may only be decided in a democratic form of public discussion which allows for participants to be 'free from any threat of domination, manipulation or control'. Habermas uses the term 'discourse' to describe the type of conversation that would take place in an ideal situation. This use may be seen to underpin the idea of a discursive ethos within which people converse with one another for the sake of the conversation and not as the means to achieve some pre-determined end.

While the ideal situation may never be realized, it may serve to guide developments in favour of those that have been subjected to the most critical and open scrutiny. We do not actually have to have participated in the ideal case in order to imagine what that case might be like and how that ideal might guide our educational decision-making.

open and genuine discussion is to be possible. Some people may object that the notion of open discourse depends upon a general ability to take part in a discourse and that not everyone is equally competent to do that. It is true that some people think quicker than others and some people may not be so confident in presenting their views, but we may make allowances for those factors. We do this not as a condescension but rather as a means of demonstrating a commitment to open discourse. In any case normal human relations involve such accommodation. Brain surgeons converse with bus conductors, legal experts with prostitutes, teachers with students. It is simply the case that if people have an interest in others then they find ways of talking to them. For example in a limited sense, foreign tourists often find ways of explaining what they want in a restaurant even though their command of the native language is minimal. Just as we do not speak in French to a German, similarly we do not speak in technical terms that we know our discursive partners do not understand.

A discursive ethos within the education system would not involve a seemingly endless number of committees either at central or local level. Nor should we imagine that a proliferation of local committees is a means of achieving the dynamic transference of power that is advocated. These committees may not promote genuine and open discourse because formally conceived bodies have a tendency to reinforce prior power relationships: the professional versus the interested parent, teachers versus managers who have some control over them. In contrast a discursive ethos supports argument and disagreement as an expected and normal part of daily activity. We may not move immediately from an elitist to a discursive ethos but we may make moves in that direction. In that way curriculum development goes beyond documentation, reconceptualization and management structure to cultural reorientation towards discourse.

SUMMARY

We have discussed some of the difficulties with the idea that educational development is best achieved through curriculum development. The product/process dichotomy was seen to amount to little more than a difference in emphasis in specifying aims or methods. That is because it is undesirable sharply to distinguish aims and methods. We have seen the futility of attempts to prescribe the activities of teachers in a detailed way and have considered the view that good teaching may be characterized by diversity that is enabled by tradition not prescription. It is worth remembering that teaching differs from many other practices in that trainee teachers have detailed knowledge of their chosen practice through their experience as students. Trainees have already observed a wide range of teachers at work before they even begin their formal induction into teaching practice. There is no equivalent of this extended demonstration in other professional practices. It seems reasonable therefore to assume that trainee teachers already have an idea of how to proceed on the basis of their experience. What they do not have an idea of is how well they are developing as teachers and how they might evaluate their idea of personal development.

The personal development of teachers may be expensive and curricular materials might appear to circumvent the sceptical problem described above. However good teaching depends upon personal engagement with a sceptical problem rather than self-satisfied acceptance of curricular authorities. It is usually assumed that educational development is achieved through some combination of staff and curriculum development and that both sorts of developments need to be managed. Yet as we have seen educational development depends upon a change in the ethos that informs educational institutions. In other words educational development ought not to be seen as a planned event or series of events during which something is done with teachers or the courses that they teach. It has become normal to accept that policy-makers should assume control of curriculum development and that that control may be made more acceptable to teachers generally if certain selected teachers are involved in the development process. It does not seem unreasonable for governments to seek some control over the development of an education system and the development of curriculum. The idea that teachers should teach what they want seems unacceptable. But so is the idea that teachers should only teach what and how they are told.

NOTES AND REFERENCES

1. Stenhouse (1975, p. 4).
2. See Nicholls and Nicholls (1978). Also Golby *et al.* (1975).
3. The Scottish Office Education Department (SOED) (1994) provides a guide to this development.
4. Kirk (1982, p. 92), describes this process.
5. SOED (1987, para 28).
6. SOED (1993a, p. 6).
7. For an account of child-centred education, see Darling (1994). Notice however that Darling seems to want to preserve some notion of child-centreness that goes beyond pedagogy, yet I am not clear that writers such as Dewey, Rousseau and Frobel do share anything that might be called 'child-centredness' in common.
8. Hirst and Peters (1970, pp. 28–32) make the point that traditional and progressive approaches are not necessarily incompatible. Indeed they argue (to Darling's apparent disapproval) that

   Education had been conceived too much in terms of a set stock of information, simple skills, and static conformity to a code. The progressives, in revolt, stressed qualities of mind such as critical thought, creativeness and autonomy. But they did not sufficiently appreciate that these virtues are vacuous unless people are provided with the forms of knowledge and experience to be critical, creative and autonomous *with*. (italics in original p. 31)

9. This is described in Stenhouse (1975).
10. Harvey-Jones (1994, p. 4).
11. OECD (1994, p. 91).
12. See Kelly (1995). Aspin, Chapman and Froumin (1995) also explore the notion of a democratic school.
13. See Bottery (1994) for an analysis of what may be transferred from business to education.
14. Harvey-Jones (1994, p. 145).
15. Scheffler (1965, pp. 39–44) discusses these theories of truth.
16. Habermas (1970) writes

   The design of an ideal speech situation is necessarily implied in the structure of potential speech, since all speech, even intentional deception, is oriented towards the idea of truth . . . in so far as we master the means for the construction of the ideal speech situation, we can conceive of the ideas of truth, freedom and justice. (p. 372)

   The ideal speech situation may be seen as a regulative ideal that is similar to the way that Popper describes truth claims in natural science as open to challenge in free debate in which only the force of the better argument prevails. This feature of 'discourse' is discussed further by Carr and Kemmis (1986, p. 143) and also by McCarthy (1978) in the course of his comprehensive discussion of Habermas's work.

Chapter 5

Aims

The previous chapter was concerned with curriculum development in general and the specification of curriculum intention in particular. It was argued that it is unhelpful to be too prescriptive in such specification and that curriculum development depends primarily upon the enthusiasm and commitment of teachers and students working within a discursive ethos. The conclusion reached was that despite the complexity and evaluative nature of educational decisions, the education system should be open to widespread scrutiny so that there is the maximum opportunity for teachers to discuss possibilities, justify their decisions and persuade others who disagree with them. Disagreement should be seen as a normal feature of a discursive ethos which informs both the aims of the education system and the way that educational professionals, students and others work.

Elitism arises out of the claim that the education system is so complex and value-laden that some form of hierarchical closed decision-making procedure is inevitable. This claim is often based on the practical difficulty of securing agreement on complex and potentially divisive issues like educational aims and methods. In this chapter it is argued that there is rather more agreement on educational aims than élitists might claim and that some of these aims may usefully be stated while others may not. According to this argument, we do not try to set out the aims of education once and for all, as it were. Instead we only set out educational aims[1] in so far as they help us to solve the problems that we have now. One of the main problems that we face, as I have argued, is to establish the democratic conditions within educational institutions that will enable us to distinguish between good and bad practice. The idea of 'education for democracy' rests not only on epistemological criteria that were discussed in the first two chapters but also on the ethical, moral and practical basis of enabling people to be committed to and to make informed decisions within a form of life that is simply accepted by most people as the best hope that we have.

Talk about educational aims is classified by many educational theorists into things that people should know, things that people should do and attitudes that they should have.[2] For example people should know why argument, persuasion and justification are important educational activities. They should be able to take part in those activities and they should recognize the importance of self doubt, of the ability to listen and of the ability to take seriously the views of those who disagree with them. In short, aims may be classified into knowing that (theoretical knowledge), knowing how (practical knowledge, ability) and attitudes (dispositions, values). Both theoretical and practical knowledge seem to be related to the product approach to curriculum development because it seems to be easy to assess whether someone knows in these ways. For example people may be asked to write down reasons or perform activities. It is much more difficult however to assess whether someone has certain attitudes or values or even what it means to have certain attitudes or values. A process approach is often suggested as the best way of characterizing aims of this latter sort.

Despite the popularity of this threefold classification of aims in the practical matter of communicating curriculum intention, the classification has been heavily criticized on the grounds that it offers no advantages over the specification of aims in ordinary language. The purpose of setting down aims may not be as an aid so much to the construction of an elaborate model for curriculum development as to widespread conversations and justifications about education. For example there is unlikely to be much disagreement about wanting children to learn how to read and write, to be interested in their history, science and art, to be able to mend and clean things, to be prepared for some kind of work, to be honest and thoughtful and to respect other people's views. In the remaining part of this chapter we examine what might usefully be specified about the aims of various sectors of education. First though, let us consider an exemplar which highlights the way that compulsion to attend school need not imply that there is a need to specify educational aims in great detail.

Arguments in favour of a core or compulsory curriculum usually rest on the idea that some education to a foundation level of capability is needed to sustain the motivation to continue learning and to promote social cohesion through common experiences at school.[3] Both aims are widely believed to be worthwhile in themselves. Therefore, the arguments go, all children should attend school and be inducted into some common practices. The best way of ensuring commonality, it is assumed, is to specify those aims that should be achieved by all students and to test until those aims have been achieved. It is worth noting however that in Britain, as elsewhere, parents have the right to educate their children at home and the number of these 'home schoolers' is increasing.[4]

CASE EXEMPLAR

FAMILY RESEMBLANCE AND CURRICULUM CHOICE

Children who are brought up in homes in which it is normal to discuss history, play tennis and watch television are likely to be inducted into the practices of history, tennis and television at home. These practices are not exclusive to one another however. Plainly some television programmes are about tennis and history. Tennis itself has a history as does television. Moreover these practices overlap with other practices through common activities such as reading, rule-following, telling the truth, recounting an observation and trying out new ideas.

To describe learning as an induction into practices is to describe learning as a form of socialization since practices do not exist apart from people who act in ways characteristic of the practice. Such socialization is not limiting however because practices overlap.[5] It is a mistake to assume that the conception of education as initiation necessarily leads to what has been called the balkanization of practices or the teachers of practices.[6] It is also a mistake to assume that this conception implies a military-style form of teaching or training in which the notions of play and experimentation are otiose. No practice follows entirely from the application of a set of rules as if such a set could be prescribed in advance of the practice or as if one set of rules governed one practice, another set governed another practice and so on. Nevertheless some form of training may well be a prerequisite for further induction into some practices. Moreover for formal educational purposes, certain practices are to be preferred rather than others not only because some practices may be degenerating but also because certain practices involve activities that are obviously common to many other progressive practices in which we have an educational interest.

That is why generally we prefer to induct students as a priority into those practices that are termed the humanities rather than practices such as swimming or bricklaying. The former include activities such as imagining, writing, reading and discussing what it is to be human, whereas the latter include these activities to a lesser degree. That is not to discount the latter as less worthwhile than practices of the former type. Plainly if you want to build a wall, bricklaying is more valuable than poetry and walls may be more aesthetically pleasing than some poems. Instead it is to argue that the former sort of practice is more useful than the latter for formal educational purposes even though induction into the latter may be of some educational value.

When it comes to deciding what practices should be included in the formal educational curriculum the decision is complicated by the fact that children have already been and are continuing to be inducted into certain practices outwith school. While teachers cannot know for sure what these practices might be they and only they can plan their lessons to take account of what students do outwith school and what students are interested in doing in the future. It is unlikely for example that good teachers would plan lessons to include an excessive amount of watching television, colouring in books and playing in parks. It is worth emphasizing however that an induction into a practice may be a gateway into other practices for students who are motivated to find out more. In that way children who learn to read novels may go on to read about history, geography and other practices.

From this exemplar we can see that there is an essential indeterminism about the formal curriculum. That does not mean however that there can be no justification for compulsory schooling. Nor does it mean that parents and guardians ought not to want to send their children to schools. Without some form of compulsion however some parents and guardians may not provide any opportunities at all for their children to take part in social practices that involve more than two or three people or that involve their children looking beyond their immediate environment. The school offers a different sort of communal involvement to that which is on offer at home though many home schoolers argue that communal involvement within the school amounts to little more than a repressive form of induction into a particularly deformed set of practices. For them the opportunities for students to share ideas, to learn the give and take of conversations are outweighed by exposure to bullying, inadequate teachers and the repression that might arise out of the compulsion to attend. Whether or not children attend schools, it seems uncontentious to suggest that all children should learn certain practices to a sufficient depth for them to at least have a reasonable chance of going on on their own. Principal among this latter sort of practices are surely those that enable children to read, write and perform simple arithmetic calculations. For many people a primary education should be concerned first and foremost with these abilities.[7]

PRIMARY EDUCATION

The formal primary curriculum is often divided into something like the following: language, mathematics, environmental studies, expressive arts and religious and moral education.[8] It is not possible to list here, or possibly anywhere, the detailed objectives that might comprise each of the above mentioned areas though these areas are taken by curriculum designers to constitute some sort of balance in the primary curriculum. However it is unlikely that someone not involved in education professionally would categorize the aims of primary education in that way. I suspect that these people are much more likely to talk in terms of the three Rs, reading, writing and arithmetic, physical education of some sort, knowledge of the world and the values of honesty, creativity and diligence.

We might expect there to be widespread agreement on the desire for children to learn to read, write, add up, multiply and divide. Moreover the recognition of stages within these activities is reasonably unproblematic. For example difficulty with texts, size of print, ability to use dictionaries, encyclopaedias, adding two digit numbers, three digit numbers, multiplication and division are things that are easily understood and easily describable. In the case of mathematics it is possible to be quite precise in detailing educational outcomes because of the lack of ambiguity in the use of basic mathematical language and the ease of assessing whether those outcomes have been achieved. The context for achievement is clear and is implicit within the statement of the desired outcome. The same precision may be achieved in the case of knowledge about language. For example a statement detailing an ability to check spelling using a dictionary is in need of little further elaboration since the context for achievement is clear.

Similarly the statement that children should be able to multiply two 2-digit numbers using pencil and paper is fairly unambiguous. Again the context is clear. Many more examples could be given. There might be minor disagreement about some issues like the importance of mental arithmetic for the multiplication of large numbers but this disagreement is not likely to be serious. In short there does not seem to be much of a problem in explaining in ordinary language the stages that children go through in learning the so-called three Rs. Moreover testing procedures are easily established, easily verifiable by anyone without the need for special resources.

It is worth noting that an ability in language is not so easily defined as an ability in mathematics or knowledge of language which includes grammar and syntax. This is due to the fact that activities like reading aloud and discussion are influenced very much by the context in which these activities take place. For example, it is much more difficult to read well out loud if the audience is bored or hostile. In addition the use of particular expressions and accents may be quite acceptable in one area but incomprehensible elsewhere. Moreover language is changing all the time. It is not possible to stop linguistic development by trying to describe once and for all correct usage. An education in the use of language is situated in the flux of changing experience not fixed in some immutable prescription.

Just as we can see that some balance between product and process approaches is appropriate to curriculum development associated with the three Rs, so the balance is appropriate to the teaching of other things. For example the teaching of expressive art seems most suited to a process approach because logically art seems to include the idea of something original. On the other hand techniques may well be described and technical proficiency may be developed alongside aesthetic awareness. Recognition of the importance of narrative and awareness of self may be seen as part of the wider project of induction into a cultural inheritance. An ability to talk about pictures, plays and operas may be a practical consequence of such an induction but it is neither necessary nor appropriate precisely to specify which pictures or plays should be studied in abstraction from the interests of those who are taking part in the study.

Again in the case of environmental studies, it seems not to matter so much whether children study the solar system, plants, energy sources or any other related topic so long as they develop an interest in the ways that the environment is commonly conceptualized. Nor does it matter so much whether television, newspapers, books or leaflets are used in this development. The point is that children come to see that it is possible to relate many seemingly incoherent features of the environment through the adoption of taxonomies and the study of theories. Since there are many ways of forming this relationship it makes little sense to try to prescribe one way. Instead good teachers will try to build upon childrens' prior interests to engage them in a new area of study. There is no way that these interests can be described in advance of the particular engagement.

For the primary curriculum then it may well be useful nationally to set down certain statements of intent for the areas of mathematics and knowledge about language. For particular schools it may also be helpful to set down certain statements of intent for other areas of the curriculum as well. This local specification would function more as an aid to professional and non-professional debate about curricular content rather than precise guides to teaching. There are some areas of the curriculum however where teachers might be trusted on the basis of their experience and training to select appropriate activities in which students engage. Of course teachers may wish to seek advice on their selection of activities. Moreover a specialist might produce good arguments for choosing particular activities and these arguments might be supported by exemplar learning materials. That is a long way however from the present kind of centralist prescription from government of what teachers should teach and the materials that they should use.

The more prescription there is, the more room there is for interpretive difficulties and for the main point of agreement to get lost in debate about the details of guidelines and prescription. Hence there is more room for the appointment of experts to provide a definitive interpretation and to bolster elitism. On the other hand there are instances where ordinary and specialized language coincides and it is possible and useful to specify a curricular aim. For example, few parents would want their children to do nothing else other than exercises designed to improve an ability in the three Rs. Most parents are likely to want their children to be taught other things that were mentioned earlier as constituents of a broad primary education. However I suspect that most parents are happy to leave the precise curricular content and method for teachers to decide.

We have here an example where the idea of diversity within tradition is reflected in a balance between product and process approaches to curriculum development. A common objection to this balanced approach is that teachers are led to place all their effort on achieving the product three Rs because such achievement is easily monitored by the number of children who achieve the required outcomes in a certain time. The process approach may then become a time-filler consisting of colouring exercises and the like. The effort required to teach in a process way is considerable. Not only does the teacher have to prepare activities that might engage the interests of pupils but also the unpredictability of the pupils' responses makes for demanding lessons. In a situation in which a teacher might have thirty children in a group for twenty-two hours a week, teaching of this sort may not take place.[9]

Where the notion of a learning process becomes conflated with the notion of a time-filler for pupils or a breathing space for teacher, pupils may become bored. Parents may come to doubt the teacher's authority and they may come to wonder whether they could not themselves organize more stimulating processes for their children to engage in, leaving teachers with more time to concentrate on the product areas of curriculum. In a situation in which great emphasis has been placed on the idea of value for money from public services, the emphasis on product approach is reinforced. This is particularly the case where a school's catchment area is predominantly middle class. These parents often have the resources to fund their childrens' activities of the process kind outwith school.

Many teachers have been relieved therefore to be given directives on the proportion of their time that they should spend on various curricular areas. As we have seen in the last chapter however such a directive cannot ensure a balance, merely a means of appealing to the notion of a curricular authority to legitimize a desire to spend time on activities other than practice in the three Rs. Moreover the more that a consumerist ethos is promoted in schools, the more the balance will be distorted in favour of those things that concerned parents cannot provide at home. Therefore the tight prescription of curricular balance may actually work against achieving that balance overall. It is paradoxical that a lack of prescription might actually stand a better chance of achieving some curricular balance.

A catalogue of worthwhile activities could be assembled to inform the selection of particular activities and support could be offered to teachers to exchange ideas about their judgements. The tendency for teachers to concentrate on the achievement of prescribed products may best be countered not by trying to prescribe all parts of the primary curriculum in great detail, but by spending more time actually planning interesting activities within which children practise the three Rs. It should not be imagined that learning the three Rs need necessarily be dull, whereas engaging in creative and other activities is always exciting. There are a variety of imaginative ways of getting children to practise just as there are a lot of boring things for children to do. Moreover some form of training in activities may be an essential prerequisite to any worthwhile future engagement in the activity.

CASE EXEMPLAR

WITH AN EYE ON THE MATHEMATICAL HORIZON: DILEMMAS OF TEACHING ELEMENTARY SCHOOL MATHEMATICS[10]

This exemplar is taken from the work of Loewenberg Ball who grapples with two dilemmas that are central to this book. First she explains how subject matter knowledge is important for effective elementary school teaching but that that knowledge should be related to knowledge of other practices in which the child has an interest. Second she explains how knowledge of the expert need not conflict with the idea of authentic engagement with the experience of the child. She outlines her overall approach as follows:

> Teaching and learning would be improved, the argument goes, if classrooms were organized to engage students in authentic tasks, guided by teachers with deep disciplinary understandings. Students would conjecture, experiment, and make arguments; they would frame and solve problems; they would read and write and create things that mattered to them.[11]

Taking her inspiration from Bruner's oft-quoted assertion that 'any subject can be taught effectively in some intellectually honest form to any child at any stage in development',[12] she argues that she seeks to induct children into the practice of mathematics by doing what mathematicians do.

Instead of doing worksheets and memorizing facts, children engage in serious mathematical problems, discussions, investigations and projects. They are led away from practices in which they are familiar like counting money and riding on escalators towards the more abstract practice of mathematics. As they make progress they are corrected when they have obviously gone wrong but allowed to push their ideas as far as the teacher's subject knowledge will allow. Loewenberg Ball puts it this way, 'with my ears to the ground, listening to my students, my eyes are focused on the mathematical horizon'.

She explains that she teaches negative numbers through the use of analogies. First there is the analogy of monetary payments (+) and debts (−). Second she uses the analogy of a lift that is moving up (+) and down (−) a building that has many floors including underground floors. She asks the children to represent what happens if they start on the fourth floor and come down six floors. They construct a diagram. She goes on to introduce more abstract ideas like the idea of an infinite number of ways of getting to a particular floor and of the sense in which −5 is a larger number than −2. This leads on to consideration of notions such as net worth and balances.

Throughout these lessons she describes how the teacher is walking a sort of tightrope between telling the students that they are wrong and allowing them to go on just far enough to know why they are wrong. Now no one even begins to walk a tightrope if they do not know what is on either side of it. Teachers therefore need to be absolutely confident of their subject and themselves to walk that tightrope. For example, Loewenberg Ball recalls how the children began to question the concept of number itself and to invent unconventional conceptions of number. Teachers have to be able to 'show the children the way back' to convention and they are only able to do this if they have a thorough knowledge of the 'track' themselves through their mathematical training.

Loewenberg Ball presents her dilemma as follows: 'Surely I am responsible for ensuring the content of the third grade curriculum' and 'Might I not be confusing some students by teaching in this open way?' Moreover someone might reasonably complain that it is unfair to leave students floundering instead of giving them the right answer? Fortunately she is able to report that all students have completed the assessment successfully and she goes on to argue that she believes she is responsible for more than this minimum. She concludes that she is committed to trying to get students to see that understanding and sensible conclusions come from hard work and some frustration and pain.

This exemplar illustrates a central dilemma that good teachers face: on the one hand learning involves following how things are done and it is tempting to break things down into easily assessable steps so that student progress may easily be checked; on the other hand following does not necessarily mean replicating behaviour. Rather following sometimes means coming to the right answer having worked things out for one's self as an accomplished practitioner might work things out for themself. There is a danger however that teacher and children develop their own criteria for what is to count as right and wrong rather than coming to understand criteria that are based on the practice of mathematics. That is why some form of external assessment of students is important. The point is not to try to remove curricular guidelines altogether – they serve a purpose as Loewenberg Ball illustrates. The point is to avoid making those guidelines so specific that teachers like her are put off from taking risks to the detriment of the authenticity of their teaching. Loewenberg Ball can justify her practice both in terms of the set criteria for third grade mathematics and by referring to the desirability of a discursive ethos, imaginative ability, cooperation, listening to others and other aims related to apparently non-mathematical areas of the curriculum.

Teaching of this type is demanding and involves a shift of resources away from management, administration and inspection towards lesson preparation, publishing of ideas, consulting about and justifying curricular decisions. The shift of resources also involves the strengthening of a tradition of teaching against a constant stream of imposed changes. Tradition however does not mean stagnation and for a tradition to develop it is important that the members of a tradition are themselves engaged in an educative enterprise – that they learn from one another. This means the same values of honesty, compassion and fairness that teachers try to encourage in their pupils also inform the tradition of teaching itself and the administrative development which supports that tradition.

Recently it has become common practice for parents to help out in primary schools in what is referred to as cooperative teaching. On the face of it this practice is entirely commendable: the school is open to scrutiny; the value of cooperation is demonstrated.

Yet the nature of the partnership between teacher and parent is not entirely clear in this venture. In the first case one party is a paid employee, the other party is not. In the second case one party has a professional interest in teaching, the other party may be seen to have a partisan interest in the teaching of their child. Cooperative teaching may be seen to favour the child of the co-opted parent. There are good reasons therefore to be wary of the move to increase the amount of cooperative teaching however cost effective this may appear to be. Instead parental expertise may be utilized in a much less problematic way if a distinction is drawn between statutory provision for which teachers assume primary responsibility and non-statutory provision that takes place in school buildings. This latter type of provision may be staffed by parents and may be supervised on a voluntary basis.

CASE EXEMPLAR

SUPPORTED STUDY[13]

It is widely acknowledged that students learn at different rates and that while it may be organizationally and educationally effective to learn in classes within school, some students are unable to keep up with the class for one reason or another. It is also acknowledged that all students benefit from some additional help with their study. In both cases there is the idea that formal learning within a class should be supplemented with some form of supported study. In mainstream schools, it is common to have learning support teachers who operate either within or without the class to help particular students who have special educational needs. The idea that children with special needs are somehow in a separate category to those in the mainstream has come to be replaced by the idea of a spectrum of need emphasizing that most children need support at some stage in their learning.

In some schools schemes of supported study are established within which volunteers offer support to any students that want their help. For example, one school in Edinburgh[14] involves secondary pupils befriending primary pupils, helping them with their homework and any other issues of concern to them. In Eastern Europe[15] there is a strong tradition of supported study which is voluntary and is seen to be particularly helpful to people who have no encouragement or facilities at home in which to study. Supported study schemes are now also common in certain parts of Britain and America. There are of course a host of other initiatives of a voluntary nature which teachers and others undertake so that their expertise might be passed on to students through activities organized outwith school. For example, hill walking, sailing, archaeology are not typically taught at school but supported through initiatives of a voluntary nature.

SECONDARY EDUCATION

The secondary curriculum may be seen to be influenced by at least four considerations: a continuation of the primary curriculum; a subject-based or academic curriculum with areas such as maths, science, history, geography, physical education, music, languages;[16] a vocational curriculum with areas such as technical education, business studies, work experience and technology;[17] and those other areas that interested groups have managed successfully to promote such as environmental studies, peace studies and social education.[18] For many people, all this is seen as a sort of preparation for a grand trial by examination which takes place towards the end of secondary education and which is the single most important determinant of success in later life.

Success in the academic sector of this examination is the preferred route to a desired aim of profitable and meaningful employment. Partly this route is preferred because of the prestige in which success in academic examinations is held. Partly too it is preferred because of the view that an academic education is the best means for individuals to fulfil their aspirations and potential in a general sense. Recently however in order to reverse what is seen to be a prejudice against the so-called practical or vocational subjects, governments have tried to raise the status of a vocational education through schemes like the Technical and Vocational Education Initiative (TVEI) in the UK[19] and the 'Tech Prep' initiative in the USA.[20] Representatives of these governments claim that an academic education is unsuitable for many students and that their nation's post-war economic decline arose partly as a result of an overemphasis on the academic. Despite the resources that have been directed into the attempt to raise the status of the vocational, it is not yet clear that the prestige of success in academic examinations has been seriously dented.

It seems that many employers and others do not trust the idea of a general vocational education. Even recruitment policies in British further education colleges, which might be expected to be biased in favour of the vocational, are often based on academic success. Some subjects such as computing and business studies have established themselves in secondary schools alongside academic studies on the back of the vocational initiative and it is likely that other subjects will follow the same route to establish themselves. At the same time other subjects such as classics have been marginalized in secondary schools.

The relationship between education and work is complex. On the one hand there is the simple idea that people need to be trained to do certain specific things. On the other hand there is the idea that people need to be educated so that they can choose between a range of occupations and move easily between occupations as commercial conditions change. Presently the latter sort of transferability seems best to be achieved by those who are able to succeed academically. These students often realize both the liberal ideal of curricular breadth and the vocational ideal of preparing to do specific jobs that might arise in the future. Unfortunately the vocational curriculum is still dominated by instrumentalism as a result of an empiricist ethos and so those students who are not academically inclined are very often presented with an impossible choice; either they partake of something non-academic that is intellectually impoverished or they join an academic race that is at best irrelevant and at worst harmful. Of course some lucky students of this type manage to find vocational courses that are not intellectually impoverished and they go on to realize both liberal and vocational ideals in similar ways to those of their academic counterparts.

Since secondary education is the immediate precursor both to work or unemployment for many pupils and to further or higher education for others, then it is hardly surprising that instrumental concerns dominate this sector of education. In particular so long as some form of student assessment takes place in secondary schools then the published results of that assessment are likely to be used to select for future employment or study. There is no way of avoiding this conclusion. However no one can be entirely happy with the idea that the main outcome of 10–12 years of schooling is marks on a piece of paper which have a particular currency in the job or education market.

Moves have been made to try to dissolve the vocational/academic distinction by encouraging collaborative arrangements between secondary schools and technical, further and community colleges. Such arrangements might seem to imply even larger secondary schools than those that exist to date. However this implication does not necessarily follow. Every vocational area need not be staffed separately. For example, the technology of electrical contracting is closely related to the teaching of science. Similarly catering and home economics need not be taught as if they were entirely different activities. Hairdressing and beauty therapy are not unrelated to personal and social development. Horticulture is closely connected with biology. In short all practices may be considered to be academic or vocational depending upon the purposes of those who are describing them.[21]

Someone may object that an attempt to dissolve the academic/vocational distinction is seriously misleading. They may suggest that the former is predominantly linguistic and disinterested, the latter non-linguistic and interested. To that objection we may reply that in both cases an ability to speak and act in particular ways characterizes the practice in question. So just as a plumber acts and speaks in certain ways so too philosophers act and speak in certain ways. The interest of the former may be more immediate than the interest of the latter but it is a mistake to suggest that the interests are different in kind or that either is entirely disinterested. Language and interests do not exist in a vacuum apart from the communities of practitioners who use language for particular purposes in which they have an interest. There are vocations like journalism in which the use of language is central. On the other hand it is possible to do joinery as a hobby and for the sake of values that are the intrinsic to the practice of joinery. Just as one might expect a journalist to be familiar with different ways of writing so one might expect a plumber to be familiar with different ways of bending pipe. If secondary education is to be concerned to dissolve the distinction between the vocational and the academic then it is unhelpful to think in instrumental terms only. Rather it is helpful to try to re-orient such thinking towards an authentic appropriation of intrinsic values. Let us see how this argument may be applied to the teaching of technology.

CASE EXEMPLAR

TEACHING TECHNOLOGY

I use the term technology to refer to those subjects that involve students making things. In Britain some of these subjects used to be referred to as craft, design and technology. This term was introduced to counter the low status that subjects like woodwork and metalwork were supposed to have. It was assumed that these crafts were somehow not cognitive enough and not sufficiently oriented to the future which, it is usually assumed, is bound to be 'high tech' in all aspects. The notion of a design process was introduced to try to raise the profile of cognition within making and some workshops were either converted into counselling suites or modified so that they could be used as classrooms within which the design process could be carried out.

Academic drift may be detected in this move to elevate the notion of design as the primary focus for making something. This move may be confirmed in the British National Curriculum specification for technology which emphasizes not the range of materials that are to be used, nor the type of machines that should be involved, but stages in the technological process. The curriculum designers here seem to have decided that curriculum intention is best communicated as a series of stages in *the* technological process, as if it were obvious that there was just one such process consisting of the stages of identifying needs, generating a design proposal, planning and making, and appraising the result.[22]

Readers will notice the similarity between these stages and the stages in the model of curriculum development that was discussed in the last chapter. Just as it was argued there that we need to build in some notion of value into the curriculum design process, so too here I argue that we need to build in the notion of intrinsic value to technology. As Walsh explains:

> activities such as curing the patient, repairing a machine, building a house, cooking a meal or tending a garden may require from us and reward us with a great deal in the way of intellectual effort, audacity and fulfilment . . . What we have yet to find is even the hint of a good general reason for the omission of technical subjects from the liberal curriculum.[23]

To which we may add that we can find many excellent reasons for the inclusion of the technical subjects within the liberal curriculum. For example, it is not just that woodwork has its own standards of goodness that are intrinsic to the practice, but also that wooden artefacts enable us to do all kinds of basic things like pegging out washing that constitute part of what it is to be human. There is nothing liberalizing about an inability even to mend the simplest of things or to recognize that technical artefacts may also be more or less aesthetically pleasing according to criteria that are internal to the technical practice as well as aesthetic non-technical factors.

Just as I argued that it is a mistake to imagine that art does not involve some balance between technique and creativity so too crafts like woodwork and metalwork involve a similar balance. Once we start to see all practices as potentially liberalizing in this way then the possibilities open up for all kinds of inter-disciplinary studies that attempt to solve basic problems that students face. For example, the present lack of opportunity to engage in serious consideration of legal obligations and rights seems to me to be a serious omission from many curricula. It may also be advantageous to be able to distinguish between good and bad in those everyday practices such as building, plumbing and joinery upon which we all depend.[24]

It is worth noting however that practices in which tools other than pens are used, tend to be rather expensive to support. I suspect that the implications for resources have hindered the development of those practices that are most commonly associated with the vocational as much as any academic drift. For example, technical and further education colleges find it difficult to keep pace with innovations in equipment that are taking place within the industries that these colleges were meant to serve. Put simply paper and pens are considerably cheaper than blow torches and bending machines.

As with primary education, prescription of curricular balance may be unimportant so long as students are encouraged to consider a number of possibilities rather than those that might immediately appeal to them. It is also important that their depth of engagement with a practice is sufficient for them to understand something of the internal norms that govern good conduct within that practice. Depth of engagement is important because it enables students to learn to identify goodness within a practice and to come to an appreciation of goodness more generally. The idea that a liberal education may only be achieved through induction into certain forms of knowledge may be replaced by the idea that a liberal education may be achieved through induction into any practice in depth and through which the student comes to value intrinsic goodness.

Proponents of the former idea might argue that the life of the mind may not be developed by an in-depth induction into the practice of plumbing and that, important though plumbing might be, it does not encapsulate all those modes of experience and understanding that mankind has progressively made meaningful. To argue this way is to assume however that a liberal education is something that is achieved all at once, as it were, as if an interest in plumbing might not be connected to an interest in metals which is unconnected with science. It may be slightly whimsical, even romantic, to suggest that there is something authentic about working with materials rather than working with pens. Yet there is something basic and fundamentally satisfying about getting a feel for the material and changing it while respecting its qualities.

All these considerations lead me to conclude that within some schools, the equipment necessary for making and mending things should be maintained. It is also necessary to ensure that there are teachers with a sufficiently broad range of expertise to engage the interest of most students. Finally it is necessary to provide some choice of curricular options. There may be a variety of ways that teachers can try to engage the interest of students but if all of them fail then it seems preferable for students to try again in another subject rather than to put in time simply to meet some notion of prescribed curricular balance.

Flexible timetables that facilitate a core and options system need not lead to administrative confusion. Smart cards and other technological advances provide an easy way of registering student interest. Truants who fail to find any options to be of interest provide an indication that, for them at any rate, the system is failing. That does not mean that the system overall is failing however. We may have to accept that for some students at some periods in their lives, an educational opportunity fails to interest them. At a later stage they may well seek to rejoin the formal education system as many adults do. Moreover the system may come to involve not only schools, colleges and universities but any institutions within which practical expertise and equipment are found such as factories and other sorts of commercial enterprise. The ideal of life-long learning which many national and international agencies are promoting may well involve a conception of the education system that is considerably broader than the system that informs present institutions.[25]

FURTHER AND HIGHER EDUCATION

I include under this heading colleges of technical and further education, community colleges, polytechnics and universities. Until recently further and higher education in the UK were considered separately – one devoted primarily though by no means exclusively to non-degree vocational education and the other devoted primarily to degree-awarding vocational and academic education. Vocational here refers to the idea that the prime purpose of studying at this level is to secure meaningful and gainful employment. Academic refers to the idea that while employment prospects are important, these prospects are not the only or main reason for engaging in education at this level.

Recently there have been mergers between different sorts of institutions within this sector. All institutions are able to offer pathways to degrees, albeit through different mechanisms. In the UK as elsewhere new universities have been created out of the old polytechnics and there has been an increase in the range of qualifications available at degree level. There has also been an increase in the number of students who undertake courses of further and higher education. Such developments have led some cynics to claim that these increases and mergers are not so much the result of a further drive to educate people as a way of keeping them off the unemployment register. Even if this cynicism were partly justified that would not preclude further and higher educational institutions from having an educative function. Moreover it would not preclude the possibility that that function might enable some form of economic development. Certainly the claim is widely made that an increase in the numbers of students in higher education is a necessary prerequisite for national economic prosperity.

The idea that a university education is worthwhile in itself has tended to be displaced by the idea of a specific vocational education.[26] Such an education often includes long periods of work experience during which both students and employers have the opportunity to get to know one another without there being a commitment on either side to continue the relationship. For some commentators such as members of the present British government, this vocationalism in higher education was long overdue. These people believe that it is not justifiable for the state to provide an academic education for the few while most people were prepared for a purely instrumental role at work. Instead an academic education may be considered to be a sort of luxury for which individuals might fund themselves.[27] Public funding for higher education, such people argue, should now be tied more tightly to the criterion of vocational relevance. No longer, they claim, should a majority in work support the liberal education of a leisured class.

An egalitarian ethos may be seen to inform these reforms of higher education and it might be imagined that promoters of a discursive ethos would support these reforms fully. Unfortunately such egalitarianism is not without its problems and I am not sure that promoters of a discursive ethos like me can support these reforms fully. That is because these reforms seem to be based exclusively on an instrumentalist conception of education. As we have seen, an exclusive concern with instrumentalism is neither vocationally or academically rewarding. A new binary divide may be opening up in further and higher education between a group in each country of ten or so universities with strong traditions in research, liberal arts, pure sciences and practices like law and medicine, which tend to be related to high status occupations, and other institutions of further and higher education. It has been suggested that some of these other institutions might become sites for teaching only rather than places where academic practitioners develop through research and teaching. Such institutions would become sites for the delivery of a fixed curriculum that is aimed primarily at securing employment. Unfortunately we do not know what sort of activities will promote vocational competence in the future. That is because we do not know just how industry, commerce or work in the public sector will develop in the future. Moreover it is not clear just what sort of research could be carried out to see whether particular educational activities were vocationally efficient in securing permanent employment for graduates. We do not know just what occupations are going to be in demand in the future.

We may conclude that the threefold problem of predicting the numbers and types of jobs on offer, of predicting those activities that might promote success in those jobs, and the related problem of knowing just what sorts of jobs promote economic success may be leading policy-makers in further and higher education astray. Instrumentalism is very tempting both for policy-makers and for students. Students are attracted to courses of this type in the belief that they lead to lucrative employment. In a climate of financial stringency, in which loans are replacing maintenance grants, students whose parents are relatively poor may well not wish to gamble that their course will lead to employment that in turn will enable them to repay the loan. For such students it is tempting to take a so-called vocational course with the likelihood of reasonably paid employment at the end of it. A course in the liberal arts may well be perceived to be more of a financial gamble.

Students whose parents are rich however are not so constrained in their choice. Not only can they apply to the top universities confident that they can meet any financial burdens that such institutions might place upon them but also their choice of course can be guided more by their interest than by the logic of gambling. Moreover the success of these students is enhanced by their study in an area in which they have a particular interest. If it turns out that a course that is less obviously vocational is the best form of vocational preparation then the egalitarian ideal behind the vocational initiative begins to look hollow. The net result of these vocational initiatives may be that a prestigious academic education is given to the few while a low-status vocational education is given to most others. An ability to conform in an unquestioning way might be encouraged by such a vocational education rather than an ability to innovate and challenge. In the situation in which employers do not seem to be expanding sufficiently quickly to take up the supply of graduates on offer, innovation may be more valuable than conformity.

A vocational education need not be like this. Specialist degrees may follow the pattern of apprenticeships in a similar way to the supervision of research degrees. Apprenticeships may appear to represent a narrowing of insight and opportunity. However it should be remembered that masters and supervisors are not only philosophers and physicists; they are sometimes also parents, business people, plumbers and other kinds of practitioners. As with teaching generally the greater the range of forms of discourse and practice with which a teacher/supervisor is familiar, the more likely it is that the student will be able to understand. It is possible to specialize without abandoning interest in all other forms of practice.

SUMMARY

We have seen that it is possible to talk about aims in education in ordinary language without the use of jargon. We have seen that similar tensions run through all sectors of education: between process and product approaches to curriculum development, and between liberalism and economic rationalism. Those tensions are not resolved by treating all practices as if they were the same and as if the prime purpose for engaging in them was to secure employment. Nor are the tensions resolved by attempting to divorce professional from non-professional educational aims. Rather we may only set out educational aims in so far as that setting helps us to solve the problems that we face now.

We have seen that it is a mistake to conflate vocationalism with instrumentalism. The important distinction is not between the academic and the vocational, but between the instrumental and the intrinsically worthwhile. Study of practices can be both vocationally relevant and liberalizing depending on how those practices are taught. We would do better to encourage teachers at all levels to broaden their experience and to deepen their ability to participate in a chosen form of practice. We should organize things so that students have the opportunity to expand their insights and abilities on the basis of study with a number of teachers and engagement with a number of practices. In this way teachers as well as students would have the opportunity to continue to educate themselves. The development of systems of continuing or life-long learning may be important in this regard.[28] All communites of practitioners offer learning opportunities. Moreover there are no logical reasons why courses of study cannot be both vocationally useful and intellectually satisfying if means-ends curriculum development is avoided.

NOTES AND REFERENCES

1. For an account of pragmatism in the formulation of educational aims, see Aspin and Chapman (1994, Chapter 2). As described earlier, a great deal of attention used to be given to the topic of the aims of education by philosophers and curriculum theorists. In particular it was argued that if the aims of education could be grounded in some way, then it would be possible to determine the curriculum content of the different sectors of education. For an overview of three rival accounts of the aims of education, see Bailey (1984, Chapter 6). Bailey considers Hirst's (1974) 'forms of knowledge' thesis, Phenix's (1964) account of 'realms of meaning' and White's (1973) and (1982) argument in favour of a compulsory national curriculum.

   As Bailey points out however, it is possible to see Phenix's work as similar to that of Hirst 'but that his logical analysis is faulty and collapses under the criticism of Hirst' (p. 83). For Hirst, liberal education 'is an education concerned directly with the development of the mind in rational knowledge' (1974, p. 43). Knowledge, can be distinguished into seven forms roughly comprising mathematics, science, humanities, morals, aesthetics, religion, philosophy. It is important to note that Hirst has himself changed his mind about the 'forms of knowledge' thesis and has come to believe that the notion of a 'practice' is important (in Barrow and White 1993). Nevertheless the thesis remains very influential and is often used in attempts to justify any sort of differentiated curriculum. Similarly White's arguments in favour of a national curriculum may have been influential in bringing about such a curriculum in the UK. Of course neither Hirst nor White can be held responsible for what others do with their ideas to try to justify modularization or prescription in curriculum design.

2. The distinction between 'knowing that' and 'knowing how' may be traced back to Aristotle. It was Ryle (1949) however who popularized this distinction which was enthusiastically taken up by Bloom and other curriculm designers. Bloom (1956) has been particularly influential in adding the 'affective' domain to derivatives of Ryle's distinction.

3. See White (1973, p. 1).

4. Reported in the *Times Educational Supplement*, 5 May 1995, p. 3, 'Features'.

5. This directly contradicts the 'forms of knowledge' thesis and points towards pragmatic curriculum development.

6. See Hargreaves and Fullan (1992, pp. 223–6).

7. See Campbell and Little (1989).

8. Taken from SOED (1994).

9. Alexander (1992) looks at the aims of primary education and how these are working out in practice.

10. Loewenberg Ball (1990).

11. Loewenberg Ball (1990, p. i).

12. Bruner (1960, p. 33).

13. See MacBeath (1992, Chapter 3).

14. MacBeath (1992, Chapter 3).

15. Quoted in White (1973, p. 70).

16. This is very much along the lines of the 'forms of knowledge thesis'.

17. As a result of instrumental thinking about educational aims.

18. As a response to the 'societal needs' type of argument.

19. See Esland (1990) for commentary and for references to primary sources.

20. See Hull and Parnell (1991).

21. This is something like Dewey's theory of vocationalism. See his (1966) Chapter 19.

22. See MacKay *et al.* (1991).

23. Walsh (1993, p. 165).

24. Walsh (1993), see also Benyon and MacKay (1992).

25. The de-schooling movement may well be re-energized by the 'information technology' revolution. It is worth looking at Illich (1973), for example.

26. See Phillips-Griffiths (1965).

27. See Barnett (1990) for a discussion of the idea of a higher education.

28. See Ranson (1994).

Chapter 6

Methods

As we saw in Chapter 3, it used to be imagined that different teaching methods could be compared against apparently uncontroversial criteria like efficiency and effectiveness in order to determine which methods are the best for achieving certain objectives. In the previous chapter I argued that there is far more agreement about educational objectives than might be imagined by those who try to over-prescribe curricular objectives. It will come as no surprise to read that in this chapter I argue that it is also a mistake to try to prescribe the use of different teaching methods as if such methods could somehow be detached from teachers' ideas of what they are trying to achieve. I go on to argue that instead of focusing courses of teacher education on teaching methods that it would be better to focus on subject knowledge[1] and educational theory.

For me both aims and methods are interrelated in the everyday activities of those who work within educational institutions. Teachers in particular are involved in an on-going modification of aims in the light of failure of method, modification of method or a new interpretation of aims. Good teaching does not include the relentless pursuit of a particular objective with regard to the student's inability to understand. Nor does good teaching include the exclusive use of a prescribed teaching method or a standard worksheet against the teacher's practical judgement that such use is inappropriate for particular students at particular times.

The notion of good teaching embodies the idea of practical judgement as superior to the kind of technical advice about method that might be supposed to lead to effectiveness, efficiency and quality. These terms tend to suggest that objectives can be set once and for all and methods selected on the basis of speed, cost and customer satisfaction with the achievement of these objectives. As we have seen however it is not possible for the educational enterprise to be guided entirely by such objectives. In this chapter I further advance the argument that teaching is a moral activity in which the notion of practical judgement is important. The idea of practical judgement depends upon an acknowledgement of tacit knowledge and a willingness to trust people to act in a morally correct way but to demand retrospective justifications for their actions where such justifications are helpful. The easiest way to make sense of the idea of practical judgement is through the notion of a tradition.[2] Good teaching does not stem from skilful mastery of existing practical knowledge. Instead it stems from membership of a tradition which is guided by a general notion of goodness that is only realized in action. Thus good teaching can only be fully realized within an inherited and unarticulated body of practical knowledge which constitutes the practice of teaching. Practical knowledge is always reinterpreted and reviewed however as teachers not only reflect on their practice but also as they attempt to justify their decisions to others. In that way good teachers come to be practically wise in that they are able not only to pick out the salient features of a situation, but also to weigh up a range of alternatives embodying different values and to act in the most morally defensible way.

Were it the case that teachers taught only one student at a time and that this student was pretty similar to all other students, then it might just be plausible to suggest that good teaching consists in getting hold of the right materials and consulting a sort of methods manual to find out how those materials should be used. On this view learning to teach might reasonably consist in learning how to interpret the manual and in learning some 'tricks of the trade', including the location of materials and ways of introducing those materials. As it is however classes are made up typically of a wide range of students, all with different aspirations and interests. Moreover teachers typically teach a number of such classes in the course of their careers. The sheer complexity of all this means that even if there were a sort of methods manual available, teachers would not know where to look in it. They would need to be able to pick out the most important feature of their predicament in order to index the manual. Moreover their predicament might seem quite different a second later when some students developed signs of distress for example and they had to re-prioritize their evaluative commitments in order to decide where to look for guidance about what to do. In time teachers might come to memorize the manual and access it quickly on a second by second basis but they would still need a further manual to help them to interpret their predicament correctly. Where could the notion of correctness come from other than through some idea of goodness that is embedded within the way that people simply act?

The inherent uncertainty of teaching practice militates against any idea that goodness can be determined on an individual action by action basis, but that goodness is embedded within what we might call a web of actions that are themselves part of the fabric of a tradition of people trying to cope with similar uncertainties. On this view, learning to teach involves an induction into a practical tradition so that teachers come to develop a form of practical wisdom. As we have seen however educational researchers who share an empiricist ethos, have tried to explicate further this notion of practical wisdom so that trainee teachers and others might have a better idea of what they are aiming for. Yet they come up against the same difficulty time and time again of trying to account for extraneous variables in teaching contexts. This difficulty arises because it is not easy, nor even possible to decide which features of the context affect the outcome of research and which features are extraneous to that research. The large discrepancies in the results of different experiments into similar topics may be explained by reference to the particularities of different attempts to educate.[3] The success of experimental educational research is dependent upon the isolation of a set of variables like teaching method and student success during the course of an experiment and in the future identification of those variables. There are good reasons to be sceptical about the findings of researchers who are not themselves very familiar with teaching practice.[4]

It is worth wondering whether the interpretation of teaching contexts might best be left to teachers who are in the position of being able to take account of the nuances of context and histories of their students after all. Yet novice teachers might wonder how they should go about beginning to develop their practice. I suggest that they may well begin by watching others and by trying out for themselves the range of teaching methods that are commonly in use. Below I set out a number of common teaching methods along with what I believe to be uncontroversial guidelines as to their use. I aim to show that it is possible to justify the use of a range of methods in ordinary language and in a way that appeals to common sense. Instead of there being a need for a specialized language that only educational professionals have the time to understand, I argue that ordinary description and justification are perfectly adequate as a means of encouraging widespread debate.

Even though these guidelines are easy to understand that does not mean that the methods themselves are easy to practice nor that the guidelines are specially significant in themselves. These guidelines are meant to serve as a focus for discussion and basis for experimentation rather than as a series of tips on what teachers might do. Obviously while it is helpful to describe the methods individually, in practice the methods are usually combined.[5] For example the method of exposition is used to give instructions, to entertain and to inform. In the formal lecture situation, it is used extensively. In most teaching situations however it is used for short periods of time in combination with other methods and many teachers might not recognize it as a method at all. Instead they may simply talk with students clearly and in an interesting way responding normally to the students' reaction to their talk. Other teaching methods may be seen in this way, not as methods, but as things that good teachers simply do.

QUESTIONING

This method is used to check students' understanding, to gain students' attention, and to prompt students to develop a topic for themselves. In this last case, students are asked what amounts to leading questions that are structured carefully to build upon what students already know and to lead them to make connections for themselves so that they come to understand.

Questioning is used therefore both as an alternative to telling students and as a means of finding out what they know. In this latter case students may be asked to regurgitate what they have been told. In a successful instance of the former case, students will have uttered the required words for themselves in the first instance and their utterance will have been met with approval from the teacher.

In these exemplars we see the way that in teaching, it is often helpful to reverse the standard order or explanation. Instead of starting with definitions, the teacher starts with problems or applications and works back to definitions and theory. We also see how an apparent inability to come up with set answers to questions may lead to interesting learning experiences and inspire students to set their own objectives and to make connections between a range of seemingly unconnected practices.

CASE EXEMPLAR

LEADING QUESTIONS

T: Do you remember the experiment when we passed current through a wire?
S: Yes.
T: What happened to the wire?
S: It heated up.
T: Can you think of any application of this effect?
S: No.
T: What about an electric fire?
S: So an electric fire is just a coil of wire with a current running through it?
T: Yes, now think about a kettle and a light bulb.
S: So they are just made up of wire that gets very hot, so hot in fact that in the case of the bulb, it glows white.
T: Yes.

CASE EXEMPLAR

NEVER TELLING THEM THE ANSWER[6]

T: What is good teaching?
S: How are we supposed to know, that's what I came on this course to find out. You're supposed to tell us.
T: All right, let's divide into small groups for a while and see if you can answer the question in groups.
S: If we can't answer the question on our own, how are we going to do it in groups? We'll just chatter or look blank at each other.
T: Well I don't know the answer either, that's why I asked you.
S: Well you must have some idea.
T: I think I know it when I see it but I can't define it. Look at these two video clips of people teaching, which is the best?
S: The first, there's no doubt about it.
T: So you know what good teaching is?
S: Alright but we want to know how to become one.
T: Well let's look at the objectives of this course. Now if you satisfy all of these, will you be a good teacher?
S: No, you'll be someone who just follows rules in order to have an easy life and you'll expect your students to do the same. Whatever you're doing you won't be teaching well.
T: No one ever travels so high as he who knows not where he is going.
S: What do you mean? Why do you say that?
T: Well think about it.

EDUCATIONAL TECHNOLOGY

The chalkboard is probably the most widely used piece of educational technology. It is used to draw students' attention to important points, to illustrate an explanation, to give instructions, and to pace the dictation of notes where this is appropriate. The board provides a semi-permanent record that has the advantage of immediacy and freshness. For some purposes however the overhead projector has become popular as a means of displaying information because it enables the teacher to face the class while performing all the functions possible with a chalkboard. In addition it can provide a permanent record both of teacher and student work. Information can be masked and revealed at appropriate times. Overlays can be used and visual clarity can be achieved with well-produced transparencies. The overhead projector also has the advantage that a complex diagram or piece of writing can be prepared in advance of a class for later display without wasting time during the class.

Demonstrations may involve the use of educational technology such as video cameras to display intricate details of a performance. Demonstrations are used primarily to show students what to do in a practical activity: the student practises following the example shown by the teacher. Often the teacher will interrupt students while they practise in order further to demonstrate how they might improve and students may assist in the demonstration. In some cases it is too expensive or time consuming to perform a demonstration and video recordings or slides of the demonstration are used instead. These pieces of technology may also be used as an aid to dramatic presentations, role plays and simulations.

Role plays and simulations are very often used as a way of simulating vocational experience in an educational institution. It is possible to argue that all forms of vocational education may be taught in this way and that the nearer the simulation approaches reality, the better. The use of the training restaurant in a college of further education is a well-known example of the use of this method. The method may also be used however to illustrate particular points that might appear to students to be highly abstract. For example, moral dilemmas may be illustrated in this way. Imaginative teaching strategies may be devised where a clear context for the role play or simulation can be established and differentiated from the normal context within which other methods are employed.

Simulations may also be produced using computers. I refer here to the use of computers for the teaching of things other than computing. The computer is used as a tool. The development of this technology in education has not been as rapid as might be expected. Probably this is because of the expense of producing suitable software and the rate at which hardware changes – for example the different formats of interactive video. The rapid rate of change in this technology makes it very difficult for educational institutions to keep up with developments that are on display in shops and available for students to try out. On the other hand the use of word processors, spreadsheets and databases has become standardized as a means for students to report their work and to take notes. These three computer applications are probably the most important educational applications of computer technology. Moreover as on-line educational resources are developed then more good quality educational resources are likely to become available at an economic cost. For example satellite reception of foreign language channels may be down-loaded to form the basis of some lessons.

Some educationalists argue that the use of computer technology represents the future of formal schooling and that the balance in schools will shift from teachers to machines. In the future, so the argument goes, teachers might help students to plan their curriculum, but delivery will be by machine, programmed with the latest educational software that is produced on a global scale. There may well be moves in this direction, but if the argument advanced in this book is correct, then a computer can only be a constituent part of a practice and not a replacement for it. It may not be necessary physically to locate all staff in one building called a school, but learning depends upon it being possible to meet and work with people who are more accomplished in the practice than one's self.

GROUP WORK AND DISCUSSIONS

The first of these methods is used extensively in primary and further education, but not so well used in secondary or higher education. Small groups of students are given a task to perform and feedback on their success is given either individually or collectively. The method is supposed to encourage cooperative work patterns as students talk and work together. It is therefore a particularly useful method for encouraging students to practise particular forms of discourse or activities. The method is also used to encourage students to share their experiences with one another and even to get to know one another. Finally the method is a way of coping with mixed-ability classes. For example small groups in primary schools are often made up of pupils with levels of ability that are perceived to be similar. The method allows the teacher to give some individual attention to pupils while the others get on on their own or with others in their group.[7]

There are two main problems with particular uses of the method. First, students have to be shown how to use a particular form of discourse before they can practise it. Practice may be little other than gossip unless group members have a pretty good idea of what is expected of them. Second, it is very difficult to correct mistakes that a group might be making and to differentiate the contributions that the various members of the group have made. The management of small group activity is extremely difficult. Moreover the mere act of grouping students has many implications for an individual's learning opportunities. For example, to work with skilled and accomplished colleagues is likely to be preferable to working with those who are less skilled and possibly disruptive. There is also the possibility that group members come to label themselves however careful teachers might be in naming the groups. I am reminded of the joke of the naming of small groups in a primary class according to trees. Few commentators would believe that there is no difference in ability between the 'oaks', 'elms' and 'brambles'!

Sometimes it is helpful to organize larger group discussions in which the teacher takes a lead. There are two main considerations in the use of this method. The first is connected with the initiator of the discussion. The second is connected with the controller of the discussion. In both cases the connection is between student and teacher and there is a wide variety of possibilities. Teachers may want to assess their students' ability to discuss. They may want to explore a possible connection between their students' interests and a topic. They may want to justify a decision by asking the students to challenge it and by attempting to answer any challenges. They may also seek to achieve a consensus as part of their attempt to promote the idea that contestability does not involve futile argument that must be settled inevitably by some form of force.

Students too may initiate a discussion for similar reasons. However the teacher-student relationship is most at risk of breaking down in a discussion because this method allows widespread scrutiny of the teacher in an unpredictable way, whereas in the case of the other methods the teacher is able to maintain control by virtue of choice of method. In a discussion the teacher's authority may be challenged. Indeed an attempt to disrupt may be viewed as an attempt to initiate a discussion. So-called discipline problems might be viewed in this way.

To cope successfully with this method depends on teachers' ability to establish their authority with students so that students want to engage in genuine discussion with them. It is not clear precisely what is involved in the establishment of authority. However it seems to me that it is important for teachers to be acknowledged as superior in insight and knowledge in some area. Teachers should also have a broad knowledge of other activities that enables them to make connections between their students' interests and the topic under discussion. Also teachers need to have an interest in their students and a willingness to justify their decisions in open debate.

In both this exemplar and the exemplar taken from the work of Loewenberg Ball (presented in Chapter 5) some lessons in mathematics are taught by discussion. In both exemplars, the writers support the view that problem-solving in mathematics involves coming to the right answer and being able to justify one's efforts to others who are similarly engaged. For students to see the sort of knowing that mathematics involves, the teacher needs to follow students' arguments as they wander around and muster evidence to support challenges and assertions. Again we see the importance of the teacher's subject knowledge for good teaching and the way that an induction into a practice may also be considered as a form of moral education.

Lampert summarizes some of the problems that can arise with the use of the method of discussion in mathematics. First she points out that the mathematical and social purpose of the discussion needs to be clarified at the outset. That is so that the students understand that the point of the discussion is not to fill in time before the teacher gives the correct answer. Lampert reports that some students are so used to the idea that teachers should provide them with ready answers that they look to other teachers or their peers to supply them with the security that they want. She reports that some other students try to avoid the discussion altogether. Yet another group cling on to their solution against all the evidence, and end up simply shouting that they are right. The teacher needs to have thought through a strategy of how to deal with such eventualities.

INDIVIDUAL WORK

Here the emphasis is on practice and learning through doing – the maxim 'practice makes perfect' may be taken as a statement than underpins this method. For example it is generally accepted that the best way of learning to play a musical instrument is to

CASE EXEMPLAR

MATHEMATICAL KNOWING AND TEACHING

In this exemplar, Lampert[8] explains how discussion is used in the teaching of mathematics so that students come to develop certain moral qualities through authentic engagement with mathematical problems and themselves. She quotes Polya (1954) to set the scene

> In our personal life we often cling to illusions. That is we do not dare to examine certain beliefs which could be easily contradicted by experience, because we are afraid of upsetting the emotional balance. There may be circumstances in which it is not unwise to cling to illusions but [in doing mathematics] we need to adopt the inductive attitude [which] requires a ready ascent from observations to generalizations, and a ready descent from the highest generalizations to the most concrete observations. It requires saying 'maybe' and 'perhaps' in a thousand different shades. It requires many other things, especially the following three:
> INTELLECTUAL COURAGE: we should be ready to revise any one of our beliefs
> INTELLECTUAL HONESTY: we should change a belief when there is good reason to change it
> WISE RESTRAINT: we should not change a belief wantonly, without some good reason, without serious examination.[9]

This quotation is not meant to indicate that 'anything goes' in mathematics. Instead it is meant to indicate that mathematical discourse is process as well as product based and that it is possible to distinguish between good and bad processes as well as correct and incorrect answers. Certainly learning mathematics sometimes involves following rules and applying them correctly where correctness is determined unproblematically by the teacher as an expert. While this involvement may well be important, Lampert explains that she takes mathematics to involve more than this. For her it is important for students to be able to engage in mathematical discourse and come to exhibit the kind of characteristics that Polya articulates.

She explains that a discussion might begin with the statement of a problem. Students try to solve that problem through the formulation and discussion of hypotheses. The relative mathematical merits of various hypotheses set the stage for the kind of zig-zag between inductive observation and deductive generalization that is seen to characterize mathematics and that is exhibited in the give and take of discussions described by Polya. Students are responsible not only for finding a solution but also explaining the strategies behind the solution. Students' strategies yield answers to the teacher's question but the solutions are more than the answers. Students are asked not only to explain their own hypothesis but also to try to explain what they thought others were doing in coming to their hypotheses. They are asked to defend their solutions against challenges from their peers and the teacher. In that way students would rehearse the sort of intellectual courage, honesty and restraint that Polya considered was essential for doing mathematics.

practise playing pieces of increasing difficulty under decreasing amounts of super-vision. This apparently obvious teaching method has been rather denigrated recently. I suspect that this denigration has arisen partly because there has been a tendency to overestimate the importance of the process of gestalt – the idea that learning comes about 'in a flash' as it were. For example, everyone is familiar with the situation in which no matter how many times they try to do something they get no further until quite suddenly something happens and they find that they can do it. However it is important not to over-stress the importance of gestalt learning as if all learning were like this. Learning is often difficult and accomplished performance depends upon hours of dedicated practice. Moreover there are good arguments in favour of training as a prerequisite of learning.

I suspect that another reason why this method is less popular than it used to be is the increasing use of mixed-ability teaching. It is very difficult to motivate people to practice in a situation in which they always seem to be the last to finish or the worst performer. The method inevitably leads to some people feeling frustrated and others elated. Yet another reason for the present unpopularity of the method is that it has become fashionable to denigrate the idea of a teacher as an expert who inducts students into one practice. Instead as I argued in the previous chapter there has been a tendency for the curriculum to become overloaded and for teachers to be encouraged to compromise their expertise in one curricular area in favour of some notion of pedagogical expertise. That expertise is supposed to promote generic competence in students.

In order to try to avoid difficulties such as these, the idea of an integrated learning day has been suggested and implemented in some places so that students work at their own pace through prepared curricular materials. Systems of 'open learning' are also sometimes based on a similar idea. If the arguments advanced in this book are correct then the success of these systems may well depend not only on the quality of the materials that are provided, but also on the commitment and subject expertise of the supervisors and guidance personnel who work with the students.[10]

AIMS AND METHODS

Let us reconsider two central aims of schooling that were set out in the previous chapter: the ability to engage in particular practices, which includes the ability to speak and act in certain ways, and the ability to search for coherence across a range of practices so that students might affect the way that those practices develop and frame their possibilities against a background of coherence. I am attracted to one of Wittgenstein's analogies which I develop throughout the next two chapters. He compares such practices with streets and houses that make up a city and makes the point that while some streets and houses are demolished and rebuilt, others remain. Like a city that is made up of houses and streets from a variety of periods, practices too consist of words and actions that are taken from a variety of periods.[11]

According to this analogy education might be viewed as an introduction to the streets and houses that already exist so that students can find their way about. Such an activity might also involve the process of demolition, reconstruction and maintenance. Individuals might be empowered to contribute to the demolition, construction and conservation of buildings and streets according to their idea of the kind of city that they want to inhabit. In order to achieve all of these things it is necessary for individuals to develop a sort of map of the city and a means to update the map in the light of changes. The map need not cover the whole city in great detail but it is helpful to have a detailed map of one's immediate location and a general map of the rest.

The first of these aims seems to relate closely to the idea of practical knowledge or knowledge of how to do things. Here the method of individual practice under decreasing supervision and against increasingly difficult targets seems to be central. After demonstration by an accomplished practitioner students try the practice out for themselves working under decreasing supervision until they can continue on their own. Sometimes students work in groups and at other times on their own. They practice in simulations as a preliminary to the real thing when the real thing is dangerous. Good teachers question as a natural part of such activities not as conscious attempts to enable students to make connections for themselves between previous learning and some new way of speaking and acting. The second of these aims is not easily distinguishable from the first.

Questioning in a large group is difficult because it is not immediately clear just who is being addressed by the question. There is something odd about nominating questions yet an open question may lead to a variety of responses and difficulties. Teachers may direct their questions at particular students to take account of student ability or they may pitch their question at a sort of assumed average ability. In either case they may not get a satisfactory response and they may have to re-phrase the question and try to make other sorts of connections with students' prior knowledge and experience. A teacher's ability across a range of practices is likely to be an advantage here in that she has more opportunities to engage the learner in a conversation. For example analogies may be drawn from a range of practices to enable the student to understand.

If it were possible to distinguish clearly between these two aims then the distinction between aim and method might be more plausible. For example it might be decided that to achieve the first aim, all students would be inducted into a limited number of practices. It might be assumed that all students begin the induction as novices with, to use Wittgenstein's analogy, blank sheets of paper upon which to draw a map of newly built streets and houses. However the achievement of the second aim can never be so straightforward because it depends upon the precise location of existing streets and houses on the map. The precise location may vary from student to student depending on those things that have interested students in the past.

It cannot be assumed that all students begin an induction as novices with identical maps of 'open countryside'. Instead certain terrain favours certain developments and certain terrain will have been developed already. In some cases demolition may precede building and students will have to be convinced that the process of demolition is worthwhile. Moreover students do not come to the same decision about how to map buildings. These considerations led me to suggest some flexibility for students to choose which curricular areas they wish to study. On the other hand the notions of choice and interest depend upon the student having sufficient background to understand the range of options on offer. For example to present a student with a list of options is unhelpful if the student cannot read or understand the options.

Therefore my use of this analogy is not meant to imply that students develop entirely in their own way and that their developments share no similarities with the developments of others. Instead it is preferable to imagine that the 'city' is developed on the basis of general agreement in the language that people use. Unless a student's map of this development bears some relation to the 'city' then that map is useless. Students do not make their maps in abstraction from everyone else. Instead they make their maps and plans in relation to everyone else's maps and plans. While I do not wish to over-complicate the analogy, students may come to see their map as part of the 'city' itself.

It follows from this analogy that teachers not only need to have detailed knowledge of a particular part of the city but also have a wide general knowledge of the overall city so that they can show students about and lead them quickly to make their own maps and plans. Teachers need to be both specialists and generalists. To return to the analogy it is not clear that any general prescription or distinction can determine whether the commercial streets should be visited before the residential areas or vice versa. However it is clear that at some stage both sorts of development should be visited and that good teachers are likely to be familiar with both.

Over the years people have come to distinguish between traditional and modern methods of teaching:[12] traditional methods usually refer to exposition, demonstration and students performing written tasks individually; modern methods usually refer to all the other methods but with the emphasis very much upon students learning in groups by doing things that are more practical in nature. Stereotypical modern teachers may fail to correct individuals when they go wrong – they may trivialize learning into 'play school' by praising even the most facile achievement and failing to engender any degree of intellectual coherence in their teaching. Group work may disintegrate into chatter that is sustained only by whatever power modern teachers have assumed from the authority gained by their traditional colleagues. In other words in the worst case modern teachers may depend upon traditional sources of authority to legitimize the use of methods that are easy for them but useless for their students. Such teachers may have misunderstood the nature of the process approach to curriculum development. Equating process with imprecision, they proceed to employ student-centred methods whenever an objective is uncertain. They fail to appreciate that imprecision is not the same as lack of clarity and that teachers may be quite clear about what they are doing without trying to specify it.

On the other hand the stereotypical traditional teacher bores students with long lectures, dictates copious notes, insists on students working individually through difficult exercises that some students cannot complete. Praise is rarely given and student interests are treated with contempt. Moreover traditional teachers tend to concentrate on highly abstruse academic knowledge and rarely illustrate their teaching with everyday examples or examples taken from the world of work. Such teachers are only comfortable where there is a measurable educational product to be achieved. According to this stereotype it is perhaps not surprising that traditional methods went out of fashion. As one commentator recently put it: 'in my life I have on many occasions had to mend a leaking tap, saw a piece of wood and get on with people but not yet have I found a use for raising 2 to the power 6'.[13] There is much in this line of argument, yet recently there has been a backlash against modern methods. The use of such methods has been blamed for a variety of problems such as illiteracy and innumeracy among the adult population. It is widely believed that few students can spell correctly and write clearly using properly structured sentences. Industrialists have complained that these basic skills are not taught well despite their importance in securing future economic prosperity. It is also believed that modern teaching has led to a decline in moral values.

It is possible to separate two strands out of the traditional-modern debate – one which relates to method, the other to aim. Product, subject-centred academic knowledge and traditional methods have become conflated. Similarly process, practical knowledge, child-centredness and modern methods have become conflated into the kind of stereotypes described above. However this conflation is unhelpful. As I have argued it is possible to use small groups to teach both so-called vocational and academic disciplines. It is also possible to specify some vocationally specific objectives. Practical knowledge is often best taught by means of individual practice. Subjects are taught in ways that respect the interests of children. It is common sense that many things are learnt through being shown correctly how to do them and given the opportunity to practise under decreasing supervision until one is able to go on one's own. In the course of this practice one talks with others and makes connections between different sorts of activities. More educated people are able to practise in more ways and are able to explain the coherence between those ways using language that is rich in metaphor and analogy – they know a variety of routes to their destination.

In response to this common sense theory of learning, some psychologists and others claim that it is not possible to put this theory into practice in modern educational institutions. When students are taught in classes of thirty or more, it is claimed that practice based on common sense is inefficient and ineffective.[14] Instead rigorous scientific theories of learning are presumed to offer a better guide to classroom practice. As a result of this presumption, psychology of education has become an essential part of the training of teachers and an ability in this theoretical area is considered to be a prerequisite for efficient practice.

On the face of it this claim is entirely reasonable. Common sense has often proved incorrect in the past and has been modified in the light of scientific discovery. For example, common sense followed natural science when it was discovered that the earth moves round the sun rather than the other way around. Might not scientific theories of learning have led correctly to the replacement of common sense as a guide to teaching practice? As psychological theories of learning have ranged from behaviourism to cognitive theories of learning, so trainee teachers have been encouraged to practise in different ways. In the first case teachers inclined towards stimulus-response theories are likely to use praise as a reinforcement of correctly learnt behaviour. In the second case teachers devise strategies for building up what might be called a cognitive structure of concepts – they might stress relationships between the different uses of words and the importance of students establishing these for themselves.

The key question is whether these changes constitute a scientific development that actually has or is improving teaching practice or whether teachers would have been better relying on their common sense. Posing the question in this way is not meant to imply that teaching practice is an unreasoned response to unexamined assumptions. Instead it is meant to imply that common sense itself develops as teachers talk to one another and try to justify their decisions. In some cases terms that originate from supposed scientific practices such as psychology are incorporated into the way that teachers talk. 'Gestalt' and 'stage theory' might be two such terms. On the other hand I have not noticed many teachers talking about cognitive strategies.

I suggest that it is better to view psychological theories of learning more as stories about learning which teachers and others either find attractive and helpful or otherwise. Similarly teachers too invent their own stories about learning that are modified in the light of experience. Their interest in learning provides the impetus for them to continue to reformulate their stories and this in itself may be taken as a mark of an educated person. In this chapter I have presented a learning theory or story about learning that is based on an aralogy between an ancient city and the range of practices in which people engage. I do not claim that the story describes the way things really are or that the story is complete. I do claim however that the story is as worthy of consideration as any other story and that the story cannot simply be dismissed because it is not based directly on systematic observation or because its prescriptions for practice are of a tentative and provisional kind.

Even though it is possible to discuss aims and methods separately because our city presently enables us to do this, there are good reasons not to speak and act in this way. Just as it is not appropriate to try to reach a particular destination if transport difficulties present themselves so educated people do not formulate an aim and stick rigidly to its achievement despite methodological difficulties. Instead educated people formulate and reformulate aims and methods as they go along. Certainly such a search might be guided by certain values such as the search for coherence or truth in discourse but guides stand there like signposts, they do not force any one to go in a particular direction. There is nothing controversial in this view. In the course of completing a practical task craftsmen do not set out necessarily with an overall design that is rigidly adhered to. Instead they modify their ideas as the job proceeds. Certain parts of the job may be routine but others are bound to be in need of adaptation to the particular circumstances.

SUMMARY

In this chapter we have tried further to substantiate the notion that teaching practice is best viewed as a tradition that contains its own internal means of distinguishing better practice. We saw that aim and method are not as distinct as might be imagined but that good teachers modify objectives in the light of failure in method and vice versa in an ongoing reflective way. We challenged the idea that method can be determined scientifically by those not intimately concerned with teaching practice and a number of common methods were set out as a possible guide to trainee teachers. We also challenged the idea that methodological concerns were of most importance to teaching practice and argued that an engagement with stories or theories about learning was more important to trainee teachers than practice in techniques. We may wonder how far the idea of teaching methodology gets us off on the wrong foot by blinding us to certain possibilities and encouraging a manipulative conception of the teacher-student relationship.

A story was introduced that appeals to an easy-to-understand analogy and was used in order to substantiate further the status of common sense as a guide to practice. Thus further support was provided for the overall thesis that it is possible to justify educational claims in open discussion with those not professionally concerned with education. Lest it be thought that these arguments preclude any form of external check on teaching practice, the next chapter is concerned with the assessment of what students have learnt.

NOTES AND REFERENCES

1. The evidence is conclusive that a thorough knowledge of subject is an essential prerequisite for good teaching. See Brophy (1991), McDiarmid *et al.* (1990), Shulman (1991), McNamara (1993) and Bennett and Carre (1993).
2. See MacIntyre (1981) and Gadamer (1975) for discussion of the notion of a tradition.
3. That is one of the reasons why the traditional/progressive debate is far from settled.
4. This is the point that Carr and Kemmis (1986) and other supporters of 'action research' make.
5. Whole books are devoted to discussion of just one of these methods and to the way that they may be combined. See Cohen and Manion (1989) for an example of the latter.
6. This is adapted from Pirsig (1974, Chapter 17).
7. The over-zealous use of group work in primary education has been the subject of some criticism. See McNamara (1993) who argues that a teacher-centred approach is in the pupil's best interests. It is hard to see why a variety of teaching methods should not be as much a feature of primary classrooms as elsewhere, if only for the reason that students get 'fed up' with the same method of learning.
8. Lampert (1990).
9. Polya (1954, pp. 7–8).
10. In the introduction it was suggested that teaching could be regarded as an attempt to persuade students of a better way of doing or speaking about something. In that way 'traditional' teaching enables personal commitment to be shown and 'prejudices' to be modified.
11. Wittgenstein (1953, PI 18).
12. Notice the way in which method and aim interact through the notions of traditional and modern or progressive.
13. Sir Christopher Ball speaking at the annual TESS conference, Perth, 22 April 1994.
14. Bigge (1982) argues this way. See his Chapter 1.

Chapter 7

Assessment

We have seen that there has been a tendency to lose sight of the idea that in order to learn about a practice people endeavour to work with accomplished practitioners who induct them into the practice by setting graded tasks for them to achieve under decreasing supervision. We also saw that this induction not only involves the completion of tasks but also the identification of coherence between tasks so that the identity of the practice may be preserved. While the precise nature of the tasks to be completed may not be set out in advance, we can distinguish good from bad practice on the basis either of our own involvement in the practice or the overlap between the practice and our common sense. In this chapter we explore the implications for assessment of this conception of learning.

When a student is asked to complete a task, the teacher may observe and talk with the student in order to assess how well the student is doing. This assessment is a normal part of teaching for without it the teacher has no means of knowing what level of task is appropriate for a particular student. There is nothing special in this. For example simply by talking with someone or observing them we form some views about their knowledge, attitudes and capabilities. Similarly while we rarely choose to express our own assessment of our own capabilities, it seems obvious that we do in fact assess ourselves as we go along in the sense that we reflect on how well or how badly we have performed. Very often this assessment is based on a comparison of our performance with that of others. Hence as we saw, learning is logically dependent on the idea of a community which practises in established ways so that our memory of a previous attempt to do something may be checked.

In short, assessment of abilities, interests and knowledge forms part of any attempt to learn and is based on some sort of comparison. On this view all the methods of teaching which were discussed in the previous chapter are also methods of assessment.[1] In educational institutions it is sometimes useful to highlight this type of assessment and to refer to it as formative assessment. Formative assessment may be contrasted with summative assessment which is rather more contrived. Summative assessments take place at particular times and for particular purposes. Very often such assessments take the form of summary reports on a student's progress. That report might be interpreted as a kind of recognition of achievement or as a means of selecting someone for something in the future. For example, examination results are often used as a means of selecting students for places in higher educational institutions or employment.

It is important to distinguish between summative assessment and the interpretation of the results of summative assessment. For example, a student might be set a task and might be told that completion of the task has special significance in that a report of their ability will be based on the completion of that task only. However the report may be interpreted by others in a number of different ways and for a number of different purposes. The report cannot be taken as a value-neutral representation of student ability. Instead the interpretation of the report will be guided by the interest that the reader has in the student.

On the face of it formative assessment should be an unproblematic component of teaching. It has become normal however to require teachers to distinguish between teaching method and formative methods of assessment. Teachers have been required to keep records of the results of those methods of assessment and to report on them. That report has come to be used as a summative statement of student ability and has been called 'internal assessment'. I believe that this form of internal assessment is a mistake that has been made on the basis of the best intentions. Let us try to unravel the origins of this mistake.

We must remind ourselves again of the way that an empiricist ethos leads to the idea that a performance may be described in advance of the actual performance and used as a sort of ruler against which the actual performance is judged. Our common sense notion of measurement supports this idea. For example it used to be common to suppose that a metre is the length of an actual rod that is kept somewhere near Paris and that copies of this rod have been made so that other rods may be put alongside these copies and measured according to an evenly divided scale. Common sense leads us astray here as we try to adapt this idea to try to measure learning.

There cannot be an ideal 'rod' in this context because if there is such a thing as an ideal performance then it may only be located within a tradition of people who develop their practices in certain characteristic ways. Moreover it is not possible to describe their practice in ways that avoid the interpretive prejudices of those who have an interest in the measurement. Arguments such as these have not however stopped people trying to base educational assessment on a model taken from the physical sciences. Thus there have been a proliferation of assessment criteria, policies and techniques that attempt to avoid the worst effects of formal assessments while attempting to maintain some notion of an objective standard.[2] Yet many students are not helped by these attempts. A report of their adequacy cannot be interpreted in a disinterested way. The interpretation is bound to be guided by some idea of the purpose which the interpretation is to serve.

The distinction between internal and external assessment has arisen as a result of attempts to try to avoid difficulties such as the ones described above. External assessment takes place when students are asked to perform a task by those who have not been involved with their teaching. These external assessors then go on to issue a report on student ability that is based often on a comparison of the work of different students under the same or similar conditions. Of course like its internal counterpart, that report cannot stand as a neutral representation of student ability.

It remains the result of a particular set of circumstances and may be interpreted in different ways.

Internal assessment takes place when students are asked to perform a task by their teachers. The teachers go on to issue a report that is based on their professional judgement and that judgement is then moderated or verified against the judgement of other teachers, usually by some validating body which attempts to add more credibility to the report than it would otherwise have. In both the case of internal and external assessments, there remains the idea that a report on students is something more than the results of a particular set of circumstances, personal interests and prejudices. There also remains the idea that such a report may be useful either as a sort of marker of student progress or as a basis upon which to select students in the future. It is hard to see what other function formal assessment might serve.

In the case of both purposes described above, the reporting of assessment would seem to be most useful where it includes the widest possible comparison of students and where it is most credible in the sense that people believe it to be reliable and valid. It is usually believed that internal assessments are most valid but external assessments are most reliable and credible. I argue however that the interpretation of all reports of assessment invalidates to some extent all attempts formally to report any qualities other than those that include the comparison of students against each other. As the following exemplar is meant to illustrate, the logic of the discourse of assessment is based on comparison.

CASE EXEMPLAR

THE LOGIC OF THE DISCOURSE OF ASSESSMENT

P: How well is my child doing?
T: Very well.
P: Very well with reference to what?
T: The others in the group who are working within a practice in which I have some expertise.
P: How well is my child doing?
T: In What?
P: In getting to go to the university of her choice?
T: That depends upon their criteria for selection which at the moment are based on grades in an external examination.
P: How are those grades awarded?
T: On the basis of a comparison of students' performance across the country.
P: How well is my child doing?
T: In what?
P: In developing as a decent human being.
T: Very well in comparison with the rest of the people that I know!

The logic of the discourse of teaching however is to avoid making comparisons between students. Internal assessments, as I have described them, are unhelpful to learning in that they tend to lead towards the establishment of inauthentic relations between learners and teachers. For me, so long as written reports of student ability are required, external assessment remains the best basis on which to issue them. Moreover the results of such assessment form an important way of helping us to evaluate the success of an educational development. The results also provide a means of informing the judgement of those who work within the education system and those who have an interest in it.

In some countries such as Germany, there is a tradition of basing selection for further educational opportunities on the professional judgement of a teacher who knows the student particularly well and there are good reasons to wish that all selection could be based on professional judgements in this way.[3] Not the least important of these reasons is a consideration of the cost of administering systems of external assessment. On the other hand, the notion of professional judgement is closely related to élitism and we have seen the dangers associated with this in earlier chapters. In countries such as Germany it seems that professional judgements are held in high regard mainly because there is a tradition of openness which enables the democratic scrutiny of professional activities and which respects the integrity of teacher judgements because of a willingness to justify them. Elsewhere, external systems of assessment seem the only credible possibility for the time being.[4]

THE MOVE TO INTERNAL ASSESSMENT

It used to be normal in the UK as elsewhere to follow a period of study with an examination of some kind. The results of that examination were published either in the form of a number or grade. A teacher might report informally to the student or others on the student's progress prior to the examination but that report did not constitute part of the examination itself. This form of external examination had certain advantages. First, it seemed to be fair in that anyone could enter the examination irrespective of their background – it was an open competition. Second, it seemed to be objective in the sense that a teacher's formative and perhaps subjective assessment of a student played no part in the reporting of their achievement in the examination. Third, it was administratively convenient and in many cases an economical means of assessing a large number of candidates. One examination could be offered to many candidates at the same time. Criteria to govern conduct in the examination and a context for its administration were relatively clear and unambiguous. For example it was easy to replicate the context for examinations in halls across the country. Students worked in silence for an arranged time at desks spaced so that copying was not possible.[5]

In short, the external examination appears to offer a cheap, fair, convenient way of assessing student progress and produces an easy to understand comment on which to base selection for future activities – 'A' being better than 'B' and so on. Finally an external examination serves as a means of uniting students and teachers in a common pursuit of excellence that is externally monitored. The examination also offers a means of marking the end of a period of study for both teachers and students. Such a marker can be an important way of structuring time in educational institutions.

While external examinations remain popular, they also suffer from serious problems which have led to their replacement for many so-called less able students and some more able students. Many readers will recall the trauma of entering an examination hall knowing that so much depended upon that particular session. External examinations are stressful and conversation outside examination halls are often characterized by phrases such as 'my mind went blank' or 'I just could not think'. So a major problem with external examinations is that they may examine the ability to cope with stress as much as practical ability. They may be invalid in that they do not examine what they are designed to examine.

Second, the way that the examination is set and marked can be biased in favour of students who have been taught one way as opposed to another. It is often important to maintain secrecy about the examination so that students do not merely memorize the correct answers. The examination may assess the teacher's ability to prepare students for examinations rather than student ability – again some invalidity is inevitable. Third, external examinations tend to be conflated with the use of paper and pencil rather than other tools. Thus examinations tend to promote the assessment of theoretical knowledge rather than practical knowledge and attitudes. The presumed advantage of economy is negated for example in the case of oral examinations or practical examinations like music examinations which are often on a one examiner to one student basis. Finally, and most importantly, a student's performance in an examination is bound to be compared with the performance of others who took the same examination. How else could the markers proceed?

The comparison of student performance in this way is called 'norm referencing'. Norm referencing means that out of any group of students who take an examination some will do better than the norm and others will do worse. This is the basis of grading and failing. Norm referencing ensures that some students will fail and others succeed. Therefore success in a norm-referenced examination depends upon the performance of the other students who make up a particular cohort. Since it is undesirable for the same examination paper to be issued year in year out, an examining body has to institute procedures to ensure comparability between different examinations. These procedures are called moderation procedures. Over the years examining bodies have developed sophisticated statistical methods to try to ensure effective moderation. However it can never be possible to compensate entirely for a particularly good or poor group of students nor for a hard or weak examination paper. It can never be possible to substantiate the hypothetical claim that students obtaining identical marks in different examinations have equal abilities. Nor can it be possible to substantiate the claim that the same student would obtain the same mark if it were possible to sit different examinations in the same subject but in different years.

It has been argued therefore that there is nothing fair about a system of assessment which condemns a significant number of students to failure as a feature of the system rather than a feature of the students themselves. It has also been argued that there is nothing fair about a system which condemns the nervous to failure and which potentially disadvantages the members of particularly strong student groups. (That is because moderation procedures tend to be based on the maintenance of stable pass rates.) It is little surprise that internal assessment based on a summary of formative assessment became popular as a way of countering these arguments. It is supposed that the problem of stress is overcome when the student is formatively assessed. Results can be reported in a supportive and non-threatening way. No one is bound to fail as is the case with norm-referenced examinations. Practical knowledge and attitudes can be assessed by those who know the students without there being the need for expensive assessment activities that are separated from teaching and learning.

CASE EXEMPLAR

TYPES OF MODERATION PROCEDURE

Statistical comparisons

This type of procedure is used principally by examination boards in order to compare the performance of both the same student in different examination papers and different students in the same type of examination paper that has been offered over the years. While these comparisons cannot be precise, in the sense that it is never entirely clear whether particularly good results are due to particularly able students or particularly easy papers, it is possible to moderate so that wild and implausible fluctuation between students and papers are eliminated.

Use of reference tests

Essentially one external assessment is used to modify students' marks or grades to compensate for discrepancies in teachers' judgements. It is assumed that teachers are good at grading their class but that they cannot compare their judgements against other teachers' judgements elsewhere other than through a common test. This type of moderation is used in parts of Australia.

Inspection of samples of work

Here student work and the teacher's marking of it are scrutinized by others and various steps are taken to ensure that a representative sample is selected. This method is used across the UK and is particularly common in the case of vocational qualifications through a procedure known as verification.

External examining

This is a very similar procedure to the above and is common in higher education. The examiner has a good deal of discretion as to how they wish to try to ensure the maintenance of some idea of a standard.

Group moderation

This is also sometimes known as internal verification in the UK. It consists of teachers within a school or college coming to a consensus about a grade or a report that should be issued.

Even though the move to internal assessment has meant more work for teachers many of them have welcomed it on educational grounds as a means of avoiding the general loss of confidence in the educational endeavour that comes about when weaker students necessarily fail. The principle weakness with internal assessment is that it seems unduly to depend upon a personal judgement of a teacher with no possibility of any checks upon that judgement. Even though there is some evidence to suggest that teachers are good at making comparisons of ability within a group, it is hard to see how those teachers may make comparisons between groups. Those institutions that have been charged with the responsibility for administering this form of internal assessment have tried to implement moderation procedures to overcome the problem.[6]

It will be seen that each of these procedures is open to criticism. For example, just as it is hard to see how teachers can make comparisons between groups so it is hard to see how moderators can have the time to observe a sufficient number of student groups in order to make useful comparisons. Not only is it too costly to appoint moderators to oversee a manageable number of teachers but also it defeats the purposes of moderation if there is a proliferation of moderators each with his or her own idea of a typical student performance. The success of different moderation procedures may be judged partly by the fact that internally assessed awards continue to have less status than their externally assessed counterparts though as I explained earlier, credibility is closely related to tradition.[7]

CRITERIA

In an attempt to try to improve matters or as the attempt is now called, to institute procedures for quality assurance, policy-makers in the 1970s began to institute the procedure that is known as criterion-referenced assessment. No longer was it deemed appropriate for teachers to report their formative assessment in terms that they judged to be appropriate. Instead criteria for successful completion of an assessment were written at the outset which specify the desirable conditions under which success can be achieved. The public statement of these criteria was and is taken by many assessment authorities to be the best guarantee of some form of objectivity in internal assessment. However, as noted earlier, it is not easy to formulate clear and unambiguous criteria. A criterion should state what the student should be able to do, the context for the performance and the standard of the performance. The following example appears to be such a criterion:

> the student should be able to add two 2-digit numbers without a calculator but with paper and pencil. The performance should be repeated without mistake on ten occasions. Each occasion should last no longer than thirty seconds.

By observing the student completing exercises along these lines the teacher is able to judge whether or not the criterion has been met.

It is hard to imagine a more straightforward criterion than the above. Yet even in this case it is not clear just what sort of performance is required. For example, we may wonder whether the digits are to be given in written form or orally. We may wonder too whether the digits are to be laid out in columns. Moreover successful performance on ten occasions does not guarantee that the eleventh attempt will be successful. The move to objectivize the teacher's judgement in written criteria leads potentially to an infinitely long set of criteria as more and more qualifications are added to a statement of performance. In practice, criteria tend to be given as terse atomistic statements that depend upon an ability to suspend normal human conversations while these statements are interpreted.[8] In contrast to the above example of a criterion, there are less straightforward cases involving practical knowledge and values. For example, honesty does not seem to be at all amenable to criterion referencing. We may wonder about the number of occasions on which someone has to be honest before they meet the criterion of honesty. Furthermore we may wonder if there is not something dishonest about trying to be honest on say ten occasions as if the eleventh did not matter.

In the case of practical knowledge, it seems that accomplished practice cannot consist of a fixed number of performances of particular tasks. Instead accomplished practice involves the ability to continue on one's own to complete new tasks to standards that meet with the approval of a community of practitioners working within a tradition. That tradition develops and the values that guide the development do not exist apart from the tradition but as an unformalizable part of it. There is something tacit about practical knowledge that makes it impossible to make all criteria explicit. We only need to think of the difference between the 'do it yourself' attempt to hammer a nail and the accomplished joiner performing the same task. In the former case the attempt seems awkward, the wrist is held stiff, the nail does not go in at a right angle and the head of the nail may not be buried in the wood. In the latter case the performance seems effortless. It is not difficult to think of many other examples where it is not easy to specify the differences in the way that a task is completed, but we are aware of the differences none the less. Even in the case of theoretical knowledge there is a difference between the repetition of words as if those words had been memorized by rote and fluent articulation which indicates a deeper understanding. Let us illustrate this point further by considering the way in which criteria might be set out to describe the ability to tighten up an object on a screw thread. Such an ability is essential to practices which range from mending cars to closing the top on a plastic milk carton.

Criterion referencing involves the attempt to break down a complex whole into a number of discrete parts. However something important is lost in the reduction. Moreover something important is lost to the tradition of teaching when successful teaching implies the completion of a checklist of criteria that has been prepared by others for teachers to use. The language of criterion referencing implies that something has either been met or it has not. There is no room for the idea that someone may have gone as far as they can towards the achievement of a criterion. Either they have achieved it or they continue until they can achieve it. It is no wonder that many of the educational criteria that have been written recently appear to trivialize learning by attempting to rob practices of their intrinsic values.

'Better' or 'worse', 'excellent' or 'poor' are not words that feature much in the statement of criteria. These words are considered to be too subjective. It is as if the ticking of a criterion guarantees a certain standard of performance in the future no matter who observes the performance. However the act of ticking or signing that a

CASE EXEMPLAR

TIGHTENING A BOLT

Milk-tops are not exactly like bolts but they share with bolts the characteristic that unless the top or bolt is tightened up just tight enough but not too tight, the milk leaks out or the car wheel falls off. In the case of car mechanics, it is essential to be able to tighten up bolts just tight enough so that the bolt does not come loose but not too tight to strip the threads. The competent mechanic comes to *feel* the extent to which the threads are worn and the amount of pressure that can be applied to the wrench. Now the criterion-referenced approach does not help us to communicate this least problematic element of car maintenance. How do we describe a feel other than as a feel? How do we know what it feels like just to avoid stripping the threads unless we have that feel ourselves to some extent? The way mechanics act, the way they explain what they are going to do, the way they seem to care about their practice – all are indicators of their ability. But it is hard to know what further to say, except perhaps that tightening a bolt is like screwing the top on a bottle of milk!

CASE EXEMPLAR

MODULE: GENTS HAIR CUTTING[9]

At the end of the module the student should be able to

- greet the client
- gown the client
- determine the client's requirements
- know the range of tools available, their cutting effects and techniques of cutting
- devise a cutting strategy to meet requirements
- perform the cut safely and effectively
- charge the client
- thank him for his custom.

criterion has been met guarantees little other than that on a particular occasion a teacher's interpretation of an action coincides with their interpretation of a statement. The subjectivism of judgement remains. Criterion-referenced assessment offers an illusion of objectivity.

Criteria do not exist apart from a community which sustains them by constant interpretation and reinterpretation in conversations between members. Certainly such conversations are not aimless but neither are they obviously related to criteria either. For example, I doubt that anyone would recognize the above exemplar as a characterization of what goes on in a hairdressing salon. It is not surprising that many people not professionally concerned with education seem to have little patience with the extremely detailed information that is provided by criterion-referenced assessment. After all they are interested in the results of assessment for purposes other than having a record of all the things that students did in the course of a programme of study or even in the course of their life.

Supporters of criterion-referenced assessment often cite the driving test as a good example of a criterion-referenced assessment. They attempt to generalize from this example. The generalization is misleading however. That is because the context within which driving takes place is so familiar to most of us that we do in a real sense belong to a community with a tradition of motoring. As a result of this membership we interpret and reinterpret criteria for successful driving regularly as we observe behaviour on the roads. Moreover the examiners form a relatively coherent group with opportunities for regular dialogue. As a result of all these considerations the criteria for successful performance in the driving test are well-understood and accepted. There is no need for detailed statements of performance though many trainees find it prudent to take at least one or two lessons with an experienced instructor just to check that they are interpreting the criteria in a similar way to that of the examiners.

There are few practices which are taught in educational institutions that are as well known as motoring. Therefore criterion-referenced assessment is much more problematic within educational institutions for the simple reasons that only those who work within such institutions understand the way in which the criteria are interpreted. Certainly more meetings could be arranged between those who try to interpret criteria in a similar way. Here I include students, teachers, employers and other accomplished members of the tradition in which the particular set of criteria is supposed to be located.

All of this is likely to be expensive however. Teachers would not only need to meet with other teachers in order to sustain a tradition of teaching but teachers would also need to meet with accomplished practitioners in their subjects who in many cases would be university researchers and in many other cases would be trades and business people. In that way teachers and other practitioners could come to understand each other and to reach a common understanding of the standards to which students should aspire. Of course in many instances teachers actually are accomplished practitioners. That is why it is considered important for university teachers to be engaged in research. That is why it is also considered important for teachers in general actually to have relevant, recent, practical experience of whatever subject they principally teach.

However it is not clear that any of these meetings would be aided by the existence of written lists of criteria. Moreover if the purpose of these meetings is constrained by the need to verify and update criteria then several disadvantages arise. First, if the results of all these meetings are documented then there would be a proliferation of administrative detail. Second, there is a tendency for teaching to be ever more constrained by lists of criteria. The attempt to standardize the interpretation of criteria leads to the attempt to standardize the context within which the criteria are interpreted. Since teaching method and assessment are often integrated then there is a tendency to standardize teaching method. Such standardization leads to the kinds of difficulties that were discussed in the previous chapter. There is also the danger that the attempt to standardize may encourage poor teachers to omit teaching in favour of ticking a box on a checklist. Since ticking a box on a checklist cannot guarantee future performance, however good the teaching has been, then criterion-referenced assessment may be seen actually to offer a prop to poor teachers.

COMPETENCE

This apparent paradox has given rise to the use of the term 'competence' in an attempt to suggest that previous performance does guarantee future capability. The normal use of the word 'competent' implies that when someone is competent, their future capability can be at least presumed though perhaps not guaranteed. For example, we do not say someone is a competent cook if they have only boiled an egg on one previous occasion. We may say that they are competent when we have observed them over a period of time and in a variety of circumstances. It would be foolish to assume that we could pre-describe those circumstances however. Hence one would imagine that the statement of prescribed criteria can never be equivalent to the statement that someone is competent. Yet this is precisely what has happened as curriculum designers have pushed the criterion-reference system of assessment further.[10]

During the late 1980s and early 1990s a model of curriculum development has gained in importance in the UK and Australia. In an attempt to promote the idea of vocational competence, the government departments concerned with employment in both countries have developed the idea that education should primarily be a preparation for work. Groups of industrialists and others have been paid to draw up elements of competence to which students should aspire. Lists of criteria have become lists of elements of competence and performance criteria and this system of assessment is set to spread throughout all sectors of education and to include all the practices into which people might reasonably want to be inducted.[11]

In the case of work-place based assessment where an assessor has had the opportunity to observe and talk with someone over a prolonged period of time, it might be plausible for them to claim that the trainee is competent in whatever practices are conducted in that work place. However in an educational context where the student is learning to do something, the notion of occupational competence is less useful. In either case it is worth noting that work places provide no more of a uniform context for the demonstration of vocational competence than simulations within educational institutions. There is an enormous difference between work places. For example, the catering industry includes vocational contexts that vary from hot-dog trailers to multi-million pound chains of hotels. They are all work places within the catering industry but it is not clear that they share any more in common than say hot-dog trailers and freight wagons on the railway.[12]

Recently the notion of transferable competencies has been introduced to try to overcome the above difficulty. However the notion is even more problematic than the notion of a vocationally specific competence. As yet it is unclear just what a transferable competence might be other than those desirable characteristics which educated people are supposed to possess.

CASE EXEMPLAR

COMPETENCE-BASED TEACHER EDUCATION

Let us consider the example of a competence-based programme of teacher education (Strathclyde University 1994) to illustrate this point. The course descriptor lists elements of competence such as the following:

- operate within given specifications
- determine individual and group needs
- plan discrete teaching and learning experiences
- select teaching and learning resources
- modify and reproduce teaching and learning materials
- establish positive learning environments.

In turn these elements are broken down into performance criteria such as:

- appropriate learning outcomes are pursued
- appropriate administrative arrangements are complied with
- planned experiences are structured within given time allocations.

Presumably no one would deny that criteria such as these are necessary though perhaps not sufficient criteria for good teaching practice. There is more than a hint for example in recent Guidelines for Teacher Training Courses (SOED 1993b) to suggest that reflection, critical appraisal, theorizing and understanding might also be important abilities for teachers to acquire. These abilities may be taken to be the 'transferable competencies' that were referred to above. Now even if these competencies were included in the specification for courses of teacher education, under current arrangements for competence-based training in the UK, some form of evidence would need to be compiled to show that criteria such as these had been met. The problem then arises as to what sort of things could count as evidence of, for example, a reflective ability. Certainly we may recognize such an ability in others but not as the result of asking them to provide evidence for us. The ability may be seen to be based more on an appropriate set of personal values than on an ability to perform in a certain way. There are many other instances where the specification of what amounts to a set of values destroys all chance of seeing whether or not someone genuinely holds those values. 'Values' may be the nearest that we can get to making sense of the idea of a 'transferable competence' but it is hard to see what is gained by describing them in that way.

EXTERNAL ASSESSMENT

Some readers will have noticed the similarities between the specification of objectives in the product model of curriculum development and the specification of criteria for internal summative assessment. It is worth noting that assessment according to the process model may only be done formatively or by external summative assessment. Now it might be objected that any form of external assessment is inappropriate for curricula designed according to the process model. That is because outcomes and methods cannot be set out in advance of the learning situation and may only be known by those intimately concerned with it.

However this objection misses the point that those who are intimately concerned with the learning situation may choose to have student achievement recognized externally. That is not the same thing as teaching to exams or to criteria. It is simply to wish to have some external recognition of achievement. The example of music examinations is helpful. The music student is entered for the examination when ready. The student may have studied a variety of things on the way to examination. Indeed the student may not choose to enter any examination. However the possibility exists to have their achievement externally recognized in much the same way as a public performance provides a degree of external recognition.

External assessors maintain their idea of what certain grades entail by means of being part of a tradition within which assessors meet and discuss performances guided perhaps by examples of pieces that are considered to be appropriate for different levels. Within such a tradition it is unlikely to be helpful to try to get ever more accurate descriptions of satisfactory performance. Instead what is needed are economical, easily understood statements of the sort that most people would normally use. Accomplished practitioners who are prepared to act as examiners are also needed along with the means for these examiners to meet on a regular basis and to consider many examples. In that way external assessment is made on the basis of a personal judgement of student performance that is supported by many comparisons of performance made by members of a group of which the examiner is a member.

All forms of practical knowledge may be assessed externally in this way without the need for copious lists of criteria. In the case of theoretical knowledge the same considerations apply except that in this case it is even easier to arrange external assessments because these may be based on written exercises which are more economical to administer. Moreover statistical procedures may be designed by examining authorities to try to ensure some form of comparability between different examinations as described earlier.

The present situation, where external examinations tend to be limited to paper and pencil tests and internal assessment limited to the more practical subjects, has unfortunate implications. Disciplines that are externally assessed will continue to have more status than their internally assessed counterparts. Commentators will always be suspicious of a procedure that in essence involves people assessing themselves. There is a conflict of interest between teaching and formally assessing the same students. In the former case the teacher's interest is necessarily partial in favour of the student. In the latter case the teacher must somehow detach herself to act impartially. There is a difference between telling someone privately that she should improve and formalizing that advice for all to see and for all to draw whatever implication they like from the summary formalization.

CASE EXEMPLAR

RECORDS OF ACHIEVEMENT AND ACTION PLANS

The compilation of these records has, in the UK, become government policy. In essence students are asked to keep a record almost from birth onwards of what they have achieved that has not been formally recognized at school. As a recognition that this informal learning is important, and as a recognition of the idea that students should 'take charge of their own learning', the compilation of these records seems to be a good idea. Yet such compilation does give rise to similar problems to the ones discussed above. It is one thing for a student, in the privacy of the school and in the trust of her teacher, to write down those things that she thinks she has achieved as a sort of motivational device. It is quite another to then parade that record around wherever it can be compared with all other records, perhaps in an interview for a job.[13]

In the former context the student is encouraged to be honest with herself so that the process of compiling the record is an authentic experience for her. In the latter case such honesty may be a positive disadvantage. Moreover it is obvious that those children who have been brought up in an environment that is rich in educational opportunities will have more to record than those who have not and the publication of records may serve only to promote those qualities of brashness, superficiality and inauthenticity that most of us would like to suppress.[14]

Recently the British Confederation of British Industry has tried to develop further the record of achievement to include an action plan and to call the developed document a 'careership profile'. The claimed advantages of this development are set out as follows:

> Individual personal profiles are vital to the development of independent learners, motivated and able to take charge of their own careers. They need to be forward looking documents incorporating action planning as well as recording a broad range of achievement. The action plan is as important as the record. A document which simply looks back misses the point. The profile is a vehicle for promoting lifelong learning.[15]

So the familiar process of means-ends planning is advocated with the student 'reviewing achievement, setting personal goals, determining learning needs, arranging learning provision' and so on until they die. Lest all this be thought to be yet another attempt at criterion-referenced assessment upon which to base selection for limited opportunities, the CBI reassures us that the record is 'for the individual'.

It is hard to imagine that many people would keep such a record unless they were coerced into doing so. It is also hard to imagine that any one would have the time to go through the record with its author in any great detail. Moreover the record is unlikely to be as credible an instrument upon which to base selection as external methods of assessment. The danger is that those practices that the CBI and others would like to encourage as part of lifelong learning are downgraded further by being associated with an incredible method of assessment.

Practices will never gain parity of esteem with one another if the assessment of student ability in some practices is seen to be unreliable. Moreover we must be careful not to conflate ability with a specific feature of practices that are based in universities. We must avoid labelling those who happen to be good in the other practices as less able simply because the way that assessment is carried out within these practices makes it easier for more people to be deemed successful in them. Students who are not academically gifted have as much right to have their achievement in other disciplines recognized properly as anyone else. That is why the consideration of systems of assessment is fundamental to the educative endeavour.

SUMMARY

The distinction between product and process is not relevant to the assessment of student performance. From the assessor's point of view the difference is simply between attributes that may be easily described and understood and attributes that are more difficult to describe and understand. Standards of excellence exist within a community of practitioners and assessment is a normal part of practice. In so far as learning may be considered as an induction into a practice, teachers will as a matter of course assess student progress in order to decide which activity is likely to challenge students in the future without destroying their confidence.

It seems to me that this tension between challenge and confidence is essential to good teaching but that it is not possible to criterion reference this tension. It is based on a form of tacit knowledge which good teachers possess and which is essential to their membership of a tradition of teaching. In this way teaching may be viewed as a practice which contains its own norms and values like any other form of human practice in which people may discern some coherence. Despite the tacit nature of much of what is of interest in education and despite the difficulty of predicting future behaviour on the basis of past performance it is often helpful from time to time to have some external recognition of progress. Therefore it is incumbent upon governments to maintain an external system of assessment. While this incumbence might be thought expensive it should be remembered that the present attempt to objectify teacher judgement within formative assessment is also expensive as is the attempt to criterion reference all practices in the form of competencies, performance criteria or anything else. There are savings to be made here that would, I suspect, far outweigh the cost of setting up a better system.

If the resources used in this misguided effort were re-directed into maintaining the kind of external assessment system described then I believe that teachers would be able to teach free from unnecessary external constraint but with the possibility that their students could gain some external recognition of their achievement if they so wish. Of course teachers are likely to tell students where they are going wrong and what they are doing well as part of their normal conversations with them. However that is entirely separate from the external recognition of achievement. Teachers might fulfil the joint roles of teacher and external assessor but not with their own or their immediate colleagues' students. The process of meeting with colleagues and discussing performance may not only be essential for maintaining a system of external assessment but also as a form of useful personal development which informs their teaching. From time to time discussions of performance would take place with those not professionally involved in education and a teacher's judgement would be modified in that conversation.

We have to accept that it is unwise to make predictions about the likelihood of student success in the future on the basis of an assessment of ability in the past. Studies of such predictions have shown that success is not common. Employers and others may well have an interest in making this sort of prediction. However it is for them to assemble the evidence available to them and to make judgements based on that evidence. It is not up to teachers to try to make those predictions. That is not to negate the importance of education to the economy or societal harmony or whatever. It is simply to recognize that the outcome of the education system cannot be the cause which has the effect of ensuring other desirable ends.

The phrase 'the assessment tail wags the curriculum dog' is commonly used to suggest that teachers are bound to teach to any formally recognized examination. This is even more likely in a situation in which examination success rates are taken as indicators of school effectiveness.[16] It might be supposed that the system of assessment proposed above is bound to lead to uninspiring teaching towards the test. Such a supposition would be a mistake. In the proposed system, the term 'external' refers to the person responsible for making a report on the student rather than a method of assessment that is based only on paper and pencil tests which are only appropriate for assessing progress in certain practices. If industrialists and others want to select only on the basis of paper and pencil tests, that is up to them. Even if schools did not issue reports on student progress, there would be nothing to stop industrialists and others designing their own tests, and the same difficulties that were discussed above would arise. In the next chapter I discuss evaluation in education. It should be noted that far from reducing the means for professional educators to account for their decisions, the above proposals actually increase the means of accountability.

NOTES AND REFERENCES

1. Rowntree (1977) provides a good introduction to the use of terms and assessment methods.
2. The English 'Advanced Level' examinations are often referred to as a 'gold standard'.
3. See Broadfoot in Harlen (1994, pp. 29–32, 47–9).
4. Pickard (1994) warns that internal assessment is leading to dishonesty in Scottish National Examinations. As described earlier, teachers are already under pressure to reconcile concerns with students and with subjects, without putting them under managerial pressure to boost student pass rates. Students too are under pressure to achieve in these examinations and it is little wonder that some of them choose to get their work done for them. In that way internal assessment tends to favour those who are 'well-connected'.
5. Interestingly the British Driving Test is soon to include paper and pencil tests of this sort!
6. Black in Harlen (1994) gives an example of the move to internal assessment and criteria that is based on the modularization of the 16–18 curriculum in Scotland. He reports that:

   [There] was some evidence of certain difficulties, and particularly that of persuading teaching staff that a 'national standard' of comparability between the assessments of staff in different colleges has been established. This appears to be the case despite the considerable effort which

SCOTVEC, which is responsible for the system, has put into establishing quality assurance mechanisms. (p. 98)

7. See Harlen (1994, p. 5).
8. Black in Harlen (1994) reports a college lecturer's comments who had experience of writing units in 'competence' terms:

> Writing units is a linguistic exercise. You don't simply write down what they have to do, you have to translate it into competence terms which means what language you are allowed to use. The whole language that all of us are used to – 'know' and 'understand' and being able to 'remember' – suddenly you weren't allowed to have that. And even phrases such as 'explain' and 'justify', some of that was a bit sort of stretching the language. (p. 94)

9. Adapted from Module no 93313 'Gents Cutting' of the SCOTVEC catalogue available from SCOTVEC, Hanover House, 24 Douglas St, GLASGOW, G2 7NQ.
10. See D. Carr (1993) who writes:

> to speak of a given person or performance as competent can be to say *either* that they conform to certain established standards *or* that the performance was executed in an effective and efficient way . . . the second major source of confusion about competence and competencies . . . makes the mistake of construing the moral evaluative and motivational aspects of education as separable from or additional to the technical and craft dimensions in a way that wholly distorts the logical, normative and psychological relations between them. (p. 18) (italics in original)

11. See Hyland (1994) for a further critique of the 'competence movement' and Smithers (1993) who includes some international comparisons to try to show that this 'movement' in the UK is mistaken.
12. This point was made by Jonathan (1983). Designers of the 'vocational education and training' curriculum try to ensure that induction into a specific vocational practice is somehow 'generic' so that students are not disadvantaged if it turns out that employment opportunities in that specific practice do not materialize.
13. See the report from the National Foundation for Educational Research (1994).
14. The introduction of records of achievement has ethical implications which do not seem to be recognized by their advocates.
15. Confederation of British Industry (1993, p. 21).
16. See Riddell and Brown (1991).

Chapter 8

Evaluation

We may now return to the central question that was posed in the introduction: how might we know that our educational practices are progressing? In this chapter we consider evaluation at the levels of individuals, institutions, policies and systems in an attempt to answer this question. We examine the presently popular conception of evaluation and accountability, which depends upon the idea of quality in education, and go on to examine a discursive conception of evaluation.

INSTITUTIONAL EVALUATION

By now readers are familiar with the idea that empiricism may be taken to imply that there is a world external to us which provides us with an object with which to compare statements. True statements are termed facts and are supposed to correspond to reality. For an empiricist, values do not form part of the objective world. Instead they are conceived to be subjective desires or preferences. Some of these values change as people come to prefer different things and come to speak and act differently. Facts however remain relatively constant and form the foundation of common sense. Scientific enquiry does however lead to changes in those things that we regard as facts. Such enquiry is guided by the belief that the world itself does not change, merely our way of representing it. Moreover such enquiry is believed to be based on systematic objective methods, not personal preference or power in the scientific community. There is a mass of literature concerned with the notion of empiricism in natural science and much of that literature is critical of the notion. Nevertheless, as we have seen, empiricism remains a dominant influence in our education system.

What I called an empiricist ethos supports the idea that policy-making must be elitist so that scientific procedures might be applied to determine the best theoretical, management and teaching practices. Once evaluative issues are settled in this way then, as described earlier, the selection of educational methods becomes a scientific affair. Guidelines on method are issued as educational facts that have been established

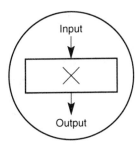

Figure 8.1

on the basis of disinterested experiment. Teachers then implement these guidelines, managed in this technical implementation by those who view teaching as an activity designed to achieve certain predetermined ends in an efficient manner. Educational managers are concerned with efficiency which is achieved by maximizing educational output over educational input. The 'value-added' to the educational process may be determined by some assessment of students before and after they undergo the process and evaluation may be conceived as the measurement of value added to the process.

An empiricist conception of individual or institutional evaluation is quite straightforward and may be summarized in Figure 8.1 where X represents whatever is to be evaluated. The inputs and outputs are measured and the difference between them is taken to be the value added by X. X is said to be progressing if the value added shows an increase.[1]

It is not clear however what 'value' means in this context. Plainly at the level of an individual teacher, it is some measure of the difference between those objectives or measurable characteristics that a student would have achieved or had prior to a course of study with the teacher and those objectives or measurable characteristics that the student achieves or has at the end of the course of study. Therefore it has become normal to issue questionnaires to students and/or to interview them after and during a course of study to discover their degree of satisfaction with the course. It has also become normal to keep records of student careers after the course of study to discover how many of them went on to secure long-term employment. At an institutional level these measures are compiled along with records of truancy rates, examination success rates and other sorts of rates into what might be called an evaluation profile. In the UK it has become normal for these profiles to be presented in newspapers and elsewhere as league tables which offer a supposed comparison between the performance of different educational institutions.

These league tables relate mainly to educational output as it were. However the measurement of educational input has not been neglected by researchers of an empiricist persuasion. Attempts have been made to work out the cost of educating different types of student attending different types of educational institution. Moreover attempts have been made to test students upon entry to an educational institution and sophisticated models have been devised to take account of students' home backgrounds. These models have included variables such as the post-code of the student's home, the number of parents the student has and the size of their home accommodation.

Without wishing to denigrate the work of those who have been given the task of trying to measure educational input and output, it is obvious that there will always be a great deal of uncertainty involved in such measurement. In the first case it is not at all clear that the notions of educational input and output make much sense since students develop in unpredictable ways because of and irrespective of the particular educational experiences that they have. For the notions to make sense there would need to be a clear way in which the educational development that took place as a result of the work of educational institutions could be differentiated from the educational development that took place elsewhere. As it is there seems to be no way that such differentiation could be achieved.

In the second case the notions of educational input and output would be useful only if there was general agreement upon the relative weight or value of the various individual measurements that were supposed to comprise input or output. Here again, empiricism needs élitism in order to remove these evaluative considerations from educational evaluation and to allow the metricians to get to work.

CASE EXEMPLAR

SCHOOL EFFECTIVENESS RESEARCH

Research of this type is well-established world-wide. Driven by political demands for accountability, indicators of school effectiveness have been derived by treating the school as a 'black box' in the way described above.[2] In order to be useful however as the OECD points out, such indicators should be

- things that can be found in some forum throughout the system so that comparisons can be made across diverse contexts
- enduring things so that trends can be analysed over time
- understandable things.[3]

As might be imagined, there is a great deal of disagreement between countries as to what the precise nature of these indicators should be. Three considerations seem to emerge as relatively incontestable:

- academic progress
- pupil satisfaction
- relationships and ethos.[4]

What also seems to have emerged from research of this type, based on measures of these three indicators, is that the effects of schools on children are not so great as the effects on them of their home, peers, community and other things that might seem to reside outwith the 'black box'.[5] This finding seems to support one of the arguments of this book that it is not helpful even to try to conceive of a school as an entity that is dislocated from the notion of a wider community.

In order to make the notions of educational input and output more plausible, there has been an attempt to merge the 'hard indicators', such as examination success rates, with 'softer' indicators, such as so-called 'ethos indicators'. Supporters of this attempt argue that they are sensitive to the criticisms that the hard indicators of educational performance are inadequate. They claim to be working towards more adequate educational indicators which include more qualitative indicators.

Such soft indicators might include qualities such as the level of honesty within the institution, the amount of time that teachers and students devote to the work of the institution on a voluntary basis, the number of questions that students ask as opposed to the answers that they give and the range of contributions that are made to staff meetings. All of these qualities might be commendable in themselves but once the attempt is made to formalize them in the form of performance indicators then something is destroyed in the formalization. For example if people know that their contribution to a meeting is being monitored then they might be encouraged to contribute even though their contribution is of little value. People might turn up just to put time in or to earn what are sometimes known disparagingly as 'brownie points'.

In short, any attempt formally to provide indicators of those things that normally are taken for granted or tacit destroys, or at least misrepresents, those things. That is not to suggest that it is impossible to talk about qualities like ethos and the like. Any attempt to measure these qualities however results in a serious distortion of them which may well have detrimental effects. These detrimental effects arise because our need to understand one another is prejudiced when people begin to talk in unfamiliar ways. For example, it would not be clear what somebody meant who said 'I'm going to increase the degree of honesty today'. Such a statement is more likely to mean the opposite to the claim that appears to be being made.

CASE EXEMPLAR

ETHOS INDICATORS[6]

- pupil morale
- teacher morale
- teacher's job satisfaction
- the physical environment
- the learning context
- teacher–pupil relationships
- discipline
- equality and justice
- extra-curricular activities
- school leadership
- information to parents
- parent–teacher consultation

It would be hard to challenge the view that lists such as the one above represent desirable indicators of school performance. It would also be hard to challenge the view that authentic human relations would be damaged if anything substantive ever came to depend upon schools maximizing their ratings on these indicators. If there is no intention to soften the hard-nosed indicators in this way then it is hard to see the point of compiling measures of performance in these softer areas. Moreover if, as the exemplar on school effectiveness was meant to show, schools cannot usefully be regarded as black boxes then the whole empiricist project of evaluation by measurement alone begins to break down.

In an attempt to move beyond the crude empiricist project of accountability through measurability, the idea of quality in education has been introduced. This move is based on an appeal to the common sense idea that goods that are cheap are often of poor quality. So, it is claimed, if educational output increases too quickly then quality will suffer. It is as if the term quality is meant to refer to all those things like ethos

---

CASE EXEMPLAR

ZEN AND THE ART OF MOTORCYCLE MAINTENANCE[7]

In this important novel published in the 1970s, Pirsig tries to elucidate the notion of quality. He begins by arguing that the art of motor cycle maintenance is really a miniature study of the art of rationality itself and that study depends upon romantic ideas of beauty. For example he argues that while the colour of the burn in the spark plug is part of the rational process of maintenance, the colour also has an aesthetic quality.[8] Moreover the motorcycle does not exist apart from the journey on which it is taken to some of the wildest and most beautiful places. Our present conception of rationality is impoverished, he explains, precisely because of the attempt to separate the knowing subject from the object (in this case the motorcycle).

In a section dealing with the difference between a craftsman and a novice, he explains how the craftsman

> is absorbed and attentive to what he is doing even though he doesn't deliberately contrive this. His motions and the machine are in a kind of harmony . . . The material and his thoughts are changing together in a progression of changes until his mind's at rest at the same time the material's right. That's Quality.[9]

> If you want to do anything you have to have a sense of what's good. That is what carries you forward. With Quality as its central undefined term, reality is, in its essential nature, not static but dynamic . . . Present culture is such that you will always be told the rationally correct way of doing things but those things would be ugly . . . A veneer of style would be overlaid to make them acceptable . . . Now the things are not just depressingly dull, they're also phoney . . . Quality isn't something you lay on top of subjects and objects like tinsel on a Christmas tree. Real Quality must be the source of the subjects and objects.[10]

In this way, Pirsig seems to liken Quality to authenticity as something that can be recognized but not defined.

indicators that are not easily specifiable or measurable. Ideally one might be able to specify educational input and output in precise ways that included the notion of acceptable standard or fitness for purpose. However given the problems with such specification then the term quality has been introduced as a sort of shorthand for all those things that are desirable but not easily measurable.

QUALITY IN EDUCATION[11]

The attempt to introduce the notion of quality in education may be contrasted with the attempt to introduce the notion of quality into motorcycle maintenance. In the latter case the attempt may be seen to be compatible with existentialist moves to dissolve the subject-object relationship. In the former case the attempt may be seen as a further plausible but doomed attempt to bolster a discredited empiricism in educational policy and practice. For the appeal to work the analogy between the normal uses of the term quality to describe goods and services and the educational use of the term would need to be convincing. Let us first discount the idea that schooling is a product. Upon enrolment for a course of study one does not purchase something additional to oneself that is separate from oneself as one would when purchasing an umbrella or a book. It is more plausible therefore (but still pretty implausible!) to compare the work of educational institutions to the work of service industries such as hairdressing. In both cases people are interested not only in the service itself but also the result at the end of the service. In both cases the result may be described though it will not conform exactly to the description. Moreover the service itself on the way to the end-product is of importance.

So what are the differences between hairdressing and education? The most crucial difference is that a student's contribution to their education is entirely different to their contribution to their haircut. It is possible to envisage a situation where a customer enters a hairdressing salon describes what she wants, sits in silence and leaves when satisfied. The corresponding educational situation is not plausible. Unless students themselves contribute within educational institutions and become engaged by whatever is on offer then whatever goes on there cannot reasonably be described as education. It is possible to have one's hair dressed after one has died!

To want quality in education amounts to little more than wanting the best in education. A quality lesson might be assumed to be better than a lesson. However the use does not solve any of our fundamental evaluative difficulties. Instead these difficulties are obscured by an inappropriate analogy that leads us astray. We are led to the view that education is a process which students undergo towards a clearly defined objective rather than as a personal engagement in which means and ends constantly interact with each other.

In summary, the conception of educational evaluation as the measurement of quality is seriously mistaken and confused because an attempt is made to merge two conflicting logics – consumerism and elitism. An attempt to untangle these logics has been made in this book and we have come up against the central difficulty for empiricists that there is no objective standard upon which to base educational policy and practice. The emphasis on standards leads empiricists to try to ensure that interpretations are guided by the same evaluative assumptions. In this way a more standard interpretation of policy is likely to be achieved and the flourishing of a variety of approaches to teaching is likely to be discouraged. Therefore our systems tend to be self referential and it is not clear just what would have to take place for systems to be changed. Even in the face of widespread misery, illiteracy or social unrest, the most likely response would be the production of yet more guidelines or more inspections or more sensitive measures. As noted previously however it is not clear that policy-making conceived in this way necessarily leads to the desired effect. The opposite may be the case.

POLICY EVALUATION

As we have seen policy is presently defined as a statement or series of statements that are designed to bring about some desired state of affairs. The success of the policy is judged according to the extent to which that state of affairs is achieved. Thus it is usual to make the distinction between the desirability of a policy and its success – between values and facts. Administrative theory is often held to be concerned with the most efficient way of achieving the desired end-state and is considered by some empirically inclined theorists to be value-neutral. The evaluation of the success of the policy is also considered by many of these theorists to be a value-neutral empirical matter which depends upon the collection of evidence. The apparent objectivity of mathematics leads them to conceptualize evidence in a quantifiable way.[12]

This way of looking at policy, theory and evidence seems to neglect the possibility that the same term may be interpreted differently according to whether that term functions as an evidential or theoretical postulate. The conceptual difficulty of quantifying evidence is also neglected. However work in the so-called post-empiricist philosophy of science has sought to question the presumption that theory and evidence are unproblematic notions to be discussed by disinterested and detached observers. Moreover the considerable body of criticism that has been directed against the fact-value distinction and positivistic theories of educational administration[13] should serve to caution those who accept the usual definition of policy in an uncritical way.

The blurring of the fact-value distinction may be illustrated by considering an account of policy evaluation from an interpretive perspective; many politicians and others support policies that are designed to increase student access to and success within higher educational institutions. In a situation of shrinking resources such policies are subject to the qualification that increased access and success should be achieved at minimum cost and without compromising educational quality. In order to judge the overall success of the policy in a quantitative way it is necessary to derive empirical measures of educational quality so that the necessary statistics relating to numbers of students, resources allocated and educational quality can be compiled. It is easy to see however that both the desirability of the policy and its success depend crucially on how the term quality is understood and measured.

Two main interpretations of the term are common[14] which seem to embody quite different conceptions of the purpose of educational institutions. In the first case quality is interpreted to mean a high standard to which all students should aspire and have equal opportunity to achieve. In the second case quality is interpreted to mean a standard that is varied according to the intended purpose of the students – quality means fitness for purpose according to this second interpretation and the meaning of purpose presents a further interpretive difficulty. Harvey and Green[15] list five definitions of quality which present even more interpretive difficulties for those who seek to measure quality in education. From an interpretive perspective the policy to fund educational institutions on the basis of their quality may be judged to be successful if a particular interpretation of the aims of the policy coincide with a particular interpretation of the results of some sort of evaluative survey. The desirability of the policy may also be judged according to whether a particular interpretation of the aims coincides with the interests of the evaluators.

In both cases interpretations are based on the interrelationship of the aims of the policy with the particular interests of the evaluators at a particular time. An empirical attempt to evaluate the success of the policy is no more value-free than a critique of the desirability of the policy. Success and desirability are not determined once and for all as if particular interpretations remain static. Nor is policy evaluation relative only to particular evaluators and their interests and power. Instead indicators of the desirability and success of a policy may emerge in the longer term according to whether people unconnected with the formation of the policy come to use the language in which the policy is framed to describe their actions. In the short term and under certain conditions people may describe their actions in a certain way and may be encouraged to proclaim the success or otherwise of a particular policy. However a policy could hardly be described as successful and desirable if its success and desirability were tied in with pecuniary rewards for using terms in approved ways or as the result of a superficial consideration. This sort of coercion and superficiality may be viewed as a crude attempt to overcome a logical disjuncture that has occurred somewhere in a chain of interpretations between policy-making and implementation.

Practical mechanisms may be devised to cope with this disjuncture which involve people learning to talk and write in particular ways that bear little resemblance to their normal ways of writing and speaking. Someone might remark that they do not say what they mean or as Trow[16] put it in connection with the use of the term quality

> coping mechanisms . . . are variously referred to as 'games' and 'scams', and involve the creative reporting of numbers and events, all wrapped in what is hoped is persuasive rhetoric that bears a somewhat loose relation to reality.

By 'reality' I take Trow to mean ways of describing actions that are normal for teachers and learners as they pursue their educative endeavours. In contrast I take 'scams' and 'games' to refer to those activities which result from a superficial and sometimes coercive attempt to get people to describe their actions as if success and desirability had to be demonstrated once and for all in order to secure funding.

In what follows, distinctions are drawn between three groups of actors concerned with educational quality: those who formulate policy and who are responsible for the allocation of funds to individual institutions; those who administer those institutions and who are primarily responsible for meeting the requirements of the funding bodies; and finally those students, teachers and others who have an interest in the development of educational institutions that is not primarily administrative.

As described earlier[17] the need for interpretation arises out of difficulties in achieving understanding in dialogue. In dialogue linguistic practices are modified. A kind of fusion of horizons has to take place for understanding to be achieved. That understanding is achieved not simply in either of the participants' prior linguistic practices, but in a kind of linguistic practice negotiated between them. The negotiated practice is not however unrelated to previous linguistic practices. Nor are all linguistic practices modified at the same time or at the same rate. Instead negotiation takes place against a background of some stability in linguistic practice.

The range of words that are commonly used in one context can be and is extended through the use of metaphor and analogy. At the same time other linguistic practices drop out of use. To return to Wittgenstein's[18] analogy between language and an ancient city; like a city that is made up of houses and streets from a variety of periods, linguistic practice too consists of words and actions that are taken from a variety of periods. The way that we speak is interwoven with the way that we act and with our form of life.

Those people and institutions that control the allocation of resources to other people and institutions have the power to influence the way that the others speak and act. This is because they can link the allocation of resources to an approved way of speaking and acting as in the example above. They have a disproportionate amount of equipment to demolish some buildings and to construct alternative streets and houses. Of course if in the longer term, other people choose to inhabit or rebuild the old streets and houses, there is not much that the powerful can do other than to try to limit access to construction equipment and demolition vehicles![19]

Policy-making might be seen as the attempt to establish certain linguistic practices as part of the stable framework that enables people to understand one another. Both the success and the desirability of that attempt may be seen to depend upon the degree to which those practices become established. To return to the earlier example, the policy to promote the use of the term quality in educational institutions may be considered to be both successful and desirable if people unconnected with the formation of the policy come to describe their actions using that term.

Before the 1980s, the coupling of the terms quality and education was rare. In many places during the 1980s, the terms began to be used together by policy-makers and administrators. Yet that use seems not to have caught on among students, teachers and those who have a non-professional interest in education. For example, few parents seem to be seeking information about educational efficiency or quality assurance procedures. Nor I suspect is much staff-room talk concerned with the use of these co-joined terms. Of course people can be coerced into speaking in a variety of strange ways. For example, teachers seeking promotion might be advised to speak as if parents are customers who demand quality education. Administrators seeking to secure funds from councils that have adopted quality criteria are also likely to interpret those criteria in an approved way.

Habermas's use of the term 'ideal speech situation'[20] might illuminate this contrast between ordinary discourse and discourse that has been systematically distorted by power relationships such as the ones operating in the case of the interview situation or funding arrangements. Let us recall that an ideal speech situation may be summarized as one in which participants are free to contribute without fear of coercion, threat or domination. For Habermas, the possibility of envisaging such situations is a necessary condition for achieving a rational consensus about truth claims. Even though ideal speech situations may never be practically realized, such situations may serve as a regulative guide to the orientation of discourse towards truth.

In the example given above, we may accept that a non-coercive discussion of the sort that occurs when teachers consider their genuine concerns among their peers is closer to the ideal speech situation than those discussions where the main point at issue is promotion prospects and power differentials. Yet the boundary between distorted and non-distorted communication is not sharp because there is a sense in which all communication is a distortion of previous forms of communication. Moreover the ability to discuss in certain specialized ways may be a useful predictive device for selecting people for certain positions as in the case of the interview.

The boundary between specialized uses and distorted uses is not entirely sharp either. It is regarded as normal for governments to use the power at their disposal to encourage people to speak and act in different ways. State-employees are encouraged to talk in different ways while they are at work through control of their wages and prospects. This is not as sinister as it might sound. Any new policy may be seen as an attempt to get people to speak and act differently. People employed by the state or a large corporation share a context based on a social tradition within which specialized uses of terms have meaning. These people are likely to have some understanding of the power relationships that have skewed their conversation in particular ways. They share a common background of linguistic practice that enables them to understand one another when they discuss a new policy. Other people unconnected with the formation and promotion of the policy may not necessarily share this background. Hence for them, the specialized or distorted uses of language may have little meaning and according to my argument the new policy may be both unsuccessful and undesirable.

In other instances however a policy is framed in terms that come to be widely accepted by those not directly concerned with the promotion of the policy. For whatever reason particular analogies, metaphors, moral resonance and arguments appeal and people come to describe their actions using the language in which the policy is framed. However it is not clear just how much time a policy should be given before the criterion is applied. Nor is the borderline between unacceptable coercion and persuasive advertising and argument clear. Most importantly of all, it is not clear how the sorts of empirical generalizations described above can be verified. On the face of it readers either agree with the interpretation or they do not. The argument appears to lead to an extreme form of relativism mediated only by an appeal to the normative notion of an 'ideal speech situation'. However Wittgenstein's discussion of ordinary language may help us to avoid this conclusion.

Wittgenstein[21] advises

> When philosophers use a word 'knowledge', 'being', 'object', 'I', 'proposition', 'name' and try to grasp the *essence* of the thing, one must always ask oneself: is the word actually used in this way in the language-game which is its original home? –
> What *we* do is to bring words back from their metaphysical to their everyday use.
> (Italics in original.)

Here Wittgenstein seems not only to be inveighing against a form of metaphysical essentialism but also to be advocating a philosophical method that gives some sort of normative force to the ordinary use of terms. His recommendation that we should bring words back from their metaphysical (or specialized) use to their everyday use is a statement of method which resonates with the ethical concern of defending ordinary language against powerful interests that might try to deform such language in particular ways. In the cases of both the philosopher's metaphysical interest and the policy-maker's interest in trying to bring about some desired state of affairs, there are limits to the meaningful use of language. Those limits are set by the rate at which ordinary language develops and changes.

We have seen how Gadamer's (1975) use of the terms 'fusion of horizons' and 'prejudice' may be helpful in explaining how ordinary language develops and changes. For Gadamer 'prejudice' is not a pejorative term. Instead the term is meant to indicate the effect of tradition which is manifest in ordinary linguistic use. According to Gadamer, linguistic development takes place as a result of the risking of prejudice in hermeneutic encounters between different interpreters or between interpreter and text. Instead of there being one final interpretation, understanding consists of a series of 'fusions of horizons' in which 'prejudice' is continually being transformed.

The concept of understanding as a fusion of horizons emphasizes the temporal nature of linguistic practices. The more that prejudices are risked, the more likely it is that understanding and linguistic development take place. Thus it makes no sense to Gadamer to argue that success and desirability, for example, can be decided once and for all in an overwhelmingly important hermeneutic encounter. Instead our understanding of success and desirability is itself located in the stream of an ongoing series of fusions of horizons. While it is not possible to predict the precise direction of that stream, it may be possible to chart its previous development. A specific example of this possibility may be provided by the attempt to achieve understanding between the three groups concerned with educational quality that I described earlier.

The family resemblance between the service model and the policy of increasing access to educational institutions may have allowed the quality debate in education to have got going. In this way the ordinary use of quality in a service context may be taken to represent the prejudice of tradition that is modified in a fusion of horizons with the educational policy-maker. Policy makers and administrators arrive at a mutual understanding of quality by a process of clarification based on this family resemblance. However those not intimately concerned with the debate – students, teachers and others have not risked their prejudices in this way. The interest in securing and allocating funds in a rational and transparent manner provides the opportunities for the ongoing fusion of horizons between policy-maker and administrator. Teachers, students and others are not so likely to have had this opportunity. Their interests are different and for them, the opportunities for understanding what is meant by quality remain rooted in the service model.

When policy-makers and others seek to reinterpret quality to mean something like fitness for purpose, then the hermeneutic distance between the ordinary use of the term quality to describe products or services and this reinterpretation is large. In this case a fusion of horizons between the prejudices of the teacher and the policy-maker is less likely. Participants in a discourse may risk their prejudices but risking does not mean jettisoning and there is a variety of other possible hermeneutic encounters which may serve to reinforce the teacher's prejudice for ordinary use. For example, teachers, students and others may be more inclined to imagine what the notion of fitness for purpose might mean in the case of a hairdressing salon than uncritically to accept that the notion forms an important guide to their interest in knowledge, truth and learning. They may wonder how a cleaner or labourer's hairstyle might differ from that of a television presenter and how the purpose of these styles should affect any description of quality. They may wonder whether the care and attention given to one style might not form a 'gold standard' for all other styles. They may then go on to reflect that no one has just one purpose in life and that the notion of fitness for purpose seems to relate more to the idea of an economic purpose than anything else.

This chain of resemblances may form a sort of 'perspicuous representation'.[22] The perspicuity links the educational use of the term quality with the idea that the purpose of educational institutions is to slot people into a particular economic vacancy which may or may not exist. In contrast there is the idea that people fulfil a range of roles in addition to their economic role. Moreover such a perspicuous representation may reinforce the prejudice that democratic societies depend upon a broadly educated population. Teachers, students and others may be unwilling to jettison this prejudice in the hermeneutic encounter with the prejudice of quality as fitness for purpose.

CASE EXEMPLAR

GOOD SCHOOLS[23]

We saw earlier some of the difficulties with research into school effectiveness and that some of the conclusions reached by researchers working within this research programme are problematic. That does not mean however that we have no idea at all what good schools look like nor what features such schools exemplify. There is a good deal of agreement on the following ten-point summary of good schools.

1. Strong positive leadership by the head and senior staff.
2. A good atmosphere of spirit, generated both by shared aims and values and by a physical environment that is as attractive and stimulating as possible.
3. High and consistent expectations of all pupils.
4. A clear and continuing focus on teaching and learning.
5. Well developed procedures for assessing how well pupils are progressing.
6. Responsibility for learning shared by the pupils themselves.
7. Participation by pupils in the life of the school.
8. Rewards and incentives to encourage pupils to succeed.
9. Parental involvement in children's education and in supporting the aims of the school.
10. Extra-curricular activities which broaden pupils' interests and experiences, expand their opportunities to succeed, and help them to build good relationships within the school.

Let us recall too that in Chapters 2 and 3 we were able to set out some of the features of good teaching and good systems of education. We cannot describe all these features in great detail, nor can we assume that these features remain constant or that their interpretation is unproblematic. While we may not know everything, we do however know some things.

One of the most persistent criticisms of hermeneutic accounts of linguistic development such as the above is that there are no clear grounds for determining which interpretation is to be preferred. After all, it might be claimed, according to the above account understanding depends simply on the empirical matter of providing opportunities for one group to talk to another. Policy-makers and teachers should have the opportunity to meet with equal opportunity to contribute to a discussion and with a symmetry in power relations so that the prejudices of policy-maker and others might both be modified. According to this argument, there is no logical reason why the policy-maker's prejudice should not be modified in a way that avoids the fitness for purpose interpretation. Perhaps the term quality may come to serve as a useful device for apportioning resources to educational institutions after all.

This kind of criticism may be met by the response offered by Bernstein (1983): a shift to an alleged hermeneutic approach to epistemology helps us to move beyond the objectivism of representations of an external reality as described earlier. The move beyond relativism however does not mean that we have to develop some other timeless criterion for demarcating once and for all between preferred and other interpretations. Instead we may encounter narratives against which we are prepared to risk our prejudices in something like the kind of ongoing conversation that Rorty (1980) describes. That conversation may be skewed in particular directions by powerful interests. However the fact that often we can recognize occasions when communication is distorted and can envisage the ideal speech situation are indications that reasons can be advanced in favour of one interpretation rather than another. Moreover the fact that in the long term so many policies come to be regarded as unsuccessful and undesirable should make us highly sceptical about any claims for the success or desirability of any new policy. We need to view policies more as attempts to move the conversation in a particular direction rather than as an attempt to bring about a state of affairs once and for all as it were.

There is a further objection which may be advanced against the theory of meaning outlined above. It may be claimed that the problem of quality in education is not so much concerned with semantics or epistemology. Instead it may be argued that all concerned with the quality debate understand each other and the epistemological implications of each others' positions perfectly well. The problem is that they do not agree. It may be suggested that governments do not trust teachers and seek to control them in various ways that are disguised under the widely accepted banner of quality. However this disguise masks a deep division between attempts externally to control teachers and their intrinsic motivation to pursue knowledge for its own sake and to induct others into that pursuit. Formulated in this way the problem becomes one of practical defence of academic values from the onslaught of managerialism. A solution to this problem might be for teachers to formulate their own procedures for quality assessment, audit and the like and to hope that governments accept those procedures rather than try to impose alternatives.

This way of formulating the problem however misses the radical implications of this interpretive account of meaning. The normal distinctions between policy, theory and practice are broken down in favour of an ongoing transformation of linguistic practice. Instead of the idea that practice needs always to be managed by the generation and application of ever more refined criteria, there is the idea that evaluative and empirical concerns are a normal part of practice. The notion of practical resistance becomes otiose as the possibility is opened up of radical transformation of the usual or normal distinctions and the theoretical framework that underpins them.

The idea that theoretical presuppositions are less relevant than practical concerns is a direct consequence of the separation of policy from theory from practice which itself results from a long tradition of logical empiricism. Embracing the fact-value distinction as it does, this tradition leads to the idea that policies embody values that are not amenable to theoretical analysis. According to this idea theoretical analysis is no more than the restating of a problem that involves different views of the value of education. So, the argument goes, practical defence is the only option for those who do not agree with the policy. It is ironic that the problem with educational institutions might not reside so much in the failure adequately to assess their own quality as to assess the quality and wisdom of government policy towards preferred criteria for the use of the term quality.

EVALUATION OF THE SYSTEM

It is obvious that we cannot establish a 'cosmic vantage point'[24] from which to evaluate a system. We are inextricably locked into the system and our position within it will inevitably affect how we see the system. Our attempts at improvement must be based as much on comparisons within the way things are now as on the way things might be. We cannot assume that there are criteria outside of the system with which to appraise it. It is at the level of system that the inadequacy of empiricist methodology is most apparent. At this level fact and value are so obviously inter-twined that it is obvious that no one individual or group can have any idea with certainty how best to proceed.

Elitism can only try to conserve the system against the fragmentation of value that seems to characterize our present predicament in the liberal democracies.[25] But such conservation only leads as we have seen, to a kind of inauthenticity in our relations with one another that is bound to increase and, if the arguments advanced in this book are correct, is bound to lead to an even further fragmentation of value. As I have argued, our cultural and social values are not yet so fragmented as to make it impossible to agree pragmatically on the best things to do in the educational institutions in which we have a prime interest. Elitism is not going to help us but things might be improved through democratic systems which encourage diversity so that we may compare institutions, people and practices. At the same time such systems might encourage reflection, criticism, authentic silence, the recognition of authority and a willingness to doubt. In that way we may have some confidence that our decisions are based on criteria that are grounded in good traditions rather than criteria that are based on an elusive notion of objective reality.

If an empiricist ethos continues to be embedded within the concepts used to describe and control public services, the tension between private interests and public values will continue to increase. In the case of public sector educational institutions, the achievement of certain predetermined and limited outcomes may become the only possible function as funds diminish and public values fragment. These outcomes may be useful in themselves and related to the educational enterprise but the sum of such achievements cannot constitute the educational enterprise. The idea of a public sector education system may become politically unachievable. Instead a basic skills training delivered in public sector institutions may be supplemented wherever possible by private effort and private capital. In reality there may develop enormous differences in cost and prestige between institutions even though they purport to offer similar courses and subject themselves to similar quality controls. Such a development could be particularly divisive and damaging because it involves the loss of an important way of legitimizing differentiated societies. It is important to maintain the idea that social mobility is possible through educational endeavour and the further idea that the precise effects and extent of that mobility are unpredictable.

It is easy to speculate now that there seems to have been an opportunity sometime in the 1950s and 1960s to articulate views of theory and practice that would have strengthened resistance to the implementation of the service model. The concentration of theoretical effort on what has been called 'Platonic' meta-theory[26] made an easy target for members of the political right who were concerned to reduce the cost of maintaining educational institutions. The work of educational institutions is, and always has been, informed by a range of perspectives and considerations. Some of these are amenable to the production or service metaphors described earlier: others however are not.

The pragmatic idea that the work of educational institutions is informed by a variety of practical strategies and theoretical interests has many attractions. Perhaps the most important of these is the unity of theory and practice as strands running through an ongoing conversation. If a lack of educational accountability is perceived to be a problem, then for a pragmatist the notion of accountability is as open to analysis as the mechanisms for achieving that accountability. Moreover if the above analysis is correct, the reduction of the complexities of institutional accountability to a series of prescribed quality indicators may well lead to a narrowing of the curriculum and a reduction in professional motivation.

To return again to the Wittgensteinian analogy, education might partly be viewed as an introduction to the streets and houses that already exist so that students can find their way about. Such an activity might also involve the observation and analysis of the process of demolition and reconstruction. Individuals might be empowered to contribute to the demolition, construction and conservation of buildings and streets according to their idea of the kind of city that they want to inhabit. It is possible that the attempt to promote the use of the term quality in educational institutions may serve limit access to demolition and building equipment.

It is also possible that the policy to derive and implement a series of quality indicators may yet turn out to be both successful and desirable according to the argument advanced in this chapter. However at the present time the omens for this do not appear to be propitious. It is worth remembering that the policy itself is not promoted and implemented without cost. An adequate system for ensuring educational evaluation would include the cost of developing and operating the system itself. Even for those with strong empiricist presuppositions the price of centrally devising, implementing and evaluating quality indicators may turn out to be too high.

SUMMARY

In this chapter we have traced the effects of an empiricist ethos in education from empirical research into institutional effectiveness through to attempts to measure quality in education. We have seen some of the problems with research and measurement of these types and have considered how policy evaluation and evaluation generally might be conceived differently. We have seen that we need to give up thinking that we can evaluate by measuring systems, people or institutions against an ideal standard. Instead we need to encourage diversity within traditions so that we may learn from one another by comparing institutions, people and practices of diverse character. We do not so much come to choose an alternative as simply to adopt better ways of doing things as part of normal practice.

In the introduction I set out the main implications of this attempt to derive a substantive theory of good teaching in advance of the derivation. These implications are not repeated in the conclusion. Instead further consideration is given to the notion of authenticity through a review of the arguments that have been advanced in this book.

NOTES AND REFERENCES

1. The 'school effectiveness' research programme tends to take this 'black box' approach. See for example the work of Coleman *et al.* (1966) and Jencks *et al.* (1972). As MacBeath (1992) points out however 'The strength of peer group and home/community effects makes the school/classroom/teacher effect marginal by comparison' (p. 12).
2. I am grateful to John MacBeath for pointing out to me that the 'black box' and ethnographic research programmes have never come together in a common main stream.
3. Quoted by Ruby in Riley and Nuttall (1994, p. 11).
4. Quoted by Nuttall in Riley and Nuttall (1994, p. 33).
5. See Rutter *et al.* (1979) and Mortimore *et al.* (1988).
6. From MacBeath in Riley and Nuttall (1994, p. 109).
7. Pirsig (1974).
8. Pirsig (1974, p. 99).
9. Pirsig (1974, p. 167).
10. Pirsig (1974, p. 284).
11. This is taken from Halliday (1994). See Ellis *et al.* (1993) for a useful overview of the 'quality debate' and Berdahl *et al.* (1991) for some international comparisons. For information relating to quality issues in Scottish educational institutions see SCOTVEC. (1993). Information relating to Scottish Higher Education may be obtained from The Scottish Higher Education Funding Council, Donaldson House, 97 Haymarket Terrace, EDINBURGH, EH12 5HD.

    Finally, I am grateful to John Fyfield of Monash University for drawing my attention to a report of the Higher Education Council, *Higher Education: Achieving Quality*, Canberra: National Board of Employment, Education and Training (1992). This document provides an excellent introduction to the 'quality debate' particular to Australian higher education institutions.
12. Many British educational institutions, particularly colleges of further education, have obtained 'BS 5750' which is the British Standards Institution's Quality Assurance Standard. Very often this is seen as the starting point to an approach known as Total Quality Managment. See Ellis (1993) for an example of this. There are a range of other 'quality standards' including 'Investors in People' and the 'Scottish Quality Managment System'.

13. For a useful discussion of these issues see *Educational Management and Administration,* 21:3, July 1993. This edition contains a number of responses to the work of Evers and Lakomski (1991). Evers and Lakomski's application of a Quinean coherentist epistemology to the justification of educational administration leads to the blurring of the fact-value distinction. For them, the distinctions between policy, theory and evidence are not sharp. Instead all three are incorporated within a network that is mediated by considerations of simplicity, comprehensiveness and other coherence criteria.
14. See Berdahl *et al.* (1991).
15. Harvey and Green (1993).
16. Trow (1993, p. 21).
17. See Taylor (1985a, p. 281).
18. Wittgenstein (1953, PI 118).
19. The work of Chomsky and Herman (1988) and other critical theorists may be explained in this way.
20. See Habermas (1973, 1984).
21. Wittgenstein (1953, PI 116).
22. Wittgenstein (1953, PI 122).
23. This account is taken from the Report of the National Commission on Education (1993, pp. 142–3).
24. This term is borrowed from Quine (1971).
25. See Jonathan (1993).
26. Elliott (1993a).

Conclusion

Social cohesion is a necessity, and mankind has never yet succeeded in enforcing cohesion by merely rational arguments. Every community is exposed to two opposite dangers: ossification through too much discipline and reverence for tradition, on the one hand; on the other hand dissolution, or subjection to foreign conquest, through the growth of an individualism and personal independence that makes co-operation impossible. In general, important civilisations start with a rigid and superstitious system, gradually relaxed and leading at a certain stage, to a period of brilliant genius, while the good of the old tradition remains and the evil inherent in its dissolution has not yet developed. But as the evil unfolds, it leads to anarchy, thence, inevitably to a new tyranny, producing a new synthesis secured by a new system of dogma. The doctrine of liberalism is an attempt to escape from this endless oscillation. The essence of liberalism is an attempt to secure a social order not based on irrational dogma, and ensuring stability without involving more restraints than are necessary for the preservation of the community. Whether this attempt can succeed only the future can determine.[1]

This quotation from Russell's *History of Western Philosophy* highlights the importance to liberal democracies of the idea of diverse practices flourishing within a tradition. The idea appears again in Kuhn's account of scientific development which is said to depend upon there being an 'essential tension' between tradition and innovation in scientific practice.[2] Rorty too develops a similar idea in his account of philosophy as a conversation between systematic and edifying philosophies.[3] In this book the idea has been used to support an account of good teaching. In this conclusion the account is further developed through an exploration of the relationship between authenticity and democracy.

As we have seen it is not possible to describe all aspects of practices, and practical development can never depend entirely upon the application of forms of discourse taken from other practices. The distinctions between progress and degeneration, better and worse, always depend upon there being some traditions within which people just act. At bottom these traditions may be underpinned, as Wittgenstein suggests, by certain primitive practices such as those that include characteristic ways of responding to pain. Normal conversations too depend upon there being tacit agreement on certain norms and social conventions. The possibility of coming to an agreement depends upon there being some touchstone that is accepted by all parties to the conversation.

As values appear to fragment within liberal democracies and problems arise, politicians are always likely to try to tighten control over tradition in order to be perceived to be doing something about a perceived malaise. Such tightening leads however as we have seen, to inauthenticity as people are led to try to say something or do something about those features of tradition which must remain tacit if they are to serve as anchors for liberal diversity. The introduction of managerialism into education may be seen as the latest attempt to hold on to the values of the Enlightenment in the face of post-modern imperatives.

We have seen how empiricist presuppositions have become embedded within educational practice and have led to an unhelpful conception of theory and practice. Instead we have discussed a conception of practice that is based on Wittgenstein's conception of a language game. The empiricist conception of theory as a text that attempts to guide practice from the outside, as it were, was rejected in favour of a conception of theory and practice as thought and action that are intrinsic to practices. We also saw however that while educational practices do not share one thing in common, they do nevertheless share a series of overlapping resemblances and that these resemblances may be shown by what Wittgenstein calls a perspicuous representation. Such representations may be the nearest that we get to the notion of theory as a way of seeing connections between a collection of seemingly disparate phenomena. On this view theories such as the one advanced in this book may be regarded as perspicuous representations that pick out a path, as it were, between practices in order to show the resemblances between them.[4]

From such vantage points, it is a short step to take to the conception of theories as no more than interesting stories that are told in the ungrounded hope that things will be better as a result of analysis of this kind. We may agree with much of the post-modern project without giving up entirely on the idea that there is something that binds us together in the pursuit of a common good. We may endeavour to get beyond the solipsism of individual existence on the one hand and on the other hand the raw struggle for power which characterizes the irrationalism of the ontology of rival forms of discourse.

We saw how the democratic form of life may enable us to carve a path between the idea that authenticity may only be known by the individual and the alternative idea that the only way that schools and other social institutions may be run is according to the values of a paternalistic elite. It was argued that authenticity unites truth and goodness through the idea of moral action. That idea may be validated by appealing to the notion of an ideal democratic consensus. Authenticity may be defined as the taking hold of the direction of one's own life and not having the direction determined for one. In that way ends and means are interwoven within social practices rather than separated into different sorts of practices.

The concept of authenticity takes on a central role within the theory of teaching outlined in this book. That does not mean however that teachers and students should 'do their own thing' nor that they should be gripped with fear of existential *angst* and become unable to do anything. The struggle for authenticity is more subtle than this. The literature surrounding existentialism and education is not vast. In particular existentialist writers have not been forthcoming in drawing implications from their philosophy for educational practice. I suggest that there may be three reasons for this reluctance: first, existentialists tend to be interested in rare occurrences in human life, not in routine problems that might be imagined to characterize the existence of teachers; second, existentialism tends to be an individualistic philosophy; third, existentialism tends to be concerned with adult existence rather than the child's mode of existence.

In some ways child-centred education might be imagined to be concerned to protect and promote the authentic existence of the child. Such a conception of education tends to emphasize the natural curiosity of children and their innate talents for creativity and discovery. Such talents, it is argued, should not be blocked by educational imperatives imposed upon them by traditionalists. They should be encouraged to 'grow', to 'develop their own interests' and to 'discover themselves'. These phrases taken from a recently published book on child-centred education[5] resonate with the existentialist's concern with authenticity. On this view teachers and students should protect their practices from the imposition of managerialist imperatives and should themselves decide what to do on the basis of the immediate interests of the child that are derived from experience. The experience required was participation in community life. Hence Dewey emphasized the educational importance of practices that include cooking, making things and cooperation.[6]

The child-centred view of education may be contrasted with the idea of education as initiation into all of the good things that have been said and done in the ascent of human-kind and that form the basis for all future endeavours.[7] Schooling may be seen as just one part of this initiation and the curriculum may be constructed on the basis of the good things that future citizens of a participative democracy will need in order to be able to participate fully in a such a democracy. Such a curriculum is not based just on ethical and moral commitment but also on an epistemological requirement to distinguish between progress and degeneration. Child-centredness as advocated by Dewey and others may be seen to cohere with the existentialist's concern with authenticity through Habermas's notion of an ideal speech situation. This situation has been characterized as an authentic ideal which promotes social solidarity. While the ideal is not realizable in itself, the degree to which the ideal is realized, may be discerned.

The child-centred and traditional views of education may be seen to come together through this notion of a democratic community guided by the ideal described above. The problem for both views of course is that if children are to be inducted into a cultural inheritance and to learn how to act authentically, then how are they to determine which parts of their cultural inheritance are worth preserving and which are worth jettisoning as inauthentic? After all, part of our project in this book has been to analyse our common inheritance in order to reject those parts that have led us astray so badly within the rationalist project. In particular means-ends rationality which informs educational developments generally has been seen to be educationally damaging.

Moreover how are we to determine whether a new vocabulary has added to our 'ascent' in encouraging progressive or degenerative practice? Recently the educational vocabulary has, in the UK for example, been extended to include standard attainment targets, grade-related criteria, elements of competence, range statements, differentiated learning, strata, levels, experiential learning and so on. How are we to know that these have progressed matters? An answer to this question was proposed in the previous chapter. We saw that we have good reason to be sceptical that the manufacture of new terms to describe familiar products and processes adds anything to the sum total of human understanding. On the contrary, such manufacture is the epitome of inauthenticity and actually serves simply to maintain communities which act as the final arbiters for the meaning of these new terms. The point is that there is no authentic context for the interpretation of these terms other than through the context that is provided by those communities. The traditions of teaching and learning themselves need to be developed to include the means of interpreting new terms and such development is bound to be imposed since the members of these traditions hardly needed such terms to practise.

We have a romantic attachment to traditions which allows us to differentiate tradition from élites. Moreover liberalism has enabled us to maintain a meaning for authenticity at home even if at work our practices are largely determined for us by others. That is why the vocationalizing project can be so damaging in schools if that project is taken to its logical conclusion. In that extreme case the only point of schooling becomes the achievement of ends that were set for children to achieve. Pushed to its logical conclusion, vocationalism denies schools any role in the development of authentic practice. We would then have reason to worry that students might become inducted into a set of undesirable practices in which it is the norm to do things under coercion rather than to discuss options in a spirit of cooperation and honest endeavour. In these practices discrimination between right and wrong may become blurred. Moreover we may begin to lose many of those things that we take for granted in the conduct of normal relationships – for example the expectation that people will tell the truth for most of the time and that they will not conspire to hurt one another.

Some people might object that talk of collegial relationships, honesty, friendship, truth and justification is commendable but largely irrelevant to a highly competitive world in which these values are not so important. They may go on to argue that educational institutions should prepare people for this harsher, more competitive world. Their objection may be countered in two ways. The first is to point out that relevance and utility are not the only criteria by which success may be judged. If they were, then we might be inclined to turn educational institutions into factories or shops with obvious relevance and utility. The second is to argue that some commercial organizations might operate more efficiently if that operation embodied some of the other values that educational institutions traditionally have sought to promote. In short we may argue that values such as truth, friendship, justice, fairness and so on form the basis for the justification of commercial competition as an enterprise that it is in everyone's interest to support.

This is in contrast to the unacceptable idea that the main justification for commercial enterprise is that certain people stand to profit by it in the short term. Moreover we may argue that the values of truth, justice, honesty and so on may form the bedrock against which sharp practice, unfair competition and coercion might be recognized. We may argue that even though these undesirable values may be a part of the real commercial world, that does not mean that we have to go about teaching people as if this were a normal part of all worlds. The point here is that it is only against a common background of what counts as right and wrong that normal commercial practice can flourish. The increasing number of commercial organizations that now adopt and apply codes of ethics provides further evidence to support this point.

We do not need to adopt the conception of authenticity that involves existential *angst* made popular by the French existentialists, as if all things were possible. Instead we may recognize that by changing our philosophical orientation we may discover new freedoms. For example Taylor uses the term 'engaged agency' to draw attention to the possibilities opened up by the dissolution of the knowing subject/known object distinction which is derived from logical empiricism:

> Engaged agency is that agency whose experience is made intelligible only by being placed in the context of the kind of agency it is . . . The context stands as the unexplicated background within which . . . this experience can be understood . . . One of the features that distinguishes a view of human agency as engaged from the disengaged picture is that the former has some space for this kind of background. On the disengaged view, and in particular on the mechanist theory that often underpins it, there is not, of course, an explicit rejection of this notion, but the entire issue to which it provides some answer does not arise. Intelligibility is assumed from the start and does not need a context to provide it.[8]

Heidegger's notion of pre-understanding and Wittgenstein's demonstration that something has already to be understood before we can ostensibly define, indicate the importance of engaged understanding and point to the compatibility of the traditional and progressive views. We are, as Heidegger points out, 'thrown' into the world. We do not engage ourselves by making what would have to be an impossible choice. That does not mean however that we have to remain where we are 'thrown' or that we can have no idea where we are going. The self may be regarded as a movement between birth and death within which we have some choice. Inauthenticity is characterized by our inevitably becoming enmeshed in ordinary life through what Heidegger calls 'falling' and 'forgetting'. We tend to 'fall' into the mundane and must to some extent 'forget' our 'fallenness' in order to act in the world.

'The self must forget itself if, lost in the world of equipment, it is to be able actually to go to work and manipulate something,' Heidegger tells us. The problem is that we tend to get so bogged down with the everyday we forget that we are called upon to take a coherent stand in a world where things genuinely are at stake. As Guignon points out in a commentary on Heidegger:

> The self-forgetfulness paradoxically tends to aggravate our own self preoccupation constantly concerned with checking our performance against public criteria into an 'extravagant grubbing about in one's soul which can be in the highest degree counterfeit'.[9]

If we follow Heidegger, authenticity may be regarded as nothing other than a fuller participation in the public form of life and some inauthenticity is inevitable. As we become initiated into the practices of our community, we soak up the 'tacit sense of what is important that circulates our world'. But of course these tacit commitments are themselves the products of our history and we can only go beyond these products if we become acquainted with them.

This brief consideration of Heidegger's work shows how an engagement with the ideas of a serious thinker such as him can help to illuminate teaching practice. That illumination does not proceed in an obvious way, but the insights gained may be all the more profound for that. With an eye on what they consider to be important, teachers try to engage the interests of students essentially by telling a series of stories. As Bruner points out however 'to tell a story is inevitably to take a moral stance'.[10]

CASE EXEMPLAR

SUPERVISION OF THE PRACTICUM

Whether or not teacher training becomes based entirely in schools, some form of practicum is bound to be included in the arrangements for the initial training of teachers. At the moment it is common for experienced teachers or university tutors to sit in on one or more of the trainee's classes during the practicum. Usually the trainee is asked to prepare some sort of plan for the lesson which is to be observed. After the lesson the tutor or experienced teacher might offer comments which range from the congratulatory to the critical.

Plainly the supervision of practicum visits is least problematic in the case of good trainees who need little more than support, encouragement and suggestions for future development. A poor performance by a trainee in the classroom is more problematic. In that case three possibilities may arise. In the first case, trainee and supervisor agree that the lesson was atypical and decide to disregard it as someone having an 'off day'. In the second case, the trainee does not agree that the performance was poor. In that case some form of reorientation would seem to be a prerequisite before any further help could be given. Somehow the way that the trainee interprets the teaching context is such that things are not picked out from that context to indicate that all is not well – the nuances of looks or the barely concealed giggles from the back of the class perhaps. The trainees view of teaching and the educational enterprise itself seem to be mistaken. In this case prior theoretical engagement with the work of people like Taylor, Heidegger and others may well help the supervisor explain concerns in a way that avoids what could turn out to be an uninformative conflict. That is because the trainee's main problem is not due to a lack of techniques. Rather the whole orientation to teaching practice is mistaken.

In the third case, the trainee knows that the performance was poor but does not know what to do to improve. Here the supervisor may well be tempted to offer suggestions as to new techniques that the trainee might try. For example, the trainee might be advised to 'vary the pitch of the voice', 'smile a little more' or 'gain control always by directing questions rather than leaving them open-ended'. The existence of books which take the form of 'tips for teachers' may be seen to satisfy a need in cases such as these. Yet by offering such suggestions supervisors risk promoting the kind of inauthenticity that by inclination they seek to avoid. As in the previous case, the supervisor might do better to try to change the orientation of the trainee rather than to offer techniques that may only serve to bolster a mistaken view of the educational enterprise.

What this exemplar is meant to highlight is that someone's perception of a problem may be misleading. To offer them techniques which they appear to want, may actually encourage the sort of inauthenticity that we can recognize in the manufactured smile of the server in the fast food restaurant or the over-use of the phrases 'Have a nice day' or 'Good morning, this is John speaking, how may I help you?' The matter of giving appropriate advice is more complex than this however. It is possible that the advice to trainees might actually serve to reorient them in a way that a long discussion about Heidegger might not. It is conceivable, for example, that the multiple use of the phrase 'Have a nice day' actually does make people feel very positive towards their existence. Such use does not obviously lead to a devaluation in human relations.

To offer advice to anyone is always a risk. To offer hope through a 'ladder' of technique is helpful only so long as the trainee comes to see the techniques as a ladder that can be thrown away once having reached beyond it. The problem with ladders of technique, as we have seen, is that presently the empiricist conception of developments is dominant and we are led to believe that running up and down ladders is all that one needs to do. The risk that the supervisor takes in offering technical advice is to further reinforce this unhelpful conception of development.

In telling a story of what has been said in the past, it is not possible to avoid pointing towards what might be. Engagement with thinkers of the calibre of Heidegger is a tall order but when considering the teacher education curriculum, it is worth considering whether such engagement may well have all kinds of unforseen benefits. Reflective practice may be empty unless there is something worthwhile against which to risk one's prejudices and come to a reoriented view of one's predicament.

I have tried to write a philosophically informed account of teaching practice which might be of interest to teacher trainees, teacher trainers and others with a non-professional interest in maintaining a tradition of good teaching. I reject the idea that teachers need a structured immersion in teaching method supplemented sometimes by more theoretical courses. Rather teaching practice for trainees as well as experienced teachers should be characterized more by informed reflection, analysis of educational values and further induction into forms of knowledge or content. In my view good teaching is characterized by a degree of scepticism about practice that cannot be avoided through the use of standard curriculum materials, national curricula, objectives or anything else. It is not desirable to try to justify practice by an appeal to the authority of an elite or by an appeal to the satisfaction of wants. In the end good teachers are authorities in some area of knowledge. That authority provides them with their only defence against a form of relativism which could become debilitating and demoralizing.

I have tried to tell a story against which readers might match their 'prejudices'. I seek to continue a conversation, to use the well-worn metaphor that underpins the idea of diversity within tradition and that informs the work of writers as diverse as Gadamer, Taylor, Oakeshott and Rorty. My own 'prejudices' are partly based on my role as a teacher educator. Many courses of teacher education over-emphasize teaching methods, psychology of education and the following of guidelines. In that way many courses (though not, it is hoped, many teacher educators who, *as educators*, must transcend or even ignore course descriptors and guidelines) actually condone the morally neutral technical view of teaching. I have noticed for example that some teacher trainees are keen to 'forget the forgetting itself' and cling to the 'prop' of course descriptors, guidelines and the like. I have heard some teachers say: 'All my students achieve the set learning outcomes. What else is there to do?' The struggle for authenticity is not helped when the authority of an official text seems to suggest that teaching is neither a moral nor an educational activity.

The last forty or so years may be characterized by the phrase 'from goodness to quality'. I believe that now there are good reasons to begin to reverse the order of that phrase. The response to a lack of trust in teachers may be the hopeless attempt to over-prescribe and control. As I have argued, over-prescription may only serve to demoralize the best for it cannot help the worst teachers. Sometimes it may be hard for good teachers to be imaginative in the case of failure of policy. To respond to widespread difficulties by promoting diversity may be difficult for policy-makers and politicians but in the end for me there is no alternative to trust, openness and commitment to one another. There is no such thing as technical morality. Personal goodness is the only hope that we have.

NOTES AND REFERENCES

1. Russell (1946, p. 22).
2. Kuhn (1977).
3. Rorty (1980).
4. See Grimmett and Neufeld (1994, pp. 4–5).
5. Darling (1994).
6. Dewey (1966).
7. See Aspin and Chapman (1994, p. 120).
8. Taylor in Guignon (1993, p. 325).
9. Guignon (1993, p. 227). This volume is an excellent introduction to Heidegger's work.
10. Bruner (1990, pp. 50–1).

Bibliography

There are two sorts of entries: works to which reference has been made in the course of the text and those, although not specifically referred to in the text, that have a close relevance.

Adorno, T.W. (1982) *Against Epistemology: A Metacritique*. Oxford: Blackwell.
Alexander, R. (1992) *Policy and Practice in Primary Education*. London: Routledge.
Apple, M.W. (1986) *Teachers and Texts*. London: Routledge and Kegan Paul.
Apple, M.W. (1993) *Official Knowledge: Democratic Education in a Conservative Age*. London: Routledge.
Archambault, R.D. (ed.) (1965) *Philosophical Analysis and Education*. London: Routledge and Kegan Paul.
Aristotle. (1953) *The Ethics of Aristotle: The Nicomachean Ethics*. Harmondsworth: Penguin.
Aristotle. (1962) *The Politics*. Harmondsworth: Penguin.
Arnowitz, S. and Giroux, H.A. (1986) *Education under Siege*. London: Routledge and Kegan Paul.
Aspin, D.N., Chapman, J.D. and Froumin, J. (eds) (1995) *Creating and Managing the Democratic School*. London: Falmer.
Aspin, D.N. and Chapman, J.D. with Wilkinson, V. (1994) *Quality Schooling*. London: Cassell.
Bailey, C. (1984) *Beyond the Present and the Particular: A Theory of Liberal Education*. London: Routledge and Kegan Paul.
Ball, D.L. (1990) *With an Eye on the Mathematical Horizon: Dilemmas of Teaching Elementary School Mathematics*. East Lansing, Michigan: The National Center for Research on Teacher Education.
Ball, S.J. and Goodson, I.F. (1985) *Teachers Lives and Careers*. Lewes: Falmer.
Barnett, R. (1990) *The Idea of Higher Education*. Buckingham: The Society for Research into Higher Education/Open University Press.
Barrow, R. (1984) *Giving Teaching Back to Teachers*. Brighton: Wheatsheaf.
Barrow, R. and White, P. (eds) (1993) *Beyond Liberal Education: Essays in Honour of Paul H. Hirst*. London: Routledge.
Barth, R. (1991) *Improving Schools from Within*. San Francisco: Jossey-Bass.
Bennett, N. and Carre, C. (eds) (1993) *Learning to Teach*. London: Routledge.
Berdahl, R., Moodie, G. and Spitzberg, I. (eds) (1991) *Quality and Access in Higher Education: Comparing Britain and the United States*. Buckingham: Open University Press.
Berliner, D.C. (1986) 'In pursuit of the expert pedagogue', *Educational Researcher*, 15(7): 5–13.
Bernstein, R.J. (1983) *Beyond Objectivism and Relativism*. Oxford: Blackwell.
Beynon, J. and Mackay, H. (eds) (1992) *Computers into Classrooms: More Questions Than Answers*. Lewes: Falmer.

Bigge, M.L. (1982) *Learning Theories for Teachers*. New York: Harper & Row.

Bloom, B.S. (1956) *Taxonomy of Educational Objectives*. 2 vols. New York: McKay.

Bottery, M. (1992) *The Ethics of Educational Management*. London: Cassell.

Bottery, M. (1994) *Lessons for Schools?* London: Cassell.

Bowles, S. and Gintis, H. (1976) *Schooling in Capitalist America*. London: Routledge and Kegan Paul.

Broadfoot, P. and Osborn, M. (1988) 'What professional responsibility means to teachers: national contexts and classroom constants'. *British Journal of Sociology of Education*, 9(3): 265–87.

Brophy, J.E. and Good, T.L. (1986) 'Teacher behaviour and student achievement', *Handbook of Research on Teaching*, New York: Macmillan.

Brophy, J.E. (1991) 'Teacher's knowledge of subject matter as it relates to their teaching practice', in J.E. Brophy (ed.), *Advances in Research on Teaching*, vol. 2. Greenwich: JAI Press.

Brown, A. and Fairley, J. (1993) 'Pressures for reform in contemporary Irish education', *Scottish Educational Review*, 25(1): 34–45.

Brown, S. and McIntyre, D. (1993) *Making Sense of Teaching*. Buckingham: Open University Press.

Bruner, J. (1960) *The Process of Education*. Cambridge, Mass.: Harvard University Press.

Bruner, J. (1990) *Acts of Meaning*. Cambridge, Mass.: Harvard University Press.

Campbell, J. and Little, V. (eds) (1989) *Humanities in the Primary School*. Brighton: Falmer Press.

Carnegie Council on Policy Studies in Higher Education (1979) *Giving Youth a Better Chance*. San Francisco: Jossey-Bass.

Carnegie Forum on Education and the Economy (1986) *A Nation Prepared: Teachers for the 21st Century. Report of the Task Force on Teaching As a Profession*. New York: Carnegie Corporation.

Carr, D. (1991) *Educating the Virtues*. London: Routledge.

Carr, D. (1992) 'Education, learning and understanding: the process and the product', *Journal of Philosophy of Education*, 26(2): 215–25.

Carr, D. (1993) 'Problems of values education', in *Values and Values Education: An Introduction*. St Andrew's: Centre for Philosophy and Public Affairs, University of St Andrews.

Carr, W. (ed.) (1989) *Quality in Teaching*. Lewes: Falmer.

Carr, W. (1995) *For Education: Towards Critical Educational Inquiry*. Buckingham: Open University Press.

Carr, W. and Kemmis, S. (1986) *Becoming Critical: Education, Knowledge and Action Research*. Lewes: Falmer.

Chalmers, A.F. (1978) *What is This Thing Called Science?* Milton Keynes: Open University Press.

Charles, D. (1984) *Aristotle's Philosophy of Action*. London: Duckworth.

Child, D. (1994) *Psychology and the Teacher*. London: Cassell.

Chomsky, N. and Herman, E.F. (1988) *Manufacturing Consent: The Political Economy of the Mass Media*. New York: Pantheon.

Chubb, J.E. and Moe, T. (1990) *Politics, Markets and America's Schools*. Washington: Brookings Institution.

Churchland, P.S. (1986) *Neurophilosophy*. Cambridge: MIT Press.

Churchland, P.M. (1989) *A Neurocomputational Perspective: The Nature of Mind and the Structure of Science*. Cambridge: MIT Press.

Clark, C.M. and Peterson, P.L. (1986) 'Teachers' thought processes', in J.E. Brophy and T.L. Goods (eds), *Handbook of Research on Teaching*. New York: Macmillan.

Cohen, L. and Manion, L. (1989) *A Guide to Teaching Practice*. London: Routledge.

Coleman, J. *et al.* (1966) *Equality of Educational Opportunity*. Washington: US Government Printing Office.

Confederation of British Industry (1993) *Routes for Success: Careership: A Strategy for All 16–19 Year Old Learning*. London: CBI.

Coolahan, J. (1994) 'Some reflections on the context and process of the national education convention', in S. McCarthy and C. Trace (eds), *Teacher's Union of Ireland, Congress Journal*. Dublin: TUI, 33–7.

Cooper, D.E. (1983) *Authenticity and Learning: Nietzsche's Educational Philosophy*. London: Routledge and Kegan Paul.

CMRS (1992) *Education for a Changing World: Green Paper*. Dublin: CMRS.

Danto, A.C. (1975) *Sartre*. Glasgow: Fontana.

Darling, J. (1994) *Child-Centred Education and its Critics*. London: Paul Chapman.

Darling-Hammond, L. (ed.) (1994) *Review of Research in Education*. Washington: American Educational Research Association.

Dearing, R. (1994) *The National Curriculum and its Assessment: Final Report*. London: School Curriculum and Assessment Authority.

Derrida, J. (1982) *Margins of Philosophy*. Brighton: Harvester Press.

Dewey, J. (1966) *Democracy and Education*. New York: Free Press. (First published 1916)

Dews, P. (ed.) (1986) *Autonomy and Solidarity: Interviews with Jurgen Habermas*. London: Verso.

Downie, R.S., Loudfoot, E.M. and Telfer, E. (1974) *Education and Personal Relationships*. London: Methuen.

Dreyfus, H.L. and Dreyfus, S.E. (1986) *Mind over Machine: The Power of Human Intuition and Expertise in the Era of the Computer*. Oxford: Blackwell.

Drucker, P.F. (1992) *Managing for the Future*. Oxford: Butterworth-Heinemann.

Dworkin, G. (1988) *The Theory and Practice of Autonomy*. Cambridge: Cambridge University Press.

Elliott, J. (1993a) 'Three perspectives on coherence and continuity in teacher education', in J. Elliott (ed.), *Reconstructing Teacher Education: Teacher Development*. Lewes: Falmer.

Elliott, J. (ed.) (1993b) *Reconstructing Teacher Education: Teacher Development*. Lewes: Falmer.

Elliott, J., Bridges, D., Ebbutt, D., Gibson, R. and Nias, J. (1981) *School Accountability: The SSRC Cambridge Accountability Project*. London: Grant McIntyre.

Ellis, R. (ed.) (1993) *Quality Assurance for University Teaching*. Buckingham: Open University Press.

Eraut, M. (1994) *Developing Professional Knowledge and Competence*. Lewes: Falmer.

Esland, G. (ed.) (1990) *Education, Training and Employment*. Wokingham: Addison-Wesley/ Open University Press.

Evers, C. and Lakomski, G. (1991) *Knowing Educational Administration: Contemporary Methodological Controversies in Educational Administration Research*. Oxford: Pergamon.

Evers, C.W. (1993) 'Analytic and post-analytic philosophy of education: methodological reflections', *Discourse*, 13(2), 35–45.

Fenstermacher, G. (1986) 'Philosophy of research in teaching: three aspects', in J.E. Brophy and T.L. Good (eds), *Handbook of Research on Teaching*. New York: Macmillan.

Feyerabend, P.K. (1975) *Against Method*. London: Humanities Press.

Fullan, M.G. (1991) *New Meanings of Educational Change*. New York: Teachers College Press.

Fullan, M.G. (1993) *Changing Forces: Probing the Depths of Educational Reform*. Lewes: Falmer.

Fullan, M.G. and Hargreaves, A. (1992a) *What's Worth Fighting for is your School: Working Together for Improvement*. Milton Keynes: Open University Press.

Fullan, M.G. and Hargreaves, A. (eds) (1992b) *Teacher Development and Educational Change*. Lewes: Falmer.

Gadamer, H.G. (1975a) *Truth and Method*. London: Sheed and Ward.

Gadamer, H.G. (1976) *Philosophical Hermeneutics*. Berkeley: University of California Press.

Gadamer, H.G. (1981) *Reason in the Age of Science*. Cambridge: MIT Press.

Gadamer, H.G. (1985) *Philosophical Apprenticeships*. Cambridge: MIT Press.

Garforth, F.W. (1980) *Educative Democracy: John Stuart Mill on Education in Society*. Oxford: Oxford University Press.

Gellner, E. (1992) *Reason and Culture*. Oxford: Blackwell.

Giroux, H.A. (1989) *Schooling for Democracy*. London: Routledge.

Golby, M., Greenwald, J. and West, R. (eds) (1975) *Curriculum Design*. Milton Keynes: Open University Press.

Goodman, N. (1978) *Ways of Worldmaking*. Brighton: Harvester.

Gray, J. (1993) *Beyond the New Right. Markets, Government and the Common Environment*. London: Routledge.

Greenfield, T.B. and Ribbins, P. (1993) *Greenfield on Educational Administration: Towards a More Humane Science*. London: Routledge.

Grimmett, P.P. and Neufeld, J. (eds) (1994) *Teacher Development and the Struggle for Authenticity: Professional Growth and Restructuring in the Context of Change*. New York: Teachers College Press.

Gross, B. and Gross, R. (eds) (1985) *The Great School Debate*. New York: Simon and Schuster.

Grundy, S. (1987) *Curriculum: Product or Praxis*. Lewes: Falmer.

Guignon, C.B. (ed.) (1993) *The Cambridge Companion to Heidegger*. Cambridge: Cambridge University Press.

Gutman, A. (1987) *Democratic Education*. Princeton: Princeton University Press.

Habermas, J. (1970) 'Towards a theory of communicative competence', *Inquiry*, 13(4): 360–76.

Habermas, J. (1971) *Towards a Rational Society*. Oxford: Heinemann.

Habermas, J. (1972) *Knowledge and Human Interests*. Oxford: Heinemann.

Habermas, J. (1973) 'Wahrheitstheorien', in H. Fahrenbach (ed.), *Wirklichkeit und Reflexion: Walter Schulz zum 60. Geburtstag*. Pfullingen: Neske.

Habermas, J. (1974) *Theory and Practice*. Oxford: Heinemann.

Habermas, J. (1984) *The Theory of Communicative Action*, vol. 1. Oxford: Heinemann.

Halliday, J.S. (1990) *Markets, Managers and Theory in Education*. Lewes: Falmer.

Halliday, J.S. (1994) 'Quality in Education: meaning and prospects', *Educational Philosophy and Theory*, 26(2), 33–50.

Hargreaves, A. and Fullan, M.G. (eds) (1992) *Understanding Teacher Development*. London: Cassell.

Harlen, W. (ed.) (1994) *Enhancing Quality in Assessment*. London: Chapman.

Harris, K. (1977) 'Peters on schooling', *Educational Philosophy and Theory*, 9: 33–48.

Harris, K. (1994) *Teachers: Constructing the Future*. Lewes: Falmer.

Hartley, D. (1991) 'Democracy, capitalism and the reform of teacher education', *Journal of Education for Teaching*, 17(1): 81–97.

Harvey, L. and Green, D. (1993) 'Defining Quality', *Assessment and Evaluation in Higher Education*, 18(1): 9–34.

Harvey-Jones, J. (1994) *All Together Now*. Oxford: Heinemann.

Haydon, G. (1991) 'Review', *Education Today*, 41(3): 127–8.

Hayek, F.A. (1960) *The Constitution of Liberty*. London: Routledge and Kegan Paul.

Hayek, F.A. (1976) *Individualism and Economic Order*. London: Routledge and Kegan Paul.

Heidegger, M. (1962) *Being and Time*. New York: Harper and Row.

Heidegger, M. (1967) *What is a Thing?* Chicago: Regnery.

Hirst, P.H. and Peters, R.S. (1970) *The Logic of Education*. London: Routledge and Kegan Paul.

Hirst, P.H. (1974) *Knowledge and the Curriculum*. London: Routledge and Kegan Paul.

Hirst, P.H. (ed.) (1983) *Educational Theory and its Foundation Disciplines*. London: Routledge and Kegan Paul.

Hodgkinson, C. (1991) *Educational Leadership – The Moral Art*. Albany: SUNY Press.

Holland, R.F. (1980) *Against Empiricism*. Oxford: Blackwell.

Horkheimer, M. (1972) *Critical Theory*. New York: Herder and Herder.

Hoyle, E. and John, P.D. (1995) *Professional Knowledge and Professional Practice*. London: Cassell.

Hull, D. and Parnell, D. (1991) *Tech Prep Associate Degree: A Win/Win Experience*. Waco, Tex: Center for Occupational Research and Development.

Humes, W. (1986) *The Leadership Class in Scottish Education*. Edinburgh: John Donald.

Hyland, T. (1994) *Competence, Education and NVQs*. London: Cassell.

HMII. (1992) *Quality and Efficiency*. Edinburgh: SOED.

HMII. (1993) *Quality Assurance in Education: Plans Targets and Performance Indicators. Current Issues*. Edinburgh: HMSO.

Illich, I. (1973) *De-schooling Society*. Harmondsworth: Penguin.

Ingvarson, L.C. (1992) *A Strategy for the Professional Development of Science Teachers*. A

Report of the Science Education Professional Development Project, funded by the Department of Employment, Education and Training. Australia.

Ingvarson, L.C. (1994) 'Teacher evaluation for a teaching profession', *Victorian Institute of Educational Research*, 72: 34–47.

Jencks, C. *et al.* (1972) *Inequality: A Reassessment of the Effect of Family and Schooling in America*. New York: Basic Books.

Jessup, G. (1991) *Outcomes: NVQs and the Emerging Model of Education and Training*. Lewes: Falmer.

Jonathan, R.M. (1983) 'The manpower service model of education', *Cambridge Journal of Education*, 13: 3–10.

Jonathan, R.M. (1990) 'State education service or prisoners' dilemma: the "hidden hand" as a source of education policy', *Educational Philosophy and Theory*, 22(1): 16–24.

Jonathan, R.M. (1993) 'Liberal philosophy of education: a paradigm under strain', *Journal of Philosophy of Education*, 29(1): 93–107.

Kelly, A.V. (1995) *Education and Democracy: Principles and Practices*. London: Paul Chapman.

Kenny, A. (1984) *The Legacy of Wittgenstein*. Oxford: Blackwell

Kirk, G. (1982) *Curriculum and Assessment in the Scottish Secondary School: A Study of the Munn and Dunning Reports*. London: Ward Lock Educational.

Kuhn, T.S. (1962) *The Structure of Scientific Revolutions*. Chicago: University of Chicago Press.

Kuhn, T.S. (1977) *The Essential Tension*. Chicago: University of Chicago Press.

Lakatos, I. and Musgrave, A. (eds) (1970) *Criticism and the Growth of Knowledge*. Cambridge: Cambridge University Press.

Lakatos, I. (1976) *Proofs and Refutations: The Logic of Mathematical Discovery*. New York: Cambridge University Press.

Lakatos, I. (1978) *The Methodology of Scientific Research Programmes*. Cambridge: Cambridge University Press.

Lampert, M. (1990) 'When the problem is not the question and the solution is not the answer: mathematical knowing and teaching', *American Educational Research Journal*, 27(1): 29–63.

Loewenberg Ball, D. (1990) 'With an eye on the mathematical horizon: dilemmas of teaching elementary school mathematics', *Craft Paper 90–3*. Michigan: The National Center for Research on Teacher Education, Michigan State University.

MacBeath, J. and Weir, D. (1991) *Attitudes to School*. Glasgow: Jordanhill College.

MacBeath, J. (1992) *Education In and Out of School: The Issues and the Practice in Inner-cities and Outer Estates*. London: Scottish Office, Central Research Unit Papers.

MacBeath, J. (1994) 'A role for parents, students and teachers in school self-evaluation and development planning', in K.A. Riley and D.L. Nuttall (eds), *Measuring Quality: Education Indicators – United Kingdom and International Perspectives*. Lewes: Falmer.

McCarthy, T. (1978) *The Critical Theory of Jürgen Habermas*. London: Hutchinson.

McDiarmid, G.W., Loewenberg Ball, D. and Anderson, C.W. (1990) 'Why staying one chapter ahead doesn't really work: subject-specific pedagogy', in M.C. Reynolds (ed.), *Knowledge Base for the Beginning Teacher*, Oxford: Pergamon.

MacIntyre, A. (1981) *After Virtue*. London: Duckworth.

Mackay, H., Beynon, J. and Young, M. (eds) (1991) *Understanding Technology in Education*. Lewes: Falmer.

McMahon, A. (1993) 'Teacher appraisal in England and Wales', in L.C. Ingvarson and R. Chadbourne (eds), *Valuing Teachers' Work: New Directions in Teacher Appraisal*. Hawthorn, Victoria: Australian Council for Educational Research.

McNamara, D. (1993) *Classroom Pedagogy and Primary Practice*. London: Routledge.

McNeil, L. (1986) *Contradictions of Control*. New York: London: Routledge.

Macquarrie, J. (1968) *Martin Heidegger*. Cambridge: Lutterworth.

Malcolm, N. (1972) *Problems of Mind: Descartes to Wittgenstein*. London: Allen and Unwin.

Marland, M. (1975) *The Craft of the Classroom*. Exeter, NH: Heinemann.

Mendus, S. (ed.) (1988) *Justifying Toleration: Conceptual and Historical Perspectives*. Cambridge: Cambridge University Press.

Mortimore, P. *et al.* (1988) *School Matters: The Junior Years*. Salisbury: Open Books.

Munn, P. (1993) *Parents and Schools: Customers, Managers or Partners?* London: Routledge.

Murdoch, I. (1970) *The Sovereignty of Good*. London: Routledge and Kegan Paul.
Murdoch, I. (1992) *Metaphysics as a Guide to Morals*. Harmondsworth: Penguin.
National Board for Professional Teaching Standards. (1989) *Toward High and Rigorous Standards for the Teaching Profession*. Detroit: NBPTS.
National Commission on Education (1993) *Learning to Succeed*. Oxford: Heinemann.
National Foundation for Educational Research. (1994) *Records of Achievement in the Marketplace: The Views and Practices of Employers, Managing Agents, College Admission Tutors and Careers Officers*. Slough: NFER.
Nias, J. (1989) *Primary Teachers Talking: A Study of Teaching as Work*. London: Routledge.
Nicholls, A. and Nicholls, H. (1978) *Developing a Curriculum: A Practical Guide*. London: Unwin.
Oakeshott, M. (1959) *The Voice of Poetry in the Conversation of Mankind*. London: Bowes and Bowes.
Oakeshott, M. (1962) *Rationalism in Politics*. London: Methuen.
O'Dea, J. (1993) 'Phronesis in musical performance', *Journal of Philosophy of Education*, 27(2): 233–43.
Organisation for Economic Cooperation and Development. (1991) *Reviews of National Policies for Education: Ireland*. Paris: OECD.
Organisation for Economic Cooperation and Development. Centre for Educational Research and Innovation. (1994) *Quality in Teaching*. Paris: OECD.
Peters, R.S. (1959) *Authority, Responsibility and Education*. London: Unwin.
Peters, R.S. (1966) *Ethics and Education*. London: Allen and Unwin.
Peters, R.S. (ed.) (1967) *The Concept of Education*. London: Routledge and Kegan Paul.
Phenix, P. (1964) *Realms of Meaning*. New York: McGraw-Hill.
Phillips-Griffiths, A. (1965) 'A deduction of universities', in R.D. Archambault (ed.), *Philosophical Analysis and Education*. London: Routledge and Kegan Paul.
Pickard, W. (1994) *Times Educational Scottish Supplement*, 4 February.
Pirsig, R.M. (1974) *Zen and the Art of Motorcycle Maintenance*. New York: Morrow.
Polanyi, M. (1958) *Personal Knowledge*. London: Routledge and Kegan Paul.
Polanyi, M. (1967) *The Tacit Dimension*. London: Routledge.
Polya, G. (1954) *Induction and Analogy in Mathematics*. Princeton: Princeton University Press.
Popkewitz, T.S. (1987) *Critical Studies in Teacher Education*. Lewes: Falmer.
Popper, K.R. (1945) *The Open Society and its Enemies* (2 vols). London: Routledge and Kegan Paul.
Popper, K.R. (1961) *The Poverty of Historicism*. London: Routledge and Kegan Paul.
Popper, K.R. (1963) *Conjectures and Refutations*. London: Routledge and Kegan Paul.
Popper, K.R. (1968) *The Logic of Scientific Discovery*. London: Hutchinson.
Popper, K.R. (1972) *Objective Knowledge*. Oxford: Clarendon.
Popper, K.R. (1976) *Unended Quest*. London: Fontana.
Pring, R. (1994) 'Liberal and vocational education: a conflict of value', in J. Haldane (ed.), *Education, Values and the State*. Centre for Philosophy and Public Affairs: University of St Andrews.
Putnam, H. (1981) *Reason Truth and History*. Cambridge: Cambridge University Press.
Quine, W.V.O. (1951) 'Two dogmas of empiricism', *Philosophical Review*, 60: 20–43.
Quine, W.V.O. (1960) *Word and Object*. Cambridge: MIT Press.
Quine, W.V.O. (1971) *From a Logical Point of View*. Cambridge: Harvard University Press.
Quine, W.V. and Ullian, J.S. (1978) *The Web of Belief*. 2nd ed. New York: Random House.
Ranson, S. (1994) *Towards the Learning Society*. London: Cassell.
Rawls, J. (1972) *A Theory of Justice*. Oxford: Oxford University Press.
Rawls, J. (1993) *Political Liberalism*. New York: Columbia University Press.
Riddell, S. and Brown, S. (eds) (1991) *School Effectiveness Research: Its Messages for School Improvement*. Edinburgh: SOED.
Riley, K.A. and Nuttall, D.L. (eds) (1994) *Measuring Quality: Education Indicators – United Kingdom and International Perspectives*. Lewes: Falmer.
Rorty, R. (1980) *Philosophy and the Mirror of Nature*. Oxford: Blackwell.
Rorty, R. (1982) *Consequences of Pragmatism*. Brighton: Harvester.

Rorty, R. (1989) *Contingency, Irony, and Solidarity*. Cambridge: Cambridge University Press.

Rowland, S. (1993) *The Enquiring Tutor: Explorations in Professional Learning*. Lewes: Falmer.

Rowntree, D. (1977) *Assessing Students: How Shall We Know Them?* New York: Harper & Row.

Russell, B. (1946) *History of Western Philosophy*. London: Unwin.

Rutter, M. *et al.* (1979) *Fifteen Thousand Hours: Secondary Schools and their Effects on Children*. Salisbury: Open Books.

Ryle, G. (1949) *The Concept of Mind*. London: Hutchinson.

Sartre, J.P. (1948) *Existentialism and Humanism*. London: Methuen.

Sartre, J.P. (1957) *Being and Nothingness*. London: Methuen.

Scottish Office Education Department. (1987) *Curriculum and Assessment in Scotland: A Policy for the 90s*. Edinburgh: SOED.

Scottish Office Education Department (1993a) *The Structure and Balance of the Curriculum 5–14*. Edinburgh: SOED.

Scottish Office Education Department (1993b) *Guidelines for Teacher Training Courses*. Edinburgh: SOED.

Scottish Office Education Department (1994) *5–14: A Practical Guide*. Edinburgh: SOED.

Scottish Vocational Education Council (1993) *The Guide to Quality Audits*. Glasgow: SCOTVEC.

Scheffler, I. (1965) *Conditions of Knowledge: An Introduction to Epistemology and Education*. Chicago: University of Chicago Press.

Schon, D.A. (1983) *The Reflective Practitioner*. New York: Basic Books.

Schon, D.A. (1987) *Educating the Reflective Practitioner*. San Francisco: Jossey-Bass.

Schon, D.A. (1991) *The Reflective Turn: Case Studies in and on Educational Practice*. New York: Teachers College Press.

Schopenhauer, A. (1970) *Essays and Aphorisms*. Harmondsworth: Penguin.

Scriven, M. (1994) 'Using the duties-based approach to teacher evaluation', in L.C. Ingvarson and R. Chadbourne (eds) *Valuing Teachers' Work: New Directions in Teacher Appraisal*. Melbourne: Australian Council for Educational Research.

Shavelson, R.J. and Stern, P. (1981) 'Research on teachers' pedagogical thoughts, judgements, decisions and behaviour', *Review of Educational Research*, 51: 455–98.

Shulman, L. (1986) 'Those who understand: knowledge growth in teaching', *Educational Researcher*, 15(2): 4–14.

Shulman, L. (1991) *Final Report of the Teacher Assessment Project*. Palo Alto: Stanford University, Teacher Assessment Project.

Small, R. (1981) 'What ought to be taught? (The advantages and disadvantages of existentialism for educators)', *New Education*, 2(1): 53–60.

Small, R. (1994) 'Phenomenology and existentialism', in *International Encyclopedia of Education* (2nd edn). Oxford: Pergamon (pp. 4429–33).

Smithers, A. (1993) *All our Futures: Britain's Education Revolution*. Channel 4 Television.

Standish, P. (1992) *Beyond the Self*. Aldershot: Avebury.

Stenhouse, L. (1975) *An Introduction to Curriculum Development*. Oxford: Heinemann.

Strathclyde University (1994) *Certificate in Education: Further Education Module Descriptors*. Glasgow: Scottish School of Further Education.

Taylor, C. (1985a) *Philosophical Papers*. Vol. 1. Cambridge: Cambridge University Press.

Taylor, C. (1985b) *Philosophical Papers*. Vol. 2. Cambridge: Cambridge University Press.

Taylor, C. (1989) *Sources of the Self: The Making of the Modern Identity*. Cambridge: Cambridge University Press.

Thompson, J.B. (1981) *Critical Hermeneutics*. Cambridge: Cambridge University Press.

Tripp, D. (1993) *Critical Incidents in Teaching: Developing Professional Judgement*. London: Routledge.

Trow, M. (1993) 'The business of learning', *Times Higher Education Supplement*, 8 October, 20–21.

Turner, G. and Clift, P.S. (1988) *Studies in Teacher Appraisal*. Lewes: Falmer.

Usher, R. and Edwards, R. (1994) *Postmodernism and Education*. London: Routledge.

Walsh, P. (1993) *Education and Meaning: Philosopy in Practice*. London: Cassell.

Watson, B. (ed.) (1992) *Priorities in Religious Education: A Model for the 1990s and Beyond.* Lewes: Falmer.

White, J.P. (1973) *Towards a Compulsory Curriculum.* London: Routledge and Kegan Paul.

White, J.P. (1982) *The Aims of Education Restated.* London: Routledge and Kegan Paul.

White, J.P. (1990) *Education and the Good Life.* London: Kogan Page.

Wideen, M.F. and Grimmett, P.P. (eds) (1994) *Changing Times in Teacher Education: Restructuring or Reconceptualising?* Lewes: Falmer.

Williams, A. (ed.) (1994) *Perspectives on Partnership: Secondary Initial Teacher Training.* Lewes: Falmer.

Winch, P. (1958) *The Idea of a Social Science and Its Relation to Philosophy.* London: Routledge and Kegan Paul.

Windschuttle, K. (1994) *The Killing of History: How a Discipline Is Being Murdered by Literary Critics and Social Theorists.* Sydney: Macleay.

Wittgenstein, L. (1922) *Tractatus Logico-Philosophicus.* London: Routledge and Kegan Paul.

Wittgenstein, L. (1953) *Philosophical Investigations.* Cited from the 1967 third edition. Oxford: Blackwell.

Wragg, E.C. (1993) *Primary Teaching Skills.* London: Routledge.

Wringe, C. (1988) *Understanding Educational Aims.* London: Unwin Hyman.

Young, M. (1993) 'A curriculum for the 21st century? Towards a new basis for overcoming academic/vocational divisions', *British Journal of Education Studies*, 41(3): 203–22.

Index

UNIVERSITY OF WOLVERHAMPTON
LIBRARY